DYNAMICS OF GOVERNING
IT INNOVATION
IN SINGAPORE

A Casebook

DYNAMICS OF GOVERNING
IT INNOVATION
IN SINGAPORE

A Casebook

Gary Pan

Singapore Management University, Singapore

 **World Scientific**

NEW JERSEY · LONDON · SINGAPORE · BEIJING · SHANGHAI · HONG KONG · TAIPEI · CHENNAI

Published by

World Scientific Publishing Co. Pte. Ltd.

5 Toh Tuck Link, Singapore 596224

USA office: 27 Warren Street, Suite 401-402, Hackensack, NJ 07601

UK office: 57 Shelton Street, Covent Garden, London WC2H 9HE

Library of Congress Cataloging-in-Publication Data
Pan, Gary.
   Dynamics of governing IT in Singapore : a case book / Gary Pan, Singapore Management University.
      pages cm
      Includes index.
      ISBN 978-9814417822 (hardcover : alk. paper)
   1. Information technology--Government policy--Singapore--Case studies. 2. Informati
technology--Management--Singapore--Case studies. 3. Electronic government information--
Singapore--Case studies. 4. Technological innovation--Singapore--Case studies. I. Title.
   HC445.8.Z9I556 2013
   338.95957'06--dc23
                                                            2013001026

British Library Cataloguing-in-Publication Data
A catalogue record for this book is available from the British Library.

In-house Editor: Chye Shu Wen

Typeset by Stallion Press
Email: enquiries@stallionpress.com

Printed in Singapore

PREFACE

The primary objective of this case book is to bridge the concepts and theories students learn in their accounting/management information systems courses to actual real-life company scenarios. The focus is on issues managers need to know when governing IT innovation so as to create more efficient and effective organisations. This is an important topic because, while many would agree that innovation is the fundamental source of value creation and competitive advantage, investment in innovation is by no means a guarantee for business success. Related issues may include what existing or new processes and structures need to be put in place during IT innovation so as to maximise the value created from their IT-enabled investments? How do companies leverage on IT innovation to pursue constantly evolving strategies to seize emergent business opportunities? How do companies develop IT-enabled business network of entities with differing interests bound together in a collective whole, to attain enterprise agility? How do companies overcome challenges faced during the implementation of IT innovation? And what are the important organisational characteristics needed to create and sustain successful IT innovation? 13 case studies are presented in this book and they are contextualised within the framework of Singapore. The writing style and presentation of discussion questions at the end of each case study allows students to compare these Singaporean initiatives with other countries' methods of governing IT innovation. Such comparisons can elevate general levels of analysis and will help students get a better grasp of the principles behind IT governance.

CONTENTS

ABOUT THE CONTRIBUTORS

Barney TAN is a Lecturer in Business Information Systems at the University of Sydney Business School. He received his PhD in Information Systems from the National University of Singapore. Dr. Tan's research interests include strategic information systems, enterprise systems implementation, electronic commerce, and qualitative research methods. His research has been published in IEEE Transactions on Engineering Management, Information and Organization, European Management Journal (EMJ), and the International Conference of Information Systems (ICIS).

Calvin CHAN is a Senior Lecturer and the Head of the Business Programme in the School of Business, SIM University, Singapore. He is also the Deputy Convenor of the Cloud Security Working Group, IT Standard Committee, Singapore. He holds a PhD in Information Systems from the National University of Singapore, and a BSc (Hon) in Computer and Management Science from the University of Warwick. His research interests include e-government, information systems implementation and adoption, and case study research. His research has been published in journals such as the European Journal of Information Systems (EJIS), Government Information Quarterly (GIQ), Journal of the American Society for Information Science and Technology (JASIST), and Journal of Strategic Information Systems (JSIS).

Sathish s/o SRITHARAN is a Lecturer in the Temasek Polytechnic School of Informatics & IT, in the Diploma in Information Technology. He is also the Section Head for the Advanced Software Technology section in the diploma, and is currently a member of the Singapore Computer Society (SCS). One of Dr. Sathish's main research interests is the implementation of organization-wide integrated systems (Enterprise Systems). His emerging research interest is in the area of Interactive Digital Media (IDM) in Education, particularly related to the application of e-learning technologies and related learning pedagogies. Dr. Sathish has also co-authored two books on Information Systems Applications and has written a chapter for a case book on Managing Strategic Enterprise Systems and e-Government Initiatives in Asia.

Anand RAMCHAND is a Lecturer in Information Systems for the School of Computing at the National University of Singapore. He received his MSc and PhD in Information Systems from the same institution in 2005 and 2012. His research in graduate school focused primarily on the strategic use of information systems and technologies in transforming organizations, and the design of information architectures to realize innovative organizational changes. In his 12 years as an educator, Anand has developed pedagogical interests in the design and use of technology in delivering personalized education. He is also involved in engaging students with the professional community, and society in general.

Virginia CHA earned her Ph.D. in Innovation from the National University of Singapore and her B.S. in Information Computer Science from the University of Hawaii. She started her career as a systems programmer at Burroughs Corporation in the U.S. in 1980. She is an active mentor and angel investor to early stage startups, with focus in technology ventures at INSEAD, NUS, and SMU. She has co-authored the book *Asia's Entrepreneurs: Dilemmas, Risks and Opportunities*, and is also the chairperson of her own investment holding company with R&D office complex at Tsinghua Science Park in Kunshan, Jiangsu province, PRC.

Mahdieh TAHER is a research assistant at the Asian IT Case Series, NUS School of Computing, NUS. Her research interests are eGovernment, Analysis and Design of Information System, Information Technology Management, IT Strategic Planning. Her researches have been published in the journal of Information Technology Era, IEEE International Workshop and International Electronic City Conference. She has worked closely with Global360 Corporate.

SITOH Mun Kiat is a PhD candidate of Information Systems, School of Computing at the National University of Singapore. He has spent more than 25 years in software product creation and managed more than 100 IT projects. He is currently a business consultant for a software firm, operating in Asia. He obtained his MBA and MS in Industry Engineering from University of Houston, USA; and BS in Computer Science from University of Oklahoma, USA. He is TOGAF certified, and has received US patents for seismic tracking algorithm innovations. His primary research areas are business model, decision-making, and strategy-process.

LEONG Mei Ling is a PhD candidate of Information Systems at the School of Computing at the National University of Singapore. She obtained her MSc in Information Systems NUS in 2007 and she has about five years of working experience in system development, logistics and environmental protection. Her research interest is in the area of strategic IT issues, IT-enabled social innovation, and IT-enabled embeddedness.

Gary PAN is Associate Professor of Accounting (Education) at Singapore Management University (SMU) and the Associate Dean for Student Matters at the School of Accountancy. His research interests center on Accounting Information Systems, Corporate Governance and Accounting Education. Gary's research has been published in various premier academic journals such as MISQ Executive; Journal of the Association for Information Systems; IEEE Transactions on Engineering Management; European Journal of Operational Research (EJOR); Information & Management (I&M); Decision Support Systems (DSS); Information Systems Journal (ISJ); Journal of Strategic

Information Systems (JSIS), the Journal of the American Society for Information Systems and Technology (JASIST) and the Journal of Accounting Education (JAEd). He received the Journal of Strategic Information Systems Best Paper Honorable Mention Award in 2009. He currently serves as AE for Information & Management.

PAN Shan Ling is an Associate Professor and the Deputy Head of the Department of Information Systems, School of Computing at the National University of Singapore. He is also the academic director of the Strategic Technology Management Institute (STMI). Dr. Pan's primary research focuses on the recursive interaction of organizations and information technology (enterprise systems). He is also interested in understanding the business models and innovation of eCommerce companies. His inter-disciplinary research and education has been sponsored by multiple grants from the Ministry of Education, Workforce Development Agency and Electronic Government Leadership Centre, Singapore. Dr. Pan has published more than 70 journal papers and most of them have appeared in journals such as Information Systems Research (ISR); European Journal of Operations Research (EJOR); European Management Journal (EMJ) and International Conference on Information Systems (ICIS).

Case 1

THE EVOLUTION OF SINGAPORE'S INFOCOMM PLANS: SINGAPORE'S E-GOVERNMENT JOURNEY FROM 1980 TO 2007

Barney Tan

University of Sydney

Pan Shan Ling and Virginia Cha

National University of Singapore

SINGAPORE'S GOVERNMENT INFOCOMM PLANS

In Singapore, the use of information communication technology (ICT) in public organisations is governed by the "Government Infocomm Plans." These strategic ICT plans are based on the broader "National Infocomm Plans" of Singapore (see Figure 1.1), and set the key thrusts and strategies that provide guidelines on the use of ICT to transform the public sector. There have been four Government Infocomm Plans to date: The Civil Service Computerisation Programme (1980–1999), the e-Government Action Plan I (2000–2003), the e-Government Action Plan II (2003–2006) and iGov2010 (2006–2010). Our historical account of Singapore's e-Government journey is organised according to the four Government Infocomm Plans and presented in the subsections that follow.

CIVIL SERVICE COMPUTERISATION PROGRAMME (1980–1999)

Although the first real computer in Singapore was acquired in 1963 by the Central Provident Fund Board; a public agency that

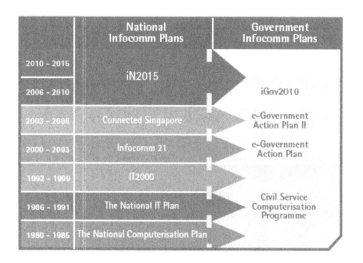

Figure 1.1:   Singapore's Government Infocomm Plans.

manages a social security savings scheme in Singapore, the first concerted effort to use ICT extensively to transform the public sector in Singapore can be traced back to 1980, when the Civil Service Computerisation Programme (CSCP) was launched in response to the Singapore National Computerisation Plan (NCP). Prior to the CSCP, public service delivery was a labour-intensive and manual process that was considerably inefficient due to the difficulty in managing the large volume of paperwork. Adhering to the directives of the NCP, 10 ICT study teams were formed with representatives from numerous ministries to examine how ICTs could be used in various public sector departments. The efforts and recommendations of the 10 ICT study teams laid the foundation of the CSCP.

The intent of the CSCP was to transform the Singapore government into an effective exploiter of emerging ICTs. The CSCP focused primarily on using transaction processing, data modeling, and data management technologies to improve the internal efficiency of the public agencies through the automation of repetitive work processes and paperwork reduction. Dr. Tan Chin Nam, Director of the Systems and Computer Organisation of the Ministry of Defense in 1979, elaborated on the aim of the CSCP, "We recognised that we had to move away from labour-intensive to capital-intensive, mechanisation and automation, in order to push up the wages.... We cannot survive on cheap labour. Computerisation was to help us to reduce manpower."

With the CSP framework in place, the Committee of National Computerisation of Singapore realised that there was a need for a central agency to coordinate and oversee the implementation of the plan. This led to the establishment of the National Computer Board (NCB) in 1981, and the agency was tasked with bringing the directives laid out by the NCP and the CSCP to fruition. Mr. Seah Kia Ger, one of the pioneers of the NCB described the challenges faced by the statutory board at that time, "You have to bear in mind that in 1981 the mindset of senior civil servants was not as open as today, although some were very positive towards and supportive of the unprecedented large-scale programme to improve the operational efficiency of the public sector.... (In addition), the structure of the civil service was not as conducive as 25 years later, to a major technological initiative. Great efforts had to be put into getting things done fast in order to push Singapore to become the first IT intelligent island state."

Despite the challenges, NCB were provided with ample resources to carry out the mandate of the Singapore government. Dr. Tan Chin Nam described how the Singapore government provided funding for implementing the CSCP, "We went to the Ministry of Finance's Permanent Secretary; George Bogaars, to ask for money. There were some discussions and negotiations. He was kind enough to say 'S$100 million (about US$70 million); that's all you need.' I would say it was very generous."

In addition, a fundamental problem with the civil service structure at the time was the lack of computing knowledge at various agencies. To overcome this problem, NCB centralised all computing personnels from various public agencies. These personnel were grouped into software and computer engineering departments under NCB. The two centralised departments began to fulfill the needs of the entire civil service. Mr. Phillip Yeo, Chairman of the

NCB at that time commented on how the initial core of computing personnel in the public sector was created: "What I did was to get the 10 ministries with their own computers. The only thing they did not own was the people. I centralised the people — the recruitment, training, supervision, and monitoring them.... But every ministry had the same priority. I told every ministry, 'tell us which project you want to implement first.' And we focused on those projects. So we spread out our people to work physically in different ministries — 30 to 40 computer guys in each ministry. That was over 300 people in all. After a year, I had 1,000 young people up and running."

NCB also undertook extensive measures to create a pool of ICT manpower to facilitate future ICT initiatives in the public sector. Training programmes were established and foreign professionals were hired to alleviate the shortage of ICT manpower. In addition, the educational system in the local universities and polytechnics was revised to offer new ICT-related courses. New technical institutes like the German–Singapore Institute and the Japan–Singapore Institute were established to train lower-level computer technicians, while the Institute of Systems Science (ISS) was set up to train top government and business leaders in the use of ICT.

By 1985, the technological achievements of the Singaporean civil service under the CSCP were impressive. 59 IT systems had been established in various agencies in the public sector, and the number of computer professionals in the civil service had risen to about 4,000. Furthermore, the number of mainframe and minicomputer installations, which stood at 350 in 1981, had risen to more than 2,000. More importantly, the CSCP demonstrated the government's resolve to transform the civil service through the use of ICT and it laid the foundation for the future use of emerging technologies in the public sector.

In 1985, Singapore was hit by a severe economic recession and the Singapore government quickly realised that there was an urgent need to re-examine the direction the economy was heading. The Singapore Economic Review Committee was established to review the strengths and weaknesses of the economy, and one of the key recommendations of the committee was to exploit emerging ICTs of the era to improve trade competitiveness, rejuvenate the key economic sectors, and create the foundation for economic growth. Dr. Tan Chin Nam, who was the General Manager of NCB, described how the committee re-conceptualised the role of ICTs in the public sector, "We are witnessing the emergence of a more comprehensive economy that requires sound business capability and IT has a contributing role in it. It is not just about national computerisation. There must be a larger meaning in our tasks."

The recommendations of the committee led to the launch of the second National Infocomm Plan called the National Information Technology Plan (NITP) in 1986. The NITP was anchored on a seven-pronged approach: developing IT professionals and experts; improving the information and communication infrastructure; promoting the ICT industry; coordinating and collaborating among various ICT-promoting organisations; establishing a culture that welcomes ICT; encouraging creativity and entrepreneurship, and increasing ICT application in workplaces. Based on the guidelines laid by the NITP, the focus of the CSCP was shifted to making public sector information accessible to the outside world and providing one-stop services through cross-agency linkages. Mr. Ko Kheng Hwa, Divisional Director of IT Application and Human resource at the NCB at the time, described the new focus of the CSCP, "No business organisation exists in isolation: it has to conduct business transactions with external entities. As long as these external transactions are based on traditional paper documents, the benefits of IT to an organisation cannot be fully achieved, no matter how extensively its internal operations are computerised."

As a result of the NITP, the CSCP began to look beyond automation using computing tools to the fusion of computer and communications technology. One of the most significant applications that emerged from the early initiative to merge computing and communications technology was TradeNet (see Appendix A). In the mid-1980s, international trade involved a staggering amount of paperwork which could result in non-value-added cost of up to 4% to 10% of the value of shipment for private sector trade companies. To improve trade competitiveness in Singapore, the NCB and the Trade Development Board (TDB) of Singapore published a set of trade data interchange standards that conformed to the international Electronic Data Interchange (EDI) standard, to standardise the process of electronic document exchange. By conforming to these standards, TradeNet enabled local companies to exchange trade documents electronically with their business partners abroad, and combine multiple trade documents into one single online form to achieve cost reduction and improved efficiency. Ms. Rosina Howe-Teo, a member of the TradeNet team, described the scope of the TradeNet initiative, "TradeNet was about integration, not just within departments but end-to-end processes. It was a massive project in that it involved 18 to 20 governmental agencies, each with its own requirements. We were moving into uncharted waters and there was a lot to adapt and adjust (to)."

Through the use of TradeNet, the trade-related sectors reaped the benefits of increased profitability and productivity as TradeNet slashed administrative costs and lowered the turnaround time for the documentation process from two days to 15 minutes. Cost savings were estimated at US$1 billion a year and by mid-1991, TradeNet was estimated to process 3.1 million import and export declarations annually. This resulted in U.S. Society of Information Management awarding "Partners in Leadership Award" to TradeNet in recognition of its achievements. With the launch of TradeNet, Singapore became the first country in the world to implement EDI nationwide.

While efforts were made to transform the trade-related sectors of the economy with TradeNet, other technological initiatives were simultaneously being developed by other public agencies in Singapore. For example, the Port of Singapore Authority (PSA) developed PortNet, which enabled shipping lines, freight forwarders, shippers, hauliers, and local government agencies to communicate with the port and each other. Similar to the context of TradeNet, the operations of the shipping industry in Singapore were filled with voluminous amounts of paperwork, and PortNet served to automate many structured, repetitive tasks in the shipping industry to reduce planning cycle time. The success of TradeNet and PortNet also led to the development of other EDI-based initiatives such as LawNet for the legal community, MediNet for the healthcare community, and BizNet for the business community. These EDI-based initiatives integrated the relevant public agencies with external private and professional organisations, which facilitated the exploitation of the ICT infrastructure developed in the earlier phase of the CSCP to create synergistic benefits for all the stakeholders involved.

The vision of ICT use in public organisations laid out by the NITP also required the consolidation of information across a number of public agencies. To this end, data hubs were established to serve as central repositories for various categories of data across multiple public agencies. For example, the Land Data Hub of the Ministry of Law was established to store information on Singapore's shareable land, while the People Data Hub of the Ministry of Home Affairs was established to store information on individual citizens that was used across various public agencies. These data hubs paved the way for inter-agency application systems such as the Integrated Land Use System and the One-Stop Change of Address Reporting System, which served to facilitate information-sharing across public agencies, provide horizontally-integrated services to the general public, and reduce data redundancy.

In addition, the NCB also undertook a number of projects that aimed to integrate the diverse information systems of various public agencies to facilitate the sharing of information. For example, the Inter-Departmental Network was established in 1989 and it linked 23 major computer centres from various organisations within the public sector. In the education sector, a project called School Link was introduced to connect the Ministry of Education to 360 schools across Singapore, facilitating communication between the schools and the Ministry, and providing support for administrative tasks such as student profiling, management, and exam scores analysis.

Although manpower reduction was expected by the late 1980s, when routine work processes in the public organisations were automated due to CSCP, it was estimated that CSCP had instead saved 1,500 jobs and created 3,500 more jobs due to the productivity gains from computerisation. By 1991, it was estimated that for every dollar invested in the CSCP, the returns on investment was US$1.87. In addition, with the exception of the Ministry of Defence which ran its own computerisation plan parallel to the CSCP, all the Ministries and Statutory Boards in the public sector had implemented their ICT initiatives in accordance to the framework laid out by the CSCP.

As Singapore entered the 1990s, the Singapore government, encouraged by their initial successes at exploiting ICT, began to perceive ICT as the means to enhance the quality of life for its citizens. Dr. Tan Chin Nam, Chairman of the NCB at that time, elaborated on the government's vision of the role of ICT in the early 1990s, "Singaporeans would be able to access and share a vast store of information. It would almost be like a giant electronic library — except technology now allows us to 'borrow' information and still leave a copy in place for other borrowers…. There would be no boundaries in the information age. Singaporeans would be able to see and talk to other people, even if they are separated by oceans, continents, time zones, geographical, and political boundaries."

To achieve this vision, the NCB and 11 sectoral groups consisting of about 200 people from the private and public sectors developed a new National ICT blueprint in 1992 that became IT2000, the third National Infocomm Plan of the Singapore government. An integral aspect of the IT2000 plan was the development of a National Information Infrastructure (NII) which comprised of three components: (1) Conduit; which refers to the physical communications pipelines, (2) Content; which refers to the information, and (3) Content; which refers to the processing of the content through mechanisms such as billing, user authentication, and permit documents. The IT2000 committee identified five strategic thrusts to leverage the NII: developing a global information hub, boosting the economic engine of Singapore, enhancing the potential of individual citizens, linking communities locally and globally, and improving the standard of living in Singapore.

Yet, the NII never came to fruition as the convergence of the deregulation of the telecommunications industry in Singapore, and the invention of the Internet enabled low-cost, high-speed public access to global information networks that went beyond what the

NII could offer. Although the economic potential of Internet technologies was apparent even during the mid-1990s, the Singapore government was concerned about the social implications of the Internet. However, the rapid adoption of the Internet by private organisations and individual citizens in Singapore eventually convinced the Singapore government that the future of ICT use in Singaporean public organisations laid in the emerging Internet technologies and not the NII. A decision was eventually made to establish a nationwide broadband network rather than to persist with implementing the NII initiative. Mr. Lim Swee Say, Chairman of the NCB in 1995, explained the rationale behind the decision to abandon the NII initiative: "Content had become multimedia. Computers had to be multimedia. The network had to change. We had to go broadband because the bottleneck was the network."

Following the decision to utilise the emerging Internet technologies, public organisations in Singapore adopted the Internet rapidly. In April 1995, the Department of Statistics of the Singapore government established the Government Resources on the Internet (GRIN) network. GRIN had two objectives: (1) providing Internet access to government officials and civil servants across all public organisations in Singapore, and (2) providing a platform to facilitate the creation of government websites. The GRIN initiative proved to be a phenomenal success. Prior to the establishment of GRIN, few public agencies had even heard of the Internet. However, within three months of its inception, all Ministries, statutory boards and organisations within the public sector were connected to the Internet. By 1996, there were an estimated 50 government websites with more than 1,500 Internet users across all public organisations in Singapore. In early 1996, an intranet was also established for the government officials and civil servants in Singapore. The intranet housed the Singapore government directory, an instructional manual, and a handbook that provided guidelines for the use of the intranet, the proceedings of the Singaporean Parliament, and various government newsletters.

The GRIN network represents the initial effort of the Singapore government at using ICT to engage individual citizens and internal government employees. Although the GRIN initiative was a resounding success, the rapid development of the network posed some unique challenges. One key challenge was that it became increasingly difficult to hire IT professionals with the relevant Internet experience as the technologies were relatively new. To overcome this problem, the NCB initiated training programmes that were similar to the programmes it conducted in the earlier phase of the CSCP. The NCB first trained its own staff centrally, who then took on the roles of Internet champions and trained IT personnel from other public agencies. In all, the NCB conducted seminars for almost 1,000 officers from the IT departments of various ministries and statutory boards to raise the awareness level and familiarity with the Internet.

Although the Internet certainly took the world and the Singaporean public sector by storm, IT2000 was not merely about Internet technologies. Singapore had also established an impressive record for service innovation through a number of high-profile initiatives that utilised other forms of technology. For example, other important nationwide technological projects carried out during this era include the development of the Electronic Road Pricing (ERP) system to manage traffic congestion, the use of radio frequency identification (RFID) chips by public libraries to eliminate queues, and the establishment of the Electronic Medical Records (EMR) system to allow doctors to retrieve patient's medical records and share information across different departments and hospitals. At the close of the 20th Century, Singapore had successfully paved the way for its citizens to live and work in a dynamic economy powered by ICTs. The dawn of the new millennium also led the Singapore government to look at ways to integrate their existing information systems for greater efficiency, and to effectively extract and analyse citizen and other business data for competitive advantage.

E-GOVERNMENT ACTION PLAN (2000–2003)

The advent of the dot.com era and the ensuing dot.com crisis that occurred at the turn of the millennium provided the impetus for the formulation of the fourth National Infocomm Plan of the Singapore government. Dubbed "Infocomm 21," the national ICT blueprint was created by the newly established Infocomm Development Authority of Singapore (IDA); a Statutory Board formed with the merger of the NCB and the Telecommunications Authority of Singapore, and aimed to "develop Singapore into a global infocomm capital with a thriving and prosperous e-economy and an infocomm-savvy e-society" (IDA, 2006a). To facilitate the attainment of this vision, four key strategies were formulated by the IDA: (1) positioning Singapore as a premier ICT hub in the Asia Pacific, (2) empowering the private, public and people sectors through the use of Internet technologies, (3) developing Singapore as an ICT talent capital and a hub for e-learning, and (4) creating a conducive pro-business and pro-consumer policy and regulatory environment.

In a parallel development, the Singapore public service embarked on a service excellence campaign called "Public Service for the 21st Century" (PS21) that aimed to inculcate an attitude of service excellence among civil servants, and cultivate a culture of continuous improvement to prepare the public sector for the future by "Anticipating, Welcoming and Executing Change" (PS21 Office, 2005). The convergence of Infocomm 21 and PS21 led to the development of the first e-citizen portal of the Singapore government in the late 1990s. Ms. Wu Choy Peng, Chief Information Officer of IDA at that time, recounted the implementation of the pioneering e-citizen portal, "... we visited a Canadian town offering local, state, and federal government services under one roof.... We built on the idea and persuaded Accenture to develop a proof of concept for Permanent Secretaries. The green light was given and the first e-citizen portal that delivered 10 different e-citizen services went live in the late 1990s."

The e-citizen portal paved the way for the e-Government Action Plan (eGAP I), the second Government Infocomm Plan of the Singapore public sector. eGAP I was conceived in 2000 with the intention of transforming the Singapore government into one of the leading e-governments in the world: one that is able to exploit the full potential of web technologies to bring about unparalleled efficiency and effectiveness in public service delivery. The primary focus of eGAP I was on facilitating the transactions between the government and its three key stakeholders groups — citizens, businesses, and employees — through the use of ICTs. Accordingly, five strategic thrusts were identified as critical to attaining the objectives of eGAP I.

The first strategic thrust was to push the envelope of electronic service delivery. The citizens' experience with private sector e-commerce and the pervasive, ubiquitous nature of Internet technologies led to increasing expectations of the government to provide its public services online, anytime and anywhere. As governments are typically perceived to be bureaucratic and inaccessible, the Singapore government believed that by adopting a citizen-centric perspective and integrating their electronic services, they could move beyond the general perception and create value for its citizens. The e-Citizen portal is a good example to illustrate the resolve of the Singapore government. The portal was designed to serve as a single access point for all government information and services. To support the development of this portal, the Public Service Infrastructure (PSI) was established to enable government agencies to rapidly develop and deliver online services to the public. In addition, to cater to the segments of the population who were unable to use the electronic services, the government set up a network of e-Citizen Help Centres to provide aid to those who are unable to use newly-created e-services and bridge the growing digital divide.

The second strategic thrust involved building new capabilities and developing new capacities. The Singapore government's focus on achieving productivity gains under the CSCP was superseded by the drive to further leverage ICTs to create value for its citizens. As the quality of e-services is directly dependent on the public organisation's ability to appreciate the implications of emerging ICTs, government officials and civil servants had to be equipped with the necessary skills, tools, systems, and infrastructure to make them effective workers in the digital economy. Consequently, an Infocomm Education Programme was established to equip public servants with the requisite ICT capabilities to extend the capacity of the public organisations they belonged to. A Technology Experimentation

Programme was also launched to provide resources for public organisations to encourage the innovative use of ICTs in their business processes and operations.

The third strategic thrust was to encourage innovation with ICTs. As citizens became increasingly sophisticated through their growing experience with Internet technology, their expectations in terms of the quality of electronic service delivery correspondingly increased. As such, experimenting with groundbreaking technologies such as emerging wireless transmission protocols and interactive broadband multimedia was imperative to the public organisations if they were to provide a similar, if not superior, online service experience. An example of a significant technological innovation in the public sector is GeBiz, the Singapore government's one-stop e-procurement portal. GeBiz was established to allow public officers to perform a wide range of procurement activities such as publishing tender notices, awarding government contracts, and allowing suppliers to respond to procurement opportunities. By 2002, it was estimated that the total value of procurements through GeBiz was about US$181 million.

The fourth strategic thrust was to develop anticipatory and sensing capabilities to become a proactive and responsive government. In order to keep pace the rapidly evolving trends in public administration worldwide, the Singapore government realised that its government officials and civil servants must be technology savvy and proactive in utilising them to develop the relevant public policy responses. Public organisations had to increasingly emulate the private sector in adopting a "sense and response" approach to anticipating new trends in public administration. Especially in the digital era where the role of customer service was becoming increasingly important, the government had to exploit the full potential of existing and emerging ICTs to churn out service innovations that added value for its citizens at "internet speed."

Finally, the fifth strategic thrust was to develop thought leadership on e-Government. To cultivate a better understanding and appreciation of the benefit of ICTs, public servants had to be equipped with the necessary knowledge and skills to use ICT tools and systems effectively. More importantly, there was a need to sensitize public officers to the impact of ICTs on the economic and social landscape so that the potential benefits that ICTs could bring would always be at the back of their mind when they make critical policy decisions.

To drive the strategic thrusts, six programmes were established. First, the Knowledge-Based Workplace programme would empower active and collaborative learning and knowledge sharing as part of the culture of continuous learning that the Singapore government hoped to nurture in the public service. Second, the Electronic Services Delivery programme would provide a one-stop interface for the government to interact with the general public through the integration of government services of individual public organisations. Third, the Technology Experimentation programme would encourage pioneering technological initiatives to better understand their capabilities and their potential for enhancing public service delivery. Fourth, the Operational Efficiency Improvement programme would facilitate a thorough re-examination of existing business functions and processes to identify possible areas for improvement. Next, the Adaptive and Robust Infocomm Infrastructure programme would develop the ICT infrastructure necessary to facilitate some of the earlier programmes and enable the creation of a knowledge-based workplace, delivery of integrated electronic services and improved operational efficiency. Finally, the Infocomm Education Programme would extend beyond teaching traditional IT literacy skills and focus on developing the capacity of each public organisation to take advantage of advancement in ICTs.

By 2003, Singapore had gained international recognition for its success in e-Government as it was consistently rated as one of the top e-Governments in the world in a number of independent studies (e.g., IDA, 2006b). In addition, the era of eGAP I witnessed the launch of several important e-Governments such as the electronic tax filing system of the Inland Revenue Authority of Singapore (see Appendix B) and the "my cpf" portal of the CPF board, which greatly enhanced the effectiveness and efficiency of public service delivery, and it resulted in massive cost savings for the public organisations.

The success of e-Government in Singapore is attributed to the e-Government development framework laid out by eGAP I, which in turn, was dependent on several critical success factors. One of the key factors was the amount of resources committed to making the programmes of eGAP I work. The Singapore government committed US$1 billion between 2000 and 2003 to the implementation of eGAP I. In addition, through the efforts of the IDA, the Singapore government demonstrated a strong commitment to transform the public sector through the use of ICT, which provided inspiration and leadership to all ministries and statutory boards in the public sector. A second factor that was instrumental to Singapore's success was the presence of an ICT champion that was influential in the hierarchy of the Singaporean Civil Service. According to Ms. Wu Choy Peng, "Mr. Lim Siong Guan, Permanent Secretary of the Finance Ministry and Head of the Civil Service at that time, played an important role in driving the eGAP I initiative."

E-GOVERNMENT ACTION PLAN II (2003–2006)

The success of eGAP I paved the way for the launch of Singapore's third Government Infocomm plan, e-Government Action Plan II (eGAP II), in 2003. Mr. Lee Hsien Loong, Deputy Prime Minister and Minister of Finance of Singapore during the time, elaborated on the economic and social forces that created the need for eGAP II in a speech during its launching ceremony (PS21 Office, 2003), "The environment is becoming more uncertain and competitive. We have to be more dynamic, entrepreneurial and self-reliant.... Singaporeans increasingly want their views on policies to be heard and the Government needs to be more consultative and open. To develop new policies and enact new laws, we must seek the views and expertise of private sector experts and various stakeholders."

The US$900 million ICT blueprint incorporated strategies that aimed to transform the Singapore public service into a networked government that provides integrated, accessible, and value-adding e-services that meet the needs of an ever-changing environment. Mr. Lee further elaborated on the objectives of eGAP II (PS21 Office,

2003), "Ultimately, eGAP II is not about IT, but about changing the approach to Government. eGAP II will deliver more one-stop, integrated services to meet the needs of our public and businesses.... eGAP II will develop the tools and help us to connect citizens with one another and with the Government. We would involve citizens in issues that they have expertise in, or issues that affect them."

Adhering to the vision of the Singapore government, eGAP II was formulated with three targeted outcomes: (1) Delighted Customers, (2) Connected Citizens, and a (3) Networked Government (see Figure 1.2). Accordingly, three sets of strategies were formulated to achieve the desired outcomes.

First, to achieve the outcome of delighting customers, the Singapore government sought to increase public awareness of its e-services and provide convenient access to its e-services. To this end, the government embarked on an ambitious project that aimed to integrate the vast array of information and services meant for different customer segments: citizens, residents, businesses and non-residents, into a single portal. The result was the re-launch of the Singapore Government Online portal (www.gov.sg) in October 2004. Integrating three existing portals for the government (SINGOV),

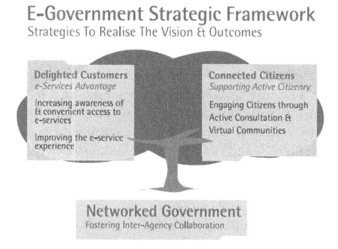

Figure 1.2:   Strategic framework of e-Government Action Plan II.

citizens (eCitizens), and the business community (EnterpriseOne), the new portal would serve as a single point of access to all government information and e-services for the various customer segments of the Singapore government. To provide convenient access to the e-services in the portal, the Singapore government undertook extensive measures targeted at three customer segments specifically. For the segment of the population that was "digitally excluded," the government provided free access to the portal at public libraries and community centres for citizens without Internet access. An eCitizen Helper Service was also established nationwide to provide aid to the segment of the population that faced difficulties in transacting with the government electronically. By April 2005, self-service kiosks were installed at all public agencies with the aim of allowing customers to help themselves to the information and transact electronically without having to queue and wait for physical services. Each public agency was also tasked to ensure that there were ample staff at hand to guide and educate customers at the self-service kiosks, so that they are able to use the e-services on their own in the future. For the business community, initiatives were established to help businesses overcome the barriers to e-service adoption. As an illustration, the government introduced the Business CARE programme in November 2004 to provide training for enterprises in using the e-services available in the portal, and lower the cost of adoption by selling computers bundled with internet access at affordable rates.

Finally, technology-savvy customers were allowed to personalise their service experience through MyeCitizen, which permits customers to subscribe to desired SMS or e-mail alerts. Examples of such alerts include reminders to return library books before their due date, and reminders to renew their annual road tax or pay for parking fines. MyeCitizen also allows users to personalise their homepage by populating it with the most frequently accessed e-services of the Singapore government. In addition to MyeCitizen, public organisations are highly encouraged to deploy feasible services on the mobile platform due to the government's belief that the mobile platform offers more extensive reach, convenience and immediacy for the technology-savvy customer segment.

The second strategy used by the government to delight its customers is to improve the e-service experience. To provide and transform e-services to meet the different and evolving needs of its customers, focus group discussions, public surveys and advisory panels were initiated by the Singapore government to obtain feedback on the needs of the citizens. In addition, a set of Web Interface Standards (WIS) was established in August 2004 to define a framework for designing government websites. The aim of the WIS was to facilitate ease of navigation and provide a consistent customer experience by standardising key features, naming conventions, and the basic layout of websites by 2007. Through the WIS, the government's need for standardisation and the individual public organisation's need for a unique identity are balanced; providing a consistent, easy-to-use interface for citizens while allowing individual public organisations flexibility in customising their suite of e-services. Another measure used to improve the e-service experience and instill customer confidence is the implementation of the national trust mark scheme, TrustSg. e-Government sites that excelled in the areas of data privacy, information disclosure, service fulfillment and best web practices adoption were accredited and awarded with the TrustSg seal on their websites. The initiative provided the impetus for public organisations to continually examine and improve their online practices and by October 2004, 78% of all eligible Government agencies had been accredited by the TrustSg scheme.

In an attempt to make their e-services as inclusive as possible, the Singapore government also identified an essential tier of e-services for enhancement in accordance to the World Wide Web Consortium Accessibility Guidelines (WCAG). The WCAG is an international standard adopted by governments worldwide, including Australia, Canada, and the United Kingdom, for the development of websites friendly to people with disabilities.

More importantly, a fundamental paradigm shift occurred in the mindset of Singapore government. The government realised that the key to improving the e-service experience is to deliver integrated services from a customer-centric perspective rather than an

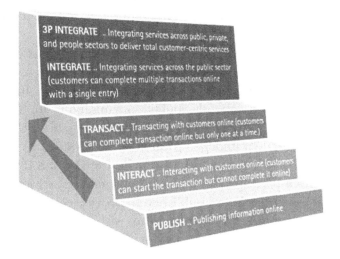

Figure 1.3:   e-Service maturity framework.

agency-centric perspective. Consequently, there was a strong drive to deliver more e-services that were horizontally-integrated across different public agencies to provide a seamless service experience for the private and people sectors. The enhanced service delivery paradigm (see Figure 1.3) was termed "Public-Private-People Integration," and the new paradigm challenged public organisations to drop their agency-centred mentality and focus on the customers' needs to generate opportunities for radical improvements in public service delivery.

To attain the objective of having connected citizens, the Singapore government actively pursued a strategy of citizen engagement through active consultation and virtual communities. The view of the government was that citizens can play a more active role in the development of the nation. Mr. Lee Hsien Loong, who became Prime Minister of Singapore in August 2004, elaborated during his inaugural National Day Rally speech, "We should have an open society which is welcoming of talent, which welcomes diverse views, yet is cohesive and has a sense of common purpose. And we should be a community where every citizen counts, where everyone can develop his human potential to the full, and everyone participates in building and repairing and upgrading this shared home which is called Singapore."

The vision of the new Prime Minister stirred the public sector into action as public organisations began to seek new ways of community building and encouraging active citizen involvement in the policy-making process. Consequently, public organisations in Singapore began to explore the ways in which ICT might be used to (1) explain public policies and their underlying rationale (2) provide new channels for public feedback on policy formulation and review, and (3) encourage active citizen participation in community building activities.

A centralised portal was established to provide electronic matching and information for citizens who wished to volunteer for community services. ICTs were also extensively used to form new virtual communities and support existing physical communities. In addition, the Singapore Public Service's launched its Consultation Portal (www.feedback.gov.sg) in April 2003 to provide a new channel for citizens to voice their opinions on national issues and public policy proposals, contributing towards a more consultative approach to policy-making. The portal provides a single access point or citizens who wish to review and provide feedback on all the new policy proposals of the Singapore government. Since its inception, the portal has been revamped to support e-polling and provide references to related policies to enable citizens to better understand public issues. Citizens are also permitted to engage in debate with fellow citizens on a myriad of policy issues in a discussion forum, or comment on Ministry-specific policy consultation papers through the e-Consultation Paper channel.

Finally, to achieve the goal of having a networked government, the Singapore government endeavoured to foster greater collaboration between different public organisations. ICT was perceived as a key enabling factor to achieving inter-agency collaboration and the government began looking at ways in which ICT could help public organisations transcend their organisational boundaries, share information, and leverage on a collective pool of knowledge to deliver consistent, integrated, and responsive services to their customers.

A Service-Wide Technical Architecture (SWTA), a technical framework comprising of principles, standards, and guidelines on the use of technology components, was established to facilitate interoperability and information sharing across agencies. The SWTA paved the way for public organisations to provide seamless, integrated e-services to their customers and its purpose was to reduce integration complexity, promote greater economies of scale, and increase re-use of components among the ICT systems of different public organisations. The SWTA was conceived as part of a broader Singapore Government Enterprise Architecture (SGEA), a blueprint that aimed to achieve complete business process and information interoperability in the public sector by 2007.

In addition, with the heightened threat to information security as a result of inter-agency information sharing, an integrated, proactive, and preventive approach was adopted to ensure the Government's preparedness for any ICT-related contingency. Government-wide security policies and guidelines; benchmarked against the best security practices of the private sector, were also established to safeguard the confidentiality and privacy of the shared information.

iGOV2010 (2006–2010)

At the end of 2006, the results of eGAP II (PS21 Office, 2006) were vastly encouraging. In 2005, 85% of the e-Government users were found to be satisfied with the overall quality of the e-services, while 9 out of 10 citizens who had the need to transact with the government opted to conduct their transactions electronically. The typical profile of an e-Government user is a white-collar worker between 20 and 39 years old. In contrast, citizens who used conventional, non-electronic means to transact with the government tended to be aged 50 and above, likely to hold blue-collared jobs, were employed, housewives or retired. An e-Government user who professed satisfaction with the quality of e-services explained, "I take advantage of e-services because they save me a lot of time and they are easy to use."

Encouraged by the success of eGAP II, as the three-year Government Infocomm Plan lapsed, the Singapore government launched a new US$1.38 billion five-year masterplan that they termed "iGov2010," which aimed to transform the Singapore government into "an Integrated Government (iGov) that delights customers and connects citizens through Infocomm" (IDA, 2006c). Mr. Raymond Lim, Minister for Prime Minister's Office and Second Minister for Finance and Foreign Affair, drew comparisons between iGov2010 and eGAP II at the annual e-Government forum in which the masterplan was unveiled, "Under iGov2010, we would invest S$2 billion to transform backend processing to achieve front-end efficiency and effectiveness. The principle to think of the 'Customer' and 'start with the user in mind' in everything we do remains the same in iGov2010. Rather, what is new is the strengthened focus and emphasis on transcending organisational structures, changing rules and procedures, to reorganise and integrate the government around customers' and citizens' needs and intentions."

iGov2010 was developed in consultation with the public sector, private organisations and the general public. As the fourth Government Infocomm Plan of the Singapore Public Sector, iGov2010 envisions an integrated government with all public organisations working as one, exploiting the opportunities of synergy and integration to exceed the expectations of the citizens it serves. The masterplan consists of four strategic thrusts (see Figure 1.4): (1) increasing reach and richness of e-services, (2) increasing citizens' mindshare in e-engagement, (3) enhancing capacity and synergy in government, and (4) enhancing national competitive advantage.

The first strategic thrust of iGov2010 seeks to increase the reach and richness of e-services with the objective of reaching even more citizens through the use of ICT. To extend the reach of its e-services, initiatives such as CitizenConnect and BizHelper were established. CitizenConnect is the continuation of a programme that was initiated during eGAP II that targets citizens without access to the Internet. CitizenConnect Centres were established at neighbourhood community clubs that provided free access to the government's e-services, while dedicated service officers were on site to educate users and assist in completing the transactions. BizHelper, on the

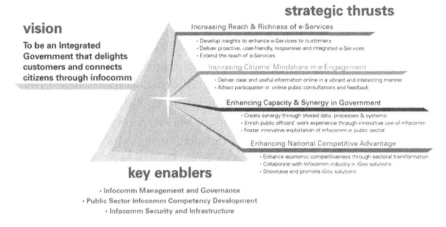

Figure 1.4:   Strategic framework of iGov2010.

other hand, was a similar service targeted at business owners that charged a nominal fee for their services at privately-run BizHelper Centres.

In addition, the trend of pushing e-services onto the mobile platform continues as the Singapore government sought to take advantage of the 100.8% mobile phone penetration rate in the country. As an illustration, the CPF board launched the mPAL service that allows employers with less than 10 employees to submit their CPF contribution details using a mobile phone in three easy steps. The use of the mobile platform is thought to be particularly attractive to busy, technology-savvy working professionals who are constantly on the move. There are also plans in the pipeline to establish a single SMS number for all government mobile services, utilising a standardised SMS format to simplify the process of trans-action. To improve the richness of its existing suite of e-services, the Singapore government sought to create more extensive feedback channels to gain further insights into their customers' needs and preferences. In addition, the government broadened their integra-tion efforts to include private organisations, with the objective of minimising the number of interactions that a citizen has to undergo in completing a single transaction.

The second strategic thrust of iGov2010 seeks to increase the citizens' mindshare in e-engagement. Under eGAP II, ICT had allowed Singaporeans all over the globe to access public information, participate in public policy consultations, and provide feedback to the government to stay connected and engaged with Singapore. The thrust seeks to go beyond eGAP II by actively engaging citizens in the policy-making process. To this end, the Singapore Government Online portal was revamped with an improved interface, designed to facilitate easy navigability and clear information presentation, in belief that an effective and aesthetically appealing interface will increase the "stickiness" of the portal, attract citizens to participate actively in online interactions and provide feedback to the government. To illustrate, animated graphics, and video snippets were used to convey information in an interesting and lively manner, while content search functionality was added to most of the existing websites of public organisations to support information search and retrieval. Separate consultation areas were also established for three specific customer segments — private organisations, youths, and overseas Singaporeans — in the Singapore government's Consultation Portal to facilitate dialogue on national issues and policy proposals from a diverse range of perspectives.

In addition to actively engaging citizens in policy-making process, web technologies were also leveraged to foster bonds and build communities within different segments of the population. For example, the Singapore government established the Youth Portal (www.Youth. sg) in February 2006. The Youth Portal is a one-stop portal for Singaporean youths to participate in community services. By offering young Singaporeans easy access to information on the community initiatives that their peers are engaged in, and information on how to start their own community activities, the Singaporean government hopes to build stronger ties between members of this population segment while creating social gains for the nation as a whole.

The third strategic thrust of iGov2010 seeks to enhance the capacity and synergy in the Singapore government. The new mantra of the public sector is "do more with less," which requires a greater extent of collaboration and integration across business processes, knowledge and information systems. The SGEA initiated under eGAP II was seen as one of the key means of bringing about integration and the corresponding efficiency gains. Under iGov2010, the scope of SGEA was expanded as extensive data and application standards were established to facilitate greater integration and coordination across agencies. An illustration of the workings of the SGEA is the establishment of the Centre of Shared Services (Vital.org), which integrates common Finance and Human Resource functions of the public organisations in Singapore to bring about economies of scale for the public sector.

ICTs were also leveraged to transform the job scope of public servants, and create solutions for the routine challenges that they typically encounter. As an illustration, mobile technologies were exploited to allow public officers to work from home, while collaborative desktop tools were used to support work across various departments and agencies. In 2006, the Singapore government also embarked on an ambitious project that sought to establish a Standard ICT Operating Environment (SOE). Targeted for completion by 2010 at a cost of US$918 million, the SOE involves the standardisation of computing and network components across the public sector, making it easier for public agencies to develop new applications on all desktops across the public sector, and establish a stronger, more consistent corporate identity.

Finally, the fourth strategic thrust of iGov2010 seeks to leverage the integrated government to create competitive advantage for Singapore on three different levels. On the industry level, the Singapore government sought to collaborate with the private ICT industry in the creation, development, and export of e-Government solutions to accelerate the growth of the private ICT sector. ICT products and services would be promoted as "Created-by-Singapore" to nations that wish to tap on Singapore's considerable e-Government expertise.

On the national level, ICT was used to bolster its macroeconomic infrastructure to attract foreign investments to Singapore. This entailed transforming various sectors in the economy through a strong collaborative effort between relevant public organisations and major players in the various industries. To illustrate, an example of one such initiative is TradeXchange, an integrated trade and logistics platform established to support the exchange of commercial and regulatory information for organisations along the entire trade and logistics value chain. It integrates public services such as the application for trade permits and customs declarations, with private sector offerings and the promotion of financial services and insurance to simplify the trade permit declaration. This integration would also reduce the number of interactions necessary to complete a transaction, and on the whole, provide the trade and logistics community with a total customer service experience. Finally, at the international level, the Singapore government sought to partner regional countries in the implementation of ICT initiatives to accelerate the rate of development. The objective is to strengthen Singapore's national competitive advantage and establish a reputation as a centre of ICT excellence. Mr. Raymond Lim elaborates, "iGov2010 is well-positioned to strengthen Singapore's national competitive advantage, as well as its reputation as a centre of excellence and a global showcase for ideas, innovation, and knowledge. Through partnerships and collaborations in the international arena, we will be a world-class city where people live, work, and play through infocomm; technologically-advanced and well-connected to the rest of the world."

While iGov2010 has not arrived at fruition, the Singapore government has established ambitious targets for its fourth Government Infocomm Plan. By 2010, the government aims to have (1) 80% of users who are very satisfied with the overall quality of e-services, (2) 90% of users who would recommend others to transact with the government through electronic means, and (3) 80% of users who are very satisfied with the level of clarity and usefulness of information published online concerning government policies, programmes, and initiatives.

APPENDIX A — TradeNet

Background

The Singapore Trade Development Board (TDB), now known as International Enterprise Singapore, was founded in 1983 for trade facilitation and promotion purposes. As a trade facilitator, TDB was providing basic information on export practices, helping traders to overcome technical barriers, and processing trade declaration documents for imports and exports. As a trade promoter, TDB actively promoted the export of goods and services, expansion into new markets, and the development of Singapore as a base for international businesses.[1] Faced with a shortage of labour in the 1980s, the turnaround time for processing trade declaration documents, which spanned from two to four days, was deemed as unsatisfactory. The 1985 recession was a catalyst for the development of TradeNet, when the Economic Review Committee proposed to leverage IT to improve trade competitiveness. Singapore was further propelled to realise this notion when Hong Kong revealed that it was working towards the creation of TradeLink, a trade-oriented electronic data interchange (EDI) system in 1986.

Paper-Based Trade Administration

The verification of trade declaration documents is a critical component of the trade administration process. This ensures that traders comply with legal requirements such as health and safety issues, and the payment of custom duties. In 1986, TDB processed an average of 10,000 trade declaration documents daily. As the volume of international trade increased, the costs of cumbersome trade procedures became increasingly visible. The paper-based trade administration process thus put both public agencies and traders in a tight spot.

From the perspective of the public agencies, the boredom and monotony of performing repetitive tasks impaired staff productivity and morale, despite constant recruitment and training by TDB to meet voluminous paper management demands. This impeded the staff's ability to carry out value-added activities as they were perpetually overwhelmed by paperwork. In addition due to their

---

[1] For details, refer to www.iesingapore.gov.sg.

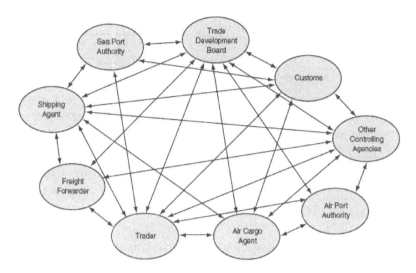

Figure 1.5:   Pre-TradeNet document flow scheme.

unconnected computer systems, the lack of coordination between TDB and the regulatory bodies led to a substantial overlap of information. Traders were often required to submit the same data in different formats to various public agencies in order to get approval for permit application. The complicated document flow scheme in the 1980s is illustrated in Figure 1.5. All in all, the paper-based administration process hindered TDB's ability to provide efficient services to the trading community.

For traders, frequent visits to different agencies in geographically dispersed locations were not only time-consuming, but also incurred significant transportation costs which could otherwise be avoided if the trade procedures were streamlined. Furthermore, the lack of coordination among public agencies attributed to the delayed clearance of documents and approval. This slowed down the movement of goods, raised customer dissatisfaction, tied up labour to maintain slack resources, and incurred additional warehousing costs to traders. As a whole, the paper-based administration process reduced the competitiveness of traders and Singapore as a premier international trading hub.

TradeNet-Based Trade Administration

The problems associated with the paper-based trade administration process prompted TDB to set up TradeNet together with the National Computerisation Board. TradeNet is an EDI system that links public agencies and the trade-related sectors to allow exchange of business documents in a structured format electronically. The ultimate purpose of this EDI system is to consolidate multiple trade documents into a single document. The simplified document flow scheme is illustrated in Figure 1.6. A 1985 study by the Swedish Trade Procedures Council showed that the costs of trade procedures corresponded to between 4% and 7% of the value of goods traded. Based on this study, it was estimated that if TDB could reduce procedural costs by 1%, it would save S$1 billion annually for the trading community.

Commitment from public agencies and traders was the key to the effective implementation of TradeNet. In light of this, CEOs of government agencies and leaders of trade associations gathered together to form an executive committee to solicit support from all trade-related parties. Although public agencies had the technical expertise, they lacked marketing skills to convince traders the

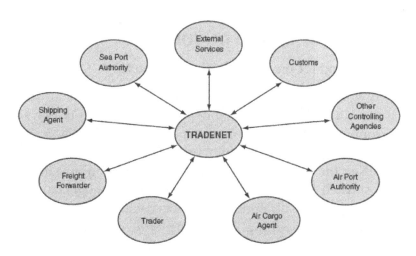

Figure 1.6:   Post-TradeNet document flow scheme.

benefits of TradeNet. TDB thus reckoned that it was important to set up a market-sensitive and performance-driven private organisation to implement and market TradeNet. This led to the development of Singapore Network Services Private Limited (SNS) by TDB, Singapore Telecoms, Port of Singapore Authority, and Civil Aviation Authority of Singapore. With its official launch in 1989, TradeNet became the first nationwide EDI in the world. TradeNet received international recognition when it won the "Partners in Leadership" award from the U.S. Society of Information Management in the same year.

TradeNet brought unprecedented changes to the trading community. It eliminated the need to submit multiple copies of trade declaration documents physically to various public agencies. Traders were only required to submit a single copy of trade declaration document through TradeNet, without any supporting documents. Once the document is validated, a notification with a permit number would be emailed to the applicant. Fees charged for document processing, custom duties, and network usage would automatically be deducted from traders' bank accounts twice a week. Notably, the trade administration process was reduced to as little as 15 minutes following the implementation of TradeNet.

THE IMPACTS OF TradeNet ON TDB

TradeNet's Impact on Organisational Structure

As a consequence of the implementation of TradeNet, the organisational structure of TDB had been re-organised in terms of unit size, unit grouping, job specification, reporting mechanism, control mechanism, and communication mechanism. Before the inception of TradeNet, there was only one trade administration unit in TDB, which consisted of over 100 staff performing homogeneous and repetitive tasks manually under close supervision. Trade declaration documents and supporting documents were examined carefully before approval was granted and communication between TDB and the trading community was mostly done via phone and mail.

After the inception of TradeNet, the trade administration unit was split into four units with a streamlined staff performing differentiated and specialised tasks without supervision. All documents were scanned to detect fraud after approval was granted. Electronic messages facilitated the communication among TradeNet participants. The widespread adoption of TradeNet led to the closure of manual processing counters, relieved the document processing staff from mundane tasks, and allowed them to perform value-added activities. In short, TradeNet reduced labour costs and boosted staff productivity.

TradeNet's Impact on Business Processes

The willingness to change the existing mindset to embrace IT was the determining factor of TradeNet's success. TradeNet had transformed public agencies from controlling bodies into trade facilitators by eliminating the need for supporting documents upon permit application through TradeNet. TDB believed that drastic improvement could only be achieved if the paperwork was reduced drastically. This explained the reason for passing the burden of responsibility to traders so as to prove their integrity. Nevertheless to prevent abuse, the outputs from TradeNet would be investigated and traders would be indicted for malpractices.

TradeNet did not only restructure TDB's business processes, but it also improved the interaction between traders and other public agencies. With the integration of TradeNet into other public agencies' systems, it changed the routine of all relevant agencies. TradeNet's one-stop, round-the-clock operation allows traders to apply for permit electronically. All related agencies would retrieve and process the trade declaration documents in a timely manner.

TradeNet's Impact on Business Network

Following the implementation of TradeNet, TDB played crucial roles in facilitating trade procedures and promoting the adoption of EDI applications. As a trade facilitator, TDB was mindful of the need to enhance the competitiveness of the trading community through a better trade administration process and wider range of services. As an EDI advocate, TDB worked hand-in-hand with SNS to explore other potential areas for EDI applications to benefit the trading community.

Apart from that, TradeNet had also helped foster stronger bonds between TDB and all the trade-related stakeholders. Prior to the implementation of TradeNet, standard linkages existed between TDB and all trade-related parties. There were no concerted efforts to improve the handling of trade transactions for mutual benefit. For effective implementation of TradeNet, all parties involved were coerced to refine business processes by overhauling obsolete procedures and installing new communication equipments. The extensive investments were thus a driving force for relevant parties to transform the previous business network to a customised one where all involved parties were mindful of the need for inter-organisational collaboration.

TradeNet's Impact on Business Scope

As a controlling body, TDB used to have no interest in investment of any kind. However, a paradigm shift occurred as a result of the implementation of TradeNet, which spurred TDB to try its hand in investment outside the organisational boundaries. Most of its subsidiaries and associated organisations were focused on EDI-related businesses. This initiative was ascribed to the profitability of SNS through aggressive marketing of TradeNet and other EDI applications.

TradeNet's Impact on Efficiency and Effectiveness

Increasing productivity in TDB and enhancing the competitiveness of the trading community were the triggers for the development of TradeNet. Therefore, the two factors to assessing the impact of TradeNet were efficiency (i.e., the ability of TDB to implement the EDI system) and effectiveness (i.e., the achievement of the intended objectives). Studies showed that there was a significant increase in trade volume handled and processing revenue earned since the implementation of TradeNet. Thus, there was no doubt that TDB had successfully boosted productivity through TradeNet. Moreover, TradeNet participants reported that they were satisfied with the TradeNet features and usage price. Hence, it was apparent that TradeNet had realised its goal by making the entire trading community more competitive internationally.

Conclusion

TradeNet has greatly facilitated trade transactions in Singapore. It has reduced the turnaround time for processing trade declaration documents and reduced procedural costs, improved inter-organisational communication, increased productivity in public agencies, and enhanced the competitiveness of Singapore as a global trading hub. More importantly, it has transformed public agencies from controlling bodies into trade facilitators, which allowed them to provide a wider range of services to benefit the trading community. In addition, TradeNet has also made fundamental changes to the organisational structure, business processes, business network, business scope, efficiency and effectiveness of TDB. In sum, the case of TradeNet is a critical part of Singapore's pioneering efforts in leveraging IT to enhance business competitiveness.

APPENDIX B — INLAND REVENUE AUTHORITY OF SINGAPORE (IRAS)

Background

Taxes are primarily collected to fund government expenditures, as well as to achieve economic and social goals. The Inland Revenue Authority of Singapore (IRAS), formerly known as Inland Revenue of Singapore (IRD), is a public agency mandated by the government to administer all aspects of taxation. The antecedent of IRAS can be traced back to 1947 when the Income Tax Ordinance was enacted. Since its independence, the pace and stability of Singapore's economy grew strongly. Faced with an escalating number of taxpayers, IRD found it increasingly hard to cope with the swelling backlog of tax cases. Meanwhile, another issue faced by IRD was the acute shortage of staff, which was about three times higher than other public agencies. IRD was thus restructured to IRAS to address these problems in 1992.[2] Being rated as one of the lowest among public organisations in terms of public satisfaction, IRAS was determined to revamp the administrative and bureaucratically aspects of tax administration process. One of the earliest attempts made by IRAS was the introduction of the phone filing service in 1995, which proved to be a catalyst to the development of the groundbreaking e-filing system in 1998.

The E-Filing System

With the launch of the new US$1.3 million e-filing system, both local and overseas taxpayers could file their income tax returns through the Internet. A significant change is the elimination of the need to submit receipts upon filing of returns. This is because the government does not want to simply overlay the e-filing system on the traditional tax filing process as they believed that drastic improvement can only be achieved if the paperwork is reduced as much as possible. Nevertheless, the changes were not applicable to high-income taxpayers who were

---

[2]For details, refer to www.iras.gov.sg.

required to post complete details of their income to IRAS for statistical purposes. Due to the simplicity of the new e-filing system, the user base was only 10% of the taxpaying population in the first year of implementation. However, as usage rates increased to 30% by 2000, Singapore decided to extend the system to self-employed individuals that comprised a significant proportion of the population of taxpayers.[3] The following section describes the evolution of the e-filing system.

THE EVOLUTION OF THE E-FILING SYSTEM

Phase I: Digitising Taxpayer Information

Prior to the creation of the e-filing system, it was estimated that nearly 50% of tax returns had yet to be assessed at the end of 1991. To put it simply, the backlog comprised of half of the collected tax returns, and this number grew exponentially each year. The imaging system was thus created in 1992 to deal with this problem. All physical returns were scanned to create digitised images for archiving purposes, thereby dispensing with the need to store paper files. Although the system was not fully automated and human labour was still required to complete the assessment of tax returns, it relieved tax officers from paper-shuffling. More importantly, with all the digital folders stored in a centralised database, tax officers were capable of locating taxpayers' information on the network to serve their enquiries instantly. In sum, the imaging system reduced administrative costs, boosted productivity, and increased public satisfaction.

Phase II: Automating Organisational Business Processes

The implementation of the imaging system paved the way for the Inland Revenue Integrated System (IRIS) in 1995. Propelled by the desire to fully automate the tax filing process, IRIS was introduced to provide an integrated one-stop service to taxpayers. According to

---

[3] Bhatnagar, S. (2000). *Modernizing Tax Administration in Singapore*, Washington, DC: World Bank.

IRAS, taxpayers can be grouped into two categories: normal taxpayers, who constitute 80% of the taxpaying population and enjoy the liberty to file returns without further validation by tax officers, and high-income taxpayers, who make up of 20% of the taxpaying population and require special attention from IRAS.

Making a decision to substantially reduce the level of human resources allocated to normal tax returns, the Workflow Management System, a subsystem within IRIS, was established to transmit unique tax returns to the specific tax officer with the relevant skills. In other words, the implementation of the Workflow Management System saves tax officers from sifting through 80% of tax returns annually.

Phase III: Developing the Phone-Filing System

The imaging system was not a panacea for solving all the problems associated with the labour-intensive legacy processes. Data entry by tax officers was still essential for the completion of tax assessment. Therefore, the next phase of re-engineering focused on the automation of the data input function. To this end, the phone filing system was revamped to involve taxpayers directly in the process of data entry to free officers from the mundane, repetitive task of data entry. A series of simple instructions was provided to familiarise taxpayers with the tax-filing process. However, despite the simplicity of the phone-filing system, it was not well accepted among taxpayers for two reasons. Firstly, it was restricted to only the portion of taxpayers with a single source of income due to security concerns. Secondly, a non-visual tax filing system was a nebulous idea and it raised resistance from most taxpayers.

Phase IV: Designing the e-Filing System

Undeterred by the lack of popular acceptance for the phone filing system, IRAS continued to persist with its efforts at enhancing the tax filing experience. Riding on the prevalence of the Internet, the Internet e-filing system was introduced in 1998 for those with employment income, which was subsequently extended to all taxpayers in later years. For effective implementation, IRAS incorporated a customer-centric perspective by adopting feedback and suggestions from tax officers and taxpayers. In addition, a one-time use of Electronic-Filing Personal Identification (EF PIN) was introduced for authentication purposes. The PIN is mailed to the taxpayer as the start of each tax cycle, and then terminated when the taxpayer has filed his returns. This saves taxpayers the hassle of trying to recall a number that would be of no use at the end of every tax cycle, and makes the e-filing system more appealing to taxpayers.

Phase V: Maintaining and Improving the e-Filing System

Precautions were taken to prevent contingencies and enhance the efficacy of the e-filing process. Firstly, an operational e-filing Helpline was opened from 8 am to 10 pm, 7 days a week during a tax cycle to answer taxpayers' enquiries. Secondly, system maintenance was carried out regularly to ensure the stability of the system. Thirdly, at the end of each tax cycle, a post-mortem was conducted to cross-examine the problems that may occur during the tax filing period. Numerous customers' queries were analysed and proposed solutions were incorporated into the e-filing system for the next fiscal year. IRAS also formed an independent Taxpayer Feedback Panel to assess and improve IRAS services. In all, the government's determination and persistency in enhancing the e-filing experience was rewarded with a growing base of e-filers from year to year.

Phase VI: Extending e-Filing Services

Another concerted effort made by IRAS to improve its e-filing services was the auto-inclusion scheme. IRAS managed to secure commitments from various government agencies and business organisations to directly transfer the income portfolio of their employees to IRAS electronically. Taxpayers are now only required to submit a series of zero returns through the e-filing system. As of 2003, this scheme supported a number of major Singaporean companies, which accounted for 46% of all employees in the country.

With the verification of tax information done by employers, IRAS is assured of the accuracy of tax returns submissions.

CONCLUSION

The evolution of the e-filing system has transformed IRAS from a bureaucratic agency to a customer-centric organisation. A number of lessons can be drawn from the case of IRAS. Firstly, the willing-ness to disregard conventional notions of treating customers as outsiders is imperative to raising customer satisfaction. A deciding factor behind the success of the e-filing system was the strategic management of customer relations. Instead of excluding taxpayers from the e-filing initiative, IRAS treats them as important stakeholders of the organisation and tries to address their needs to improve the tax administration process.

Secondly, the case underscores the ability of IT to mend the tarnished image of public agencies by improving internal operation efficiency. The rapid development of IT has resulted in increasing customer demands for an integrated one-stop service. The e-transformation for faster and efficient public service delivery is thus an inevitable consequence. Thirdly, the case demonstrates that integrative communication helps to align perceptions and concerns of public agencies with those of its stakeholders, and thus reduces apprehension towards innovations. Through constant solicitation of feedback and suggestions from all relevant stakeholders, IRAS was able to secure public confidence in the revamped tax filing system.

DISCUSSION QUESTIONS

1. By referring to the case study, please explain the importance of IT, between the underlying philosophy of governance and the level of ICTs to achieve the effectiveness of the strategic plans for ICT.
2. How do e-Government maturity and the nature of ICT lead to public sector service innovation?

REFERENCES

Infocomm Development Authority of Singapore (2006a). The Government's Infocomm Journey. Available at: http://www.igov.gov.sg/Strategic_Plans/Our_Journey.htm (accessed December 4, 2007).

Infocomm Development Authority of Singapore (2006b). Singapore: A World-Class e-Government. Available at: http://www.ida.gov.sg/doc/Infocomm%20Industry/Infocomm_Industry_Level1/Gov%20Brochure.pdf (accessed December 4, 2007).

Infocomm Development Authority of Singapore (2006c). igov2010. Available at: http://www.igov.gov.sg/Strategic_Plans/iGov_2010 (accessed December 4, 2007).

Public Service for the 21st Century (PS21) Office (2003). Delighting Customers, Connecting Citizens. Available at: http://www.ps21.gov.sg/Challenge/2003_09/hot/hot.html (accessed December 4, 2007).

Public Service for the 21st Century (PS21) Office (2005). PS21: Background. Available at: http://app.ps21.gov.sg/newps21/default.asp?id=21 (accessed December 4, 2007).

Public Service for the 21st Century (PS21) Office (2006). Rising Popularity of e-Government. Available at: http://www.ps21.gov.sg/challenge/2006_07/service/service.html (accessed December 4, 2007).

Case 2

SINGAPORE E-GOVERNMENT INITIATIVES: ENGAGING USERS

Calvin Chan

SIM University, Singapore

Pan Shan Ling

National University of Singapore

BACKGROUND

In 2000, the Singapore Government initiated the electronic government (e-Government) Action Plan to make all government services to be available online. The Government provides funding to its agencies to support their efforts to implement e-Government systems. Here, we describe the implementation of two separate e-Government systems by a single Singapore government agency. For reasons of confidentiality, the identity of this agency and the two e-Government systems are assigned the pseudonyms of SINGA, SINGA-ALPHA and SINGA-BETA, respectively.

CASE 2.1 SINGA-ALPHA

In Singapore, foreign students who wish to pursue courses offered by the local Institutes of Higher Learning (IHLs) have to apply for a student pass (STP) from SINGA. These IHLs include the local polytechnics and universities, as well as foreign universities with offshore campuses in Singapore. Prior to 2003, an applicant who had been accepted in any of these IHLs would have to visit the SINGA's Visitor Service Centre (VSC) on at least three separate occasions before he/she could be issued a STP. For a start, an applicant had to apply personally at the VSC counter by submitting the letter of acceptance issued by the IHLs and other official documents such as passports and academic certificates before being issued with an In-Principle Approval (IPA)1 letter. Then he/she had to undergo medical examination before submitting the medical report to SINGA. If all conditions were satisfied, the student would have to make a final trip to collect the STP. However it was not uncommon that an applicant had to make four trips or more as a result of misunderstanding the terminology used to describe various documents, thus resulting in inconvenience for these applicants.

During the peak period between June and July, before the start of the new academic year, officers at VSC would have to process a large number of STP applications and cope with the sudden influx of human traffic at their counters. The high volume of STP applications, coupled with the tight processing schedules, often taxed the entire customer service unit to the limit. Thus in some cases, the STP application process would take as long as five weeks before approval is given, which sometimes clashes with the academic calendar of the IHLs. An admission officer from an IHL explained, "During peak period, they cannot finish [the STP] on time. Sometimes I even have to go to [SINGA] and plead with them because these student passes have to come out on time."

In view of the government's strategic plan to develop Singapore into an education hub and increase the population of foreign students by another 10%, the SINGA-ALPHA project manager explained the rationale for the system, "we needed to improve our service and portray ourselves as a well-organised agency ready to move forward and meet, or even exceed, customers' expectations."

Diagnosing the situation, SINGA proposed an online application and registration e-service, SINGA-ALPHA. The targeted users of SINGA-ALPHA are essentially foreigners intending to study in Singapore as they need to register themselves with SINGA and get the necessary legal permit to stay in Singapore. Through SINGA-ALPHA, it was hoped that it would trim the need for excess manpower resource, reduce the frequency of trips as well as the period of waiting time for the foreign students. SINGA perceived

SINGA-ALPHA as a "significant (e-service) initiative that cut across various organisations to provide a seamless service to the applicant."

Consequently, SINGA roped in the IHLs as a surrogate to get the user requirements. The project manager mentioned, "IHLs were the ones liaising directly with the students. So they can represent the feedback and requirements of students.... If we can meet the requirements of the IHLs, we can meet the requirements of the students." Moreover, a manager in SINGA also revealed a perception that, "foreign students are a more captive audience so we just leave it to the IHLs to inform them of [SINGA-ALPHA].... No training or publicity was done for the students.... Furthermore, it makes a lot of sense for these students to submit via [SINGA-ALPHA] as it's simpler and faster."

As soon as it was decided that IHLs will be included in the implementation of SINGA-ALPHA, SINGA immediately got in touch with them. A member of the development team recalled, "We informed the IHLs that we've decided to go ahead even before we really started the project... we talked to them regarding the development of [SINGA-ALPHA] and the cooperation needed to build a common interface."

Through consultation with the IHLs, SINGA discovered that much repetition and redundancy existed in the traditional application process. For instance, a student's particulars had to be entered twice: once into the IHL's system and then again into SINGA's back-end system. The project manager remarked, "if I were to register 100 students, I would have to carry out the process 100 times. Alternatively, since the data is already residing in the IHL's system, I could simply upload the data from one system to another."

In view of these inherent inefficiencies, SINGA proposed a re-engineering of the application process. Instead of having the applicants go to SINGA to submit the letter of acceptance to obtain the IPA letter, SINGA suggested an integration of IHL admission and STP application processes. In this new workflow, the task of printing and issuing IPA letters, as well as the verification of the applicant's documents would be taken over by the IHLs. Therefore, a foreign student who had successfully applied to one of the IHLs would now receive the IPA letter with the acceptance letter. In the meantime, the particulars of successful applicants would be automatically uploaded to the SINGA-ALPHA system. Applicants would also have to liaise with the IHLs for verifications of the required legal documents, who would in turn upload the results to SINGA-ALPHA. SINGA would only start the actual processing of STP after the applicant has accepted an offer for a place in a particular IHL by applying through SINGA-ALPHA and affirmative results have been received from that IHL. The entire application process would be completed when the applicant presents the endorsed medical report at the VSC counter, whereby the STP is issued.

This new workflow would slash the approval time from five weeks to between three to ten days, depending on the applicant's nationality. In addition, the applicant would only need to make one visit to SINGA, for the collection of STP. According to the VSC's manager on the expected benefits of SINGA-ALPHA, "[SINGA-ALPHA] system would be able to handle the high workload, reduce the processing time and crowd volume at VSC. More importantly, the IHLs and foreign students could experience a straightforward, convenient and efficient system when applying for STP."

However, the IHLs were initially wary about taking over some of the work traditionally done by SINGA. For example a senior officer at an IL shared, "What would happen if a prospective student does not turn up and pass the IPA to a friend? Passports can be fabricated to match the details on the IPA so as to gain illegal entry to Singapore. Since I'm the one issuing the IPA, will I be held responsible?"

Thus, efforts were made to address the IHLs' concerns and measures were taken to seek their coorporation and commitment to SINGA-ALPHA. SINGA had to convince the IHLs of the possible benefits by participating in the implementation of SINGA-ALPHA. A member of the operational team explained, "It's really a matter of coaxing and enticing IHLs with the prospect that their process would be sped up and students would have fewer problems with their applications."

Besides highlighting the possible operational benefits, SINGA also stressed on developing a strategic convergence of interest with the IHLs by emphasising the common interest that they shared in advancing the government's long term strategic plan to develop Singapore into a premier education hub. The project manager commented, "Both [SINGA] and IHLs shared the common interest in making Singapore into an education hub…. They were helping us, helping the government by attracting foreign students to Singapore…. They will also be benefiting from this."

SINGA also adopted a give-and-take approach when dealing with IHLs during the implementation. For instance, when some of the IHLs requested for printers to print IPA letters, SINGA agreed and gave each IHL new sets of computers, printers and even reams of paper. The project manager explained, "We cannot just do a system and then impose it on them. We didn't want this type of working relationship…. We discussed a lot with the IHLs, to work out and formulate how best everyone can work together and meet everybody's needs…. There's a lot of give-and-take, like we are providing the PCs for them to do the registration because we are actually getting them to help us with screening applications and verifying documents."

An admission officer with an IHL also disclosed, "Initially, they wanted the IHLs to collect application fees and students' passport…. Then we said, "We can't be doing this." I think all the IHLs raised the concern that we don't want to be the custodian for hundreds of passports and be responsible for it. This should be [SINGA]'s job. [So] eventually it was narrowed down and we don't have to collect money nor passports."

The project manager of SINGA-ALPHA felt that such a give-and-take approach has helped in developing the IHLs' commitment to SINGA-ALPHA and offered this as evidence, "We did not demand that the IHLs participate in all progress meetings. But most of the time, they were present, sometimes even bringing in three or four people to the meetings!"

The IHLs were also involved in the testing of the prototype prior to the launch of SINGA-ALPHA. The purpose of this was to ensure that the final system matched the requirements and expectations of the IHLs. In addition, classroom style user training sessions were conducted for the IHLs' admission officers who would actually be using the system. User manuals were also prepared by SINGA and given to the IHLs for future reference. The project manager commented, "We trained them on how to check if an application has been uploaded successfully.... We explained various issues to them."

However, the foreign students were never included in any of the training. Instead, the task of training the foreign students was delegated to the IHLs. A number of IHLs did so by preparing a step-by-step guide for students.

SINGA-ALPHA was launched in January 2003 and has since consistently processed more than 90% of the total annual STP applications. In view of such remarkable and impressive take-up rate, SINGA discontinued the manual mode of application in January 2005, thus making SINGA-ALPHA the only available channel for STP application. Manual applications would only be accepted in exceptional situations whereby the foreign students are unable to apply through the online channel. The success of SINGA-ALPHA had also endeavored SINGA to extend the scope of SINGA-ALPHA to include private institutions and other lower level schools. The SINGA's Director of the Planning & Technology Division assessed the system, "[SINGA-ALPHA] has been a very good and successful story. I think it's because it is so convenient to go to this e-service... it's a win–win situation for all three parties [SINGA, IHLs and students]."

Indeed, an admission officer from one of the IHLs attested to the improvements, "... From the customer service point of view, [SINGA-ALPHA] is something I would say is really good, in the sense that it has shortened the period, so it has become more efficient in terms of operation, even for us, for the students.... It's much neater in that sense. I think they [foreign students] are happy [with the application process] and also happy with us."

Even after the initial launch of SINGA-ALPHA, the IHLs continued to raise new requirements to SINGA. An admission officer in an IHL described one such instance, "My staff noticed that the system couldn't sort the results in certain orders. We felt that the sorting function would be very useful for us. So we asked them to add in the function so that we can sort the results, etc. They agreed with no fuss."

Furthermore, SINGA also conducted post-mortem exercises with the IHLs at the end of each admission period so as to cross-examine problems and issues that might arise in an admission exercise. This feedback would form the basis of improvements to be incorporated into the system for the next year. A senior officer from an IHL commented, "The post-mortem exercises are really good because we could then present the problems we have faced, and more importantly, there is proper follow-up after that.... They send the minutes listing the things that we raised and what they have done. So we know exactly whether our suggestions are implemented or not, and the reasons behind it. This convinces me that for any project, users must feel that they are moving along with the project. For the past two years, I had very fruitful post-mortem meetings with them."

CASE 2.2 SINGA-BETA

Prior to 1999, there were only two channels available for prospective applicants who wished to apply or renew their official identification documents: (1) Applying at SINGA's Citizens Services Center (CSC) counters or (2) filling up an application form which is available in SINGA's reception desk and submitting it through the deposit boxes located in the SINGA building. After the application had been processed, the applicant would have to make another trip to collect the official identification documents. Both channels required the citizens to make two trips to SINGA, one for application and another for collection. This procedure was time-consuming and inconvenient for both the applicant and SINGA. As explained by the operational manager of SINGA-BETA, "In the past, one has to come over [to SINGA] to make an application and then a week later, he/she has to come again, to collect the [official identification documents].... It means that you need more staff to handle those that are coming to apply and those coming to collect."

In 1998, SINGA conducted a Business Process Reengineering (BPR) exercise on its operations to identify areas for improvements, in order to boost its productivity and service levels. Apart from contriving plans to revamp the current workflows, a vision of becoming a "one-stop" service centre was also conceived. As noted by the project manager of SINGA-BETA, "Over at SINGA, we have a broad strategy to reduce as far as possible the number of public interface(s). This means reducing the time needed to deal with the public, face to face. We also want to reduce the number of trips required by the public to come here to just one. This would translate to better convenience to the public."

Subsequently, a local IT solutions provider and an internationally renowned consulting firm were brought in for a full-scale consultancy study to assist in bringing the vision to life. As a result of the study, the consultants suggested the inclusion of a postage channel for the application or renewal of the official identification documents. This suggestion was accepted and eventually implemented in 1999. This meant applicants who were applying for an official identification document for the first time had the option of downloading the application form from SINGA website, completing the form, and posting it to SINGA.

For renewal cases, a renewal notice card would be sent to the applicant's residential address and because his/her personal data already resides in SINGA system, he/she only needed to attach an official identification document photo on the card and post it back to SINGA. This new channel was highly popular as it provided convenience to the public. The postage channel's success was attested by the fact that more than 75% of current annual official identification documents applications came through it. The project manager of SINGA-BETA gave his insights on the benefits of the postage channel, "For application by post, you don't need to come down to [SINGA to] apply... you just need to send in by post and come down [to SINGA] when you need to collect it. The payment can be done by cheque or they can choose to pay when they come down to collect. That means only one group of officers is needed to handle the public while the other [group] can do the processing.... This is a progression."

Two years after the BPR study, the Singapore Government initiated the e-Government Action Plan to make all government services to be available online. Through this e-Government Action Plan, agencies could apply for central government funding to support their efforts to implement e-Government systems. Given the success of the postage channel, SINGA began to look into the possibility of introducing an online application channel, which was also suggested by the consultants during the consultancy study but was not implemented. An operational manager of SINGA-BETA described the climate at that time, "It was during the dot.com boom. Dot.com was a very popular and sexy word. Everyone was saying that we should try to push everything online."

It was under such a climate that the decision to implement SINGA-BETA was made. The targeted users of SINGA-BETA were Singapore citizens who needed to apply for their official identification documents from SINGA. Through SINGA-BETA, SINGA hoped to add an additional mode of application for the citizens, which allowed them to apply and pay online anytime, and at the convenience and comfort of their homes. In addition, these applicants can also access the system to enquire about their application status, the collection date and the necessary supporting documents required for collection. Similar to the postage channel, applicants would only need to make one trip to SINGA building for collection. As noted from the senior manager of SINGA's Citizens Services Centre (CSC) on the objectives of SINGA-BETA, "[SINGA-BETA] is meant to enhance service standards… we aim to give applicants greater flexibility and convenience."

SINGA also believed that with the introduction of SINGA-BETA, operating costs could be pared down as well. For instance, postage charges and printing costs incurred by SINGA for sending out the reminder cards to inform the applicants of the collection of their official documents could be reduced since notifications would be sent via email. The project manager elaborated on the possible advantages of SINGA-BETA, "I will say the amount of attention needed for [SINGA-BETA] is definitely a lot lower than that of counter. You can probably handle 20 over cases just on

[SINGA-BETA] in an hour but it's quite unlikely that you can do that over the counter. We want to really boost up our online usage because it's of benefit to us — if we push the bulk of the applications to the internet then we could have some cost-savings such as closing down the counter or cutting back the staff that need to process the transactions. These are (our) long term goals."

During the design of SINGA-BETA, one of the key challenges was the online submission of a digital photograph. The photograph needed to be of a certain resolution, which might not be easy for a layperson to produce. The operational manager explained, "... if you take a digital photo of yourself, you may have to crop it yourself and then do touch-up to it. [However,] if you go to a photo studio to take a photo, it can be exactly the size that we require."

Moreover, it was thought that the photo studios could also act as an intermediary for those citizens who might not be IT-savvy to transact using SINGA-BETA. A SINGA officer remarked, "Not everyone uses the Internet or owns a PC.... There are groups of people you cannot reach if you offer only e-services."

In view of this issue and to make online application effortless for the applicants, SINGA tried to bring in privately owned photo studios into the project through talks with the photo studios association. In addition, the Singapore government also administrated a reward scheme, which would pay out a fee for every successful transaction on SINGA-BETA. It was hoped that through this scheme, vendors would be enticed to partake in this project thus boosting SINGA-BETA take-up rate. A member of the development team explained, "We thought that through the collaboration [with photo studios], we could at least shift 50% of the present cases over... then we could have a strong boost in the take-up rate."

Another key challenge was overcoming the security concerns in allowing online submissions of file attachments because malicious software virus could easily be uploaded into SINGA-BETA and infiltrate [SINGA's] IT infrastructure. Understandably, this became a more urgent challenge than the digital photograph and thus became a central focus throughout the implementation of SINGA-BETA. Comparatively, the digital photograph issue was sidelined and efforts to engage photo studios and citizens only occurred in the later stages of implementation, after the technical solution to counter the security concerns was found. The operational manager of SINGA-BETA described the process of engaging the photo studios, "We briefed members of the [photo] studio association before the project launch.... We wanted to alert them that it could affect their business.... We wanted to let them know our digital specifications so that they could consider rolling out digital photos and helping customers go on board [SINGA-BETA]."

None of the photo studios or the citizens was involved in the testing of SINGA-BETA. The operational manager shared, "It was our staff that actually tried out the system and gave their assessments as to which features were missing. We assessed how well they used the system in terms of user-friendliness."

SINGA-BETA was finally launched after several rounds of testing. Training for photo studios was only limited to a briefing session and a self-help CD from SINGA. Although there was no training conducted for citizens, considerable efforts were invested in publicising SINGA-BETA to them SINGA officers were sent to relevant community fairs and road-shows to promote SINGA-BETA to potential users. A member of the development team explained, "We wanted to create awareness among the people. They may not need the documents straightaway but at least we can tell them that they can actually get it online when they need it later."

As more citizens transact on SINGA-BETA, some of them also voluntarily sent their feedback to SINGA which helped to enhance the system. The project manager commented, "People who transacted on [SINGA-BETA] gave their feedback, and much of it has proven useful. Many service requests were raised in response to the feedback."

An example of such enhancements was the inclusion of a photograph editing function so that SINGA officers could edit the photographs to the required quality. Even though SINGA had already predicted possible issues pertaining to the photograph attachment, it certainly did not expect an overwhelming percentage of submitted digital photographs to fail the requirement. Through feedback from the public, SINGA realised the shortcoming and took immediate actions to rectify it. A member of the development team described the remedial action, "With the photo-editing software installed in our processing system, our officers would try to salvage the photos that may not meet our requirements. In this way, we could improve the acceptance rate."

SINGA-BETA was launched in May 2002, and to date it has only managed to garner approximately 10% of the total annual official identification documents applications. The project manager of SINGA-BETA summed up the current status of the service, "as of now, the usage [rate] is still not ideal... it's still less than 10%."

DISCUSSION QUESTIONS

1. Why did SINGA decide to implement SINGA-ALPHA and SINGA-BETA?
2. What were the differences and similarities in the way SINGA implemented SINGA-ALPHA and SINGA-BETA?
3. What were the challenges SINGA faced in implementing the two systems? Were the challenges similar?
4. In your opinion, why do you think SINGA-ALPHA has achieved a higher take-up rate than SINGA-BETA?

Case 3

DEVELOPING A CUSTOMER-CENTRIC, INCLUSIVE E-GOVERNMENT: LESSONS FROM THE CENTRAL PROVIDENT FUND BOARD OF SINGAPORE

Barney Tan

University of Sydney

Pan Shan Ling and Virginia Cha

National University of Singapore

BACKGROUND

In Singapore, all working citizens, together with their employers, are required by law to contribute a percentage of their monthly income to the Central Provident Fund (CPF), a social security savings plan established in 1955 for the purpose of providing financial security for the people of Singapore in their retirement. Today, the CPF has evolved into a comprehensive social security savings package that encompasses the retirement, healthcare, home ownership, family protection, and asset enhancement needs of Singaporeans. The money in a citizen's CPF account can be used for housing, insurance, healthcare, and investment prior to retirement, and when the citizen retires, he/she would receive a monthly retirement stipend paid out from their own accumulated CPF savings.

The government agency established to administer the CPF is the CPF Board. Positioned as the trustee of the citizens' CPF savings, its organisational mission is to enable Singaporeans to save effectively for a secure retirement. Its business activities include (1) the collection of

CPF contributions, (2) the disbursement of an individual's CPF savings for various needs, and (3) educating Singaporeans on the importance of making prudent use of their CPF savings and the need to plan for a financially secure retirement. At the end of 2006, it was estimated that the CPF Board serves 3.1 million members,[4] manages US\$83 billion of CPF savings and conducts over 31.2 million transactions a year.

My cpf is CPF's hoslistic customer service framework (see Table 3.1). Between 2005 and 2008, *my cpf* received several international awards. The multi-award winning framework leverages on ICT for the purpose of serving and educating its members, empowering them to plan and act effectively for a secure retirement through their different life stages. As a strong testimony to the effectiveness of the *my cpf* framework, a customer satisfaction survey conducted at the end of 2006 found that 99.3% of the members surveyed were satisfied with the public services provided by the CPF Board, while the complaints to compliments received ratio for the year 2007 was an impressive 1:49.

At the heart of the vastly successful *my cpf* framework is the *cpf* online portal (see Figure 3.1), a website that provides personalised, integrated online services to the members of the CPF Board. The *my cpf* online portal is recognised as one of the top public service websites in Singapore in a number of independent studies conducted by Yahoo Singapore, Hitwise, and the Singapore government. This is a

Table 3.1:   List of International Awards for *my cpf*.

Award	Year
United Nations Public Service Award Finalist	2005 and 2006
CAPAM (Commonwealth Association for Public Administration and Management) International Innovations Award and Commendation	2006
APICTA (Asia-Pacific Infocomm Technology Award) Finalist	2006
Government Technology Awards (Service Innovations) — Winner	2007
APICTA (Singapore League) — Winner	2007
Stockholm Challenge Award — Finalist	2008

[4]At the time of the case, Singapore had a total population of around 4.5 million and more than 68% of Singaporeans are members of the CPF Board.

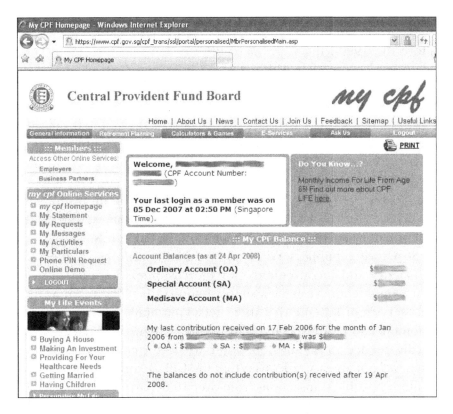

Figure 3.1:   *my cpf* online portal.

considerable achievement given that Singapore is a country that has consistently been ranked as one of the world's leading e-Government nations and has attained a high general level of e-Government maturity across the entire public sector. As of 2006, 95% of the CPF Board's transactions were conducted via the *my cpf* online portal, and according to the customer satisfaction survey conducted in the same year, 92.3% of the members surveyed were satisfied with the quality of the electronic services (e-services) provided.

While these statistics firmly attest to the effectiveness and success of *my cpf* today, prior to the introduction of the customer service framework, administration of the CPF was a process that was representative of the classic model of hierarchical bureaucracy, and was both inefficient and time-consuming.

PUBLIC SERVICE DELIVERY BEFORE *my cpf*

Before the 1990s, the CPF Board did not have an integrated customer service function within the organisation. Instead, it had a function-based organisational structure that divided the activities of the organisation according to the different CPF schemes and services available. A Customer Service Officer (CSO) who has been with the CPF Board for over 17 years described the state of public service delivery, "We had different departments on different floors (of the building). So if customers have an enquiry on housing, they'll have to go to the 35th floor. And if they have an enquiry on insurance, they'll have to go to the 36th floor.... If they have business with more than one department, they have to go to different levels."

Structuring public services along functional lines resulted in inefficiency and inconvenience for the customers because to perform a transaction or make a simple enquiry, they had to know the exact service or scheme that their needs pertained to. In addition, customers had to approach the right department that manages the specific service or scheme in order to perform the transaction, which was not an easy task given that the CPF Board provides over a hundred possible transactions from over 10 departments. And if the customers wished to perform multiple transactions or enquiries with different departments of the CPF Board, they had to join the queue at each of the departments separately.

In a bid to improve the efficiency and effectiveness of public service delivery, an integrated Customer Service department was established in June 1995. Integrating the different CPF schemes and services governed by different functional departments within the organisation, the integrated Customer Service department was structured according to three business processes: (1) Withdrawals; for CPF members who have reached the age of retirement or are leaving Singapore, (2) Schemes; that encompasses the various CPF schemes for housing, healthcare, investment and insurance, and (3) Employer Services; that provided services for the employers of CPF members. Yet, although the myriad of schemes and services offered by the CPF Board were distilled into the three business processes and housed within five "one-stop service centres" that were scattered across Singapore, customers still had to join different queues if their needs involved more than a single business process.

In a parallel development, the CPF Board established their first website in 1996. It began as an informational website that provided information on the various CPF schemes and services available at the CPF Board but within months, electronic versions of the various transaction forms of the CPF Board were made available on the website as well. The Director of Customer Relations at the CPF board described the form and function of the first CPF website, "When we started to provide things on the Internet platform, we were only 'e-enabling' our transactions and services.... So if we have a form for a transaction on paper, we will convert that transaction into an electronic format.... Our website was organised into more than 10 'handbooks' representing the various schemes that we have.... But at the end of the day, we have changed the service platform but we did not change the service experience because the customer still has to remember which department he is dealing with and go to the right platform to complete his transaction."

Structuring the website along functional lines made it difficult to navigate and use. Yet, the website was fairly well-received by the members of the CPF Board. The website processed about 200,000 transactions within the first year of its inception when the Internet penetration rate in Singapore was only 9% and by 2002, the website was handling over two million transactions a year. Although the establishment of an integrated customer service department and a website that supported electronic transactions had improved the quality of the CPF Board's services to some extent, the convergence of two significant events created a pressing need for a more efficient and effective mode of public service delivery.

DRIVERS OF *my cpf*

The first event was the appointment of the CPF Board to a new national role by the Singapore government. At the height of the Asian Financial Crisis and the global economic downturn, the

Singapore government announced the New Singapore Shares scheme in August 2001, which aimed at helping the lower income group tide over the adverse economic conditions. All eligible Singaporeans were given between US$147 and US$1,250 worth of "New Singapore Shares" which they could either redeem for cash, or retain in return for a guaranteed 3% dividend per annum. As the CPF Board was the public agency that served the broadest base of Singaporeans in the public sector, the organisation was appointed to implement the scheme. Since 2001, four other economic policies were announced by the Singapore government and similarly administered by the CPF Board: The Economic Restructuring Shares scheme between 2003 and 2005, the Progress Package in 2006, the Goods and Services Tax Offset Package in 2007, and the Growth Dividends scheme in 2008.

During the initial phase of administering the new economic policies, as the important dates for each of the schemes approached (e.g., the first day in which the shares be redeemed for cash), hundreds and thousands of Singaporeans swamp the CPF service centres, forming long snaking queues (Figure 3.2) that resulted in public dissatisfaction. The Senior Assistant Director of Service Planning and Research at the CPF Board described how the new national role of the CPF Board fueled the conviction of the organisation to further improve on the efficiency and effectiveness of its customer service, "the NSS…. is meant to be a good thing right? But you see very old ladies or gentlemen who are struggling to come to our offices just so that they can tick a form that says 'yes, we want to sign up for this scheme.'… And we feel that it is a very sad sight for an otherwise happy occasion… so is there something that we can do?" The second event was an internal review conducted as part of the organisation's drive for continuous improvement. A market study conducted as part of the review indicated that by the end of 2001, the CPF Board had become one of the leading service organisations in the Singapore public sector. Yet, as service standards across many industries were steadily improving, the study found that the customers of the CPF Board were growing increasingly sophisticated and were starting to demand for an even higher level of service quality.

In the old days at CPF

Figure 3.2:   Long queues outside a CPF service centre.

The Senior Assistant Director of Service Planning and Research elaborated, "At that time when we centralised our call centre and established our one-stop service centres, a lot of (organisations in) the public sector weren't there yet. Because we've already reached that stage and people know us for giving very good, courteous, quality, one-stop services, the question was where next to go.... We realised that, increasingly, as the population became more sophisticated and people were no longer happy with just this kind of service. So we asked ourselves... how do we take the next step?"

With the realisation that the organisation-centric, function-based mode of public service delivery adopted on both the CPF Board's website and one-stop service centres was inadequate for taking on the new national role of administering the Singapore government's economic policies and meeting the growing expectations of their customers, the management of the CPF Board was stirred into action. A committee was formally established by the management of the CPF Board to look into ways of improving the effectiveness and efficiency of the public services provided by the organisation in 2002. The recommendations of the committee led to the conception of *my cpf* customer service framework.

THE NEED FOR e-GOVERNMENT

The primary focus of the initial *my cpf* framework was to serve customers from a customer-centric perspective through concept of "Service by Life Events," which essentially integrated the vast array of services and information provided by the CPF board into bundles of services that is relevant to the various stages of life a customer may be in. The Senior Assistant Director of Service Planning and Research at the CPF Board elaborated on the rationale behind the "Service by Life Events" concept, "We realised that in our customers' mind, they come to us not based on our schemes, but it's more like 'I'm getting married... so I need to go to the CPF and do something.' A person getting married may need to buy a house or change their nomination (of the beneficiary who will receive their CPF Savings in the event of death before the age of retirement)... so if we serve them with all these related needs (at one time), it will prevent them from having to come to us repeatedly. And at the same time it saves us (time and effort), as we don't have to keep advising them on different issues (each time they come)...."

Trial implementation of the "Service by Life Events" concept was carried out in the service centres in mid-2002 as the process-based structure of the service centres made way for "one-stop service counters"; single counters that catered to all the needs of an individual customer regardless of the business processes, schemes or transactions involved. By embracing "Service by Life Events," the prior organisational-centric, function-based mode of public service delivery was replaced by a customer-centric, events-based model that is more effective in meeting the customers' needs. Yet, servicing customers by life events created a problem for the CPF Board. The Director of Customer Relations elaborated on the new problem faced by the organisation, "the initiative came at a very high cost. Our transaction costs go up because the interaction time is longer... it's easy to provide good customer service if you have endless resources... but it doesn't work that way in the public sector because excellent customer service will not get us any business returns...."

To find a solution that mitigates the spiraling costs of serving customers by life events at the service counters, the management of the CPF Board performed comprehensive analyses of their existing business processes, the external environment, and their customers. From the analyses, the management gained three critical insights. First, from their experience with providing electronic transactions through the CPF Board's website, the management realised that if a significant portion of the transactions carried out at the traditional service counters could be brought onto the electronic platform, considerable savings can be achieved. To illustrate, an internal review found that the cost of a single counter transaction was estimated at US$18.34. In comparison, the cost of a single e-transaction was estimated at only US$0.55.

Second, the management of the CPF Board realised that the population in general was becoming more Internet-savvy. The Internet Penetration Rate of Singapore had risen to 65% in 2003, and a large proportion of the population was already familiar with using and conducting electronic transactions over the Internet. Consequently, this made the provision of public services via the electronic channel more viable as the public was likely to be more receptive towards the initiative. Third, the management of the CPF Board realised that if they could move the majority of its transactions onto the electronic platform, it would allow the CPF Board to focus its resources at their service centres on the segments of their customers such as the elderly, the illiterate, and the poor, who needed it the most.

The three insights gained by the management of the CPF Board converged on a single solution: the development of an effective, customer-centric e-Government that would facilitate the migration of the majority of the customers who were using the traditional counter services onto the electronic platform. Consequently, the decision was made to perform a complete makeover of its existing website and reposition the *my cpf* framework as a predominantly online initiative with a strong emphasis on electronic public service delivery. This monumental decision marked the beginning of the CPF Board's e-Government journey.

E-GOVERNMENT DEVELOPMENT PHASE 1: EARLY 2003–EARLY 2004

In the initial phase of e-Government development, the focus of the CPF Board was on structuring the information provided on their website from a customer-centric perspective. The existing website was difficult to navigate and use as the information and services provided on the website were structured along functional lines. The Director of Customer Relations illustrated the limitations of the organisation-centric structure of the e-services on the existing website with an example, "There was this (electronic) form called 'RPS/4.' It stands for Residential Property Scheme Form 4. The form is used to change the monthly installment amount for a member's housing needs.... But even if they saw the form on our website, based on the name of the form, how would the customers know what the form was for?"

As the customers' perspective of the information and services they require stems from the life events that they are currently experiencing, the decision was made in early 2003 to replicate the "Service by Life Events" concept on the electronic channel. The first step taken by the CPF Board in December 2003 was the establishment of five major life events that typically created the highest volume of enquiries. The five life events were: starting work, getting married, having children, buying a house, and making an investment. Through a major revamp of the content on the existing website, all the information pertaining to the CPF schemes and services that were relevant to the five life events were categorised accordingly. The Director of Customer Relations at the CPF Board explained, "We started small.... Our thinking was 'Let's start off with the major life events and see the customers' reaction'... and I think the reaction was very positive..."

Guided by the objective to migrate the customers who were using the traditional counter services onto the electronic platform, besides restructuring the information on the website, the CPF Board also adopted measures to introduce the revamped website to their members. At the end of 2003, "e-lobbies"; designated areas with self-service terminals that could be used to access the CPF website, were established at all CPF service centers across Singapore. In addition, a handful of CSOs at each service center were designated as "e-ambassadors" according to a daily roster. The e-ambassadors were stationed at the e-lobbies and their responsibilities include introducing members to the revamped website, helping members conduct electronic transactions whenever possible, and educating members by highlighting the convenience and cost savings of using the electronic channel. Yet, the expanded role of the CSOs created a problem, particularly among older CSOs. A CSO described the problem and the measures adopted by the CPF Board to overcome the problem, "When the e-ambassador (initiative) first started, we were actually quite apprehensive. Especially among older CSOs… they were like 'Computers? I don't know how to use them.'… But they (the management) trained us on what is available on the website… and we are encouraged to experiment (with the website) on our own…. Soon we realised that it (the new website) is a very good thing… no more hardcopies, no more brochures to give out… and everything is updated immediately…. We no longer have to check the expiry dates of the forms and brochures…."

The initial phase of e-Government development began in early 2003 and lasted for a little over a year. At the end of the phase, the restructuring of information according to the five major life events defined by the CPF Board was completed, and an electronic transaction for the withdrawal of CPF funds was included on the website. To facilitate electronic transactions, "Singapore Personal Access" (SingPass); a confidential password of between 8 and 24 alphanumeric characters that provided a mechanism for individual customers to identify themselves, was established in March 2003. Once again, as the CPF Board was the public organisation that served the broadest base of citizens in Singapore, the SingPass was adopted by the Singapore Government as a common national password that enabled citizens to transact with different government agencies across the Singapore public sector.

The initiative to replicate the "Service by Life Events" concept on the website proved to be very successful and by the end of 2003, the number of transactions handled on the website had increased exponentially to 8 million a year while the average service cost per CPF member stood at approximately US$16.30. In addition, although a customer satisfaction survey conducted in 2003 revealed that only 62.2% of customers were satisfied with the e-services available on the website, the CPF Board received numerous positive reviews of the revamped website from their members. For instance, a member of the CPF Board described his experience with the revamped website, "I was amazed when I logged into the CPF Website today. The changes done to the website reflects exactly what I wanted to see the moment I login to CPF. (I) appreciate the effort invested in improving the website...."

E-GOVERNMENT DEVELOPMENT PHASE 2:
EARLY 2004 TO MID-2005

Encouraged by the initial success from the concerted organisational effort at developing a holistic e-Government framework, the CPF Board established two objectives in the next phase of e-Government development. First, the CPF Board sought to rebrand the CPF website to emphasise the new customer orientation of the online platform. To achieve the first objective, an extensive rebranding exercise was conducted that led to the conception of the *my cpf* website in March 2004. The Director of Customer Relations described the rationale and nature of this rebranding exercise, "Every time the customers come to our counter, they will ask 'where is my CPF?'.... We realised that this is an emotional term that we can use to connect with our customers. So we rebranded our website '*my cpf*!' With a simple change in words, you switch to a customer perspective ... From then on, all our services are rebranded from a customer perspective....

instead of calling it (an e-service) "CPF Online Statement," we call it "My Statement," "My Requests," "My Messages".... It empowers the customers and makes them feel that the CPF Board is customising everything for them."

The second objective of the CPF Board was to develop a comprehensive suite of e-services that were personalised and tailored to the needs of individual CPF members. Facilitated by SingPass, which provided a mechanism for identifying each CPF member individually, four e-services; named "My Statements," "My Messages," "My Requests," and "My Activities," were launched between August and October 2004. Collectively known as the "*my cpf* Online Services," the newly launched e-services were designed to be complementary with each other, and the informational pages (rebranded as "*my cpf* Life Events") developed in the earlier phase. In tandem, *my cpf* Online Services and *my cpf* Life Events formed a tightly integrated package of information and services that members of the CPF Board can access on "anytime, anywhere" basis. Table 3.2 provides a description of the four e-services and how they effected service transformation at the CPF Board.

The rebranding initiative and the development of a complementary suite of personalised services resulted in a phenomenal twofold increase in the number of transactions conducted online. By the end of 2004, the *my cpf* website was handling 16 million transactions a year. Yet, the rapid migration of the CPF members onto the electronic platform revealed a growing digital divide. In particular, the use of the SingPass proved to be problematic, especially among older citizens.

A member of the Innovation Committee at the CPF Board elaborated, "During a routine walkabout, one of our directors noted that many of our older members were having difficulty remembering their SingPass.... Some of them would go to the counters to reset their SingPass, but by the time they make their way to a (self-service) terminal, they would have forgotten the new SingPass that they were given just moments ago! So he (the director) sent us an email saying 'You know this SingPass, you don't expect older people to use it. Have you thought of other solutions?'"

Table 3.2:   *my cpf* online services.

My Statement (Implemented in August 2004)	*Before "My Statement"*: CPF Members had 24 different CPF statements for the various CPF schemes. To retrieve the statements, they had to request for the different statements to be mailed or navigate through layers of information on the website to retrieve the desired statement.
	With "My Statement": All the statements are integrated in a single, easy-to-read page, with an easy-to-use interface that enables customers to drill down to the required level of detail for each of the different CPF statements.
My Requests (Implemented in September 2004)	*Before "My Request"*: The CPF Board had more than 10 different schemes and offered over a hundred different transactions. Consequently, locating the right application form in order to enact the correct transaction with the CPF Board required effort and knowledge on the part of the customers.
	With "My Request": The hundreds of transactions from the various CPF schemes are organised according to a comprehensive step-by-step guide. Navigating a series of easy-to-understand options, customers are able to drill down through layers of information to the desired online form that enables them to transact electronically with the CPF Board.
My Activities (Implemented in September 2004)	*Before "My Activities"*: After submitting a form to the CPF Board, customers are not updated with the status of their transactions. As a result, some customers may forget about the transactions or services they had requested.
	With "My Activities": "My Activities" tracks the status of the transactions conducted and informs the customers of the latest status of all their electronic or paper-based transactions with the CPF Board. At a glance, customers would be able to tell immediately if their transactions have been received, processed, rejected or approved.
My Messages (Implemented in October 2004)	*Before "My Messages"*: The CPF Board took a passive approach to public service delivery. Requests for information and services had to be initiated by the consumer before a transaction could be completed. Efforts aimed at educating CPF members to actively plan for their retirement are limited on the electronic channel as they have to be initiated by the customers.
	With "My Messages": Based on information on the customer and their transaction history, "My Messages" provides customers with personalised messages encompassing all the schemes and services that are relevant to the life stages they are in. This promotes better retirement planning for the members of the CPF Board as they can now make informed decisions relating to their retirement.

At that point in time, a team from the IT department happened to be studying biometric technology and evaluating its applicability to the services of the CPF Board. The email from the top management that highlighted the problems with the use of SingPass thus struck a chord with the team, and a proposal for a biometric solution to the problem was pitched and eventually approved and implemented in March 2004. The solution took the form of a biometric e-counter, a self-service terminal that would allow a user to log into his CPF account using his thumbprint.

The leader of the biometric e-counters team detailed the problems encountered during the implementation and described how the problems were overcome, "We initially thought of linking our biometric system with the national database. But the ICA[5] said that the national database cannot be used for 'mere enquiries'.... There were many security concerns.... But we realised that we can match thumbprints on the fly using our NRICs....[6] The security risks are minimal... and if the NRIC is defective, there is no match. And that won't matter because it is just an alternative. They can still go to the counter to use SingPass, or we'll advise them to replace their NRIC."

The second phase of e-Government development began in early 2004 and was completed by mid-2005. At the end of the phase, the organisational website was rebranded from a customer's perspective as the *my cpf* website. In addition, the CPF Board developed a suite of personalised e-services that was complementary to the "*my cpf* Life Events" informational pages developed in the earlier phase. By the end of 2004, the estimated average service cost per CPF member had decreased to US$15.70, and the number of physical service counters operated by the CPF Board was reduced by almost 20% as a result of the large-scale migration of customers onto the electronic platform. In addition, according to a customer satisfaction survey conducted in 2004, the percentage of members who were

---

[5] Immigration & Checkpoints Authority (ICA) is the public agency responsible for immigration and citizen registration in Singapore.

[6] National Registration Identity Cards (NRICs) refers to the official identity document of Singapore Citizens that is imprinted with the thumbprint of the citizen.

satisfied with the quality of the e-services had risen to 74.3%. The overwhelming success of the first two phases of e-Ggovernment development attests to the immense potential of e-Government for improving the efficiency and effectiveness of the public services of the CPF Board. Yet, despite the success, the management of the CPF Board realised that e-Government remained inadequate in meeting the needs of certain customer segments. In the third phase of e-Government development, the objective of the CPF Board was on extending the reach of their e-services, so as to cater to the segments of customers whose needs have not been adequately met thus far.

E-GOVERNMENT DEVELOPMENT PHASE 3: MID-2005 TO EARLY 2007

A particularly challenging aspect of e-Government implementation at the CPF Board lies in the breadth of its customer base. Its members can range from 18 to 90 years old, and span a wide range of education and income levels, with each demographic group having their unique needs and requirements. The Chief Information Officer of the CPF Board described the various customer segments that the CPF Board has to cater to, "We have a very broad spectrum of customers. At one end we have the teenagers; most probably very IT savvy having learnt all about IT in school.... They are into social networking, Web 2.0 (technologies) and all that.... Then we have the other end... those who are not IT savvy... those with lower education levels... our older members; aged 55 and above, those who cannot afford computers.... We have to reach out to all of them. We cannot, just because we are providing e-services, ignore the other (non-IT savvy) groups."

Unlike a private organisation that can focus on the needs of its most profitable customers, the CPF Board has a public mandate to serve all customer segments. Thus, while closing all its traditional service counters and mandating the use of its e-Government framework would achieve the goal of reducing the costs of customer service and drive all of its existing customers onto the electronic platform, this was not an option as there were segments of customers that would be excluded from receiving the services. Therefore, in the third phase of e-Government development, the challenge to the management of the CPF Board was to make e-Government inclusive so as to cater to the needs of a diverse array of customer segments.

Based on a comprehensive analysis of their existing customer base, the CPF Board identified five major customer segments. The customer segments are labelled: (1) Young and IT Savvy, (2) Teenagers and Kids, (3) Non-IT Savvy, (4) Senior Citizens, and (5) On-the-move and Busy. Table 3.3 provides a brief summary of the characteristics that define the five customer segments.

By defining the five customer segments, the CPF Board was able to conduct a thorough analysis of their existing services to identify the service gaps in the current mode of public service delivery. Through the identification of the service gaps, the management of the CPF Board developed a holistic customer service philosophy

Table 3.3: A Summary of the characteristics of the five customer segments.

Customer Segment	Characteristics
Young and IT Savvy	• Age below 55 • Familiar with using the Internet and conducting transactions online
Teenagers and Kids	• Age below 20 • Extremely IT Savvy • Limited attention span • Familiar with social networking tools and playing games online
Non-IT Savvy	• Age below 55 • Unfamiliar with using the Internet and conducting transactions online
Senior Citizens	• Age above 55 and have already retired • Unfamiliar with using the Internet and conducting transactions online • Face difficulty in learning how to use the Internet
On-the-Move and Busy	• Typically busy professionals or employees of Small and Medium Enterprises (SMEs) • IT Savvy but have limited access to computers

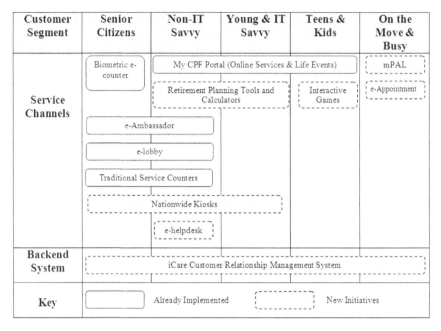

Customer Segment	Senior Citizens	Non-IT Savvy	Young & IT Savvy	Teens & Kids	On the Move & Busy
Service Channels	Biometric e-counter	My CPF Portal (Online Services & Life Events)			mPAL
		Retirement Planning Tools and Calculators		Interactive Games	e-Appointment
	e-Ambassador				
	e-lobby				
	Traditional Service Counters				
	Nationwide Kiosks				
	e-helpdesk				
Backend System	iCare Customer Relationship Management System				
Key	Already Implemented		New Initiatives		

Figure 3.3:   Identification of service gaps and the planning of new e-Government initiatives.

that was referred to as "Different Strokes for Different Folks," which provided an overarching framework to guide the development of new applications, functions, and service delivery mechanisms in the third phase of e-Government development. Figure 3.3 provides an illustration of how the service gaps in the existing mode of public service delivery were identified and how new initiatives were developed to fill these gaps. Table 3.4 provides a brief description of the new initiatives implemented in the third phase of e-Government development.

The third phase of e-Government development began in July 2005 and was completed by early 2007. Through the new initiatives implemented as part of the phase, the CPF Board had services and service delivery mechanisms that catered to the needs of its 5 major customer segments. By the end of 2006, the average service cost per CPF member had decreased to approximately US$13.54 and as reported earlier, a customer satisfaction survey found that the

Table 3.4:   e-Government initiatives developed in the third developmental phase.

Initiative	Targeted customer segment	Description
Nationwide Kiosks (Implemented in Sep 2005)	Senior citizens, Non-IT Savvy, Young and IT Savvy	By facilitating CPF transactions via the AXS commercial kiosk network, this initiative allows CPF members with no access to the Internet to perform electronic transactions with the CPF Board 24/7. As of June 2007, there are more than 463 AXS Stations strategically located all over Singapore.
Retirement Planning Tools and Calculators (Implemented in Jul 2005)	Non-IT Savvy, Young and IT Savvy	Web-based applications that calculate the amount of monthly CPF contributions, housing installments, the amount necessary for retirement. The purpose of the planning tools and calculators is to educate visitors to the CPF website on the importance of retirement planning.
e-Helpdesk (Implemented in Sep 2005)	Non-IT savvy	e-Helpdesk is a downloadable application that enables the CPF CSO to see the same screen on the computer as the customers and take control of their screen if the need arises. The main purpose of this initiative is to educate non-IT savvy users on the use of the *my cpf* Portal and help in the navigation of the portal.
Interactive Games (Implemented in Jul 2005)	Teens and Kids	Interactive, Flash-based games were designed to educate young Singaporeans on the importance of planning early for their retirement. For example, the "Voyage of Life" game was a monopoly-styled board game that lets players go through significant life events such as working, making investments, buying insurance, and buying a home. By playing the game, key retirement planning concepts are instilled in the players, who become aware of the implications of their decisions that affect financial security.

(*Continued*)

Table 3.4:   (*Continued*).

Initiative	Targeted customer segment	Description
mPAL (Implemented in Oct 2005)	On-the-Move and Busy	mPAL is a suite of Java-based applications harnessing mobile technologies. It is targeted at busy professionals or employees of Small and Medium Enterprises (SMEs) with limited access to the internet and computer. With mPal, CPF's e-services can be accessed via mobile phones anytime, anywhere.
iCare CRMS (Implemented in Jan 2006)	All Customer Segments	Previously, all the records of the CPF members were stored in various systems maintained by different departments, with minimal integration between the different systems. If a customer had enquiries that crossed more than one scheme or service, the CPF CSO would have to toggle between systems to retrieve the relevant information. The iCARE is a central repository of customer information across the CPF Board's various contact points that provides the CPF Board with the ability to profile their customers and provide personalised service to individual CPF members.
e-Appointment (Implemented in Jul 2005)	On-the-Move and Busy	e-Appointment is an application that enables busy professionals to schedule an appointment with the CSOs of the CPF Board via an SMS. SMS reminders of the appointment are sent prior to the appointment date. The CPF Board pledges to attend to the CPF members within 10 minutes of the appointment time.

percentage of customers who were satisfied with the quality of the CPF Board's e-services had risen to 92.3%. These statistics attest to the sustained improvements in terms of the efficiency and effectiveness of its public services. In addition, the volume of electronic transactions handled by the CPF Board continues to grow. At the end of the third phase of e-Government development, it was estimated that the CPF Board handled more than 32 million electronic transactions a year.

E-GOVERNMENT DEVELOPMENT PHASE 4: EARLY 2007 TO PRESENT

Facilitated by an effective e-Government, the CPF Board has nurtured a culture and organisational mindset for service excellence. Seeking the next improvement in service quality and efficiency, the present objective of the CPF Board is to extend the breadth and depth of e-Government by improving the reach and richness of its e-services. A senior executive at the CPF Board elaborates, "It (service improvement) is like an S-curve. When you are doing so well, whatever you do next is incremental. After a while, you've got to ask yourself: 'What do I need to do to break the status quo and go into the next S-Curve?'... For the less IT illiterate and the elderly, I think more can be done to reach out to them... we are also continuously looking for new ways of leveraging technology."

To this end, the present phase of e-Government development centres on three key strategies. The first strategy is to proactively reach out to the segments of the population that have traditionally been excluded from the services of the CPF Board. In particular, the management of the CPF Board is aware that there is a segment of customers that face immense difficulties in receiving public services from the CPF service centres, let alone latching onto the Internet platform to conduct electronic transactions. This customer segment includes four main demographic groups: (1) citizens with lower income who cannot afford computers or Internet access, (2) citizens who are illiterate or lack education and consequently, have no knowledge of the CPF schemes and services available and do not know where to seek help, (3) citizens with disabilities who face immense difficulties in traveling to the CPF service centres, and (4) senior citizens that lack proper care and social support.

To reach out to this segment of customers, the CPF Board launched the mobile-Ambassador (m-Ambassador) service in April 2007. The m-Ambassador Service utilises wireless technologies to enable CPF CSOs to serve customers using Ultra Mobile Personal Computers (UMPCs). Through a letter of authorisation, a member can authorise a CSO to access his/her CPF account and conduct online transactions on his/her behalf via the UMPCs, effectively gaining access to the entire suite of *my cpf* Online Services. To date, the CPF Board has partnered various grassroot organisations in organising road shows and visits to the homes of the elderly and the disabled, delivering the public services of the CPF Board to the point of need, reaching out to the segments of the population that arguably need the services of the CPF CSOs the most.

The second strategy is to further enhance the richness of their e-services. Specifically, the management of the CPF Board realised that despite the increased efficiency and effectiveness that resulted from providing services over the Internet, there were some limitations to the existing form of online transactions. The Manager of the E-Services at the CPF Board described these limitations, "Traditionally, (electronic) forms come with pre-determined fields which you must complete. There's a field for you to fill up everything, which is a good thing…. In fact, many of our forms are that way. It helps a lot in our operations…. But we don't want to be constrained by the fact that we need a pre-defined form to do everything…."

This critical management insight led to the conception of the "*My e-Concierge*" service in November 2007. My e-Concierge is an online application that consists of a simplified, open-ended form. Designed to be used like the email, My e-Concierge allows the user to key in their requests in an unstructured form, and is intended for use by customers who are unable to locate the information or e-services relevant to their needs on the *my cpf* portal. The Manager of the E-Services at the CPF Board described the function and benefits of My e-Concierge, "You see a lot of open-ended forms on the banking websites. They don't even call it a form; they're just open-ended email requests that will be processed anyway.... We brought this concept to the public sector, and it makes things really convenient for the customers. This form is especially useful for requests that are uncommon because it's not cost effective for us to create an online form for every service or request that's available at the CPF Board. Short of making the customer come to our counters, we now have My e-Concierge for them to submit their uncommon requests."

The third strategy centres on integrating the services of the CPF Board with the services of public and private organisations to bring about one-stop services and greater convenience to the customers. While data sharing agreements between the CPF Board and public organisations such as the Housing and Development Board[7] (HDB) have existed since the 1960s, the CPF Board is seeking a greater extent of collaboration and integration with external organisations towards the aim of providing seamless, cross-organisational services to their customers. Yet, the objective of integration brings a fresh set of challenges to the CPF Board.

The Deputy Director of Service Planning and Development described these challenges and the steps taken to overcome these challenges, "It's about agreeing on the terms and conditions and knowing where are the boundaries. With the private organisations, it's much easier because they are all profit-driven; they look at what is in it for them in terms of profit and if they see value, they will participate with us, and they are quite flexible in terms of accepting the conditions that we lay down. For government bodies, it's a little bit complex because we have our own rules and regulations. The data that we own individually; we are not allowed to share.... But Infocomm Development Authority of Singapore (IDA)[8] is pushing for it constantly and they help us by identifying the potential services

---

[7]The Housing and Development Board (HDB) is Singapore's public housing authority. HDB plans and develops public housing towns with the aim of providing citizens with quality homes and living environments.

[8]Infocomm Development Authority of Singapore (IDA) is a Statutory Board tasked with overseeing Infocomm technology development, deployment, and usage in Singapore.

that can be integrated…. And if we have some ideas for collaboration, we will go through our colleagues in the Housing Department, who will discuss it with their HDB counterparts…."

Through the three strategies, the present phase of e-Government development that began in early 2007 seeks to raise the standard of the CPF Board's services to an even higher level. While the latest phase has not arrived at fruition, and new challenges will inevitably arise, the well-honed service system of the CPF Board and the relentless drive towards service excellence stands the organisation in good stead in the foreseeable future. In any case, the successful e-Government experience of the CPF Board up to this point in time certainly attests to the momentous potential of e-Government for enhancing the quality and delivery of public services, and underscores the important role of information and communications technology in the course of public administration.

THE PROCESS OF E-GOVERNMENT DEVELOPMENT AT THE CPF BOARD

Defining Four Phases of e-Government Development

By constructing a timeline of the e-Government initiatives implemented (refer to Figure 3.4), a pre-implementation phase and four e-Government development phases in the process of e-Government development at the CPF Board can be defined based on the different strategic objectives of each phase.

The strategic objectives, the key initiatives developed, and the organisational impact of the use of Information Technology (IT)/ e-Government in each phase are summarised in Table 3.5.

DIFFERENCES FROM EXISTING MODELS OF E-GOVERNMENT DEVELOPMENT

By distinguishing between the various phases of e-Government development, a comparison between the process of e-Government development that unfolded in the case of the CPF Board

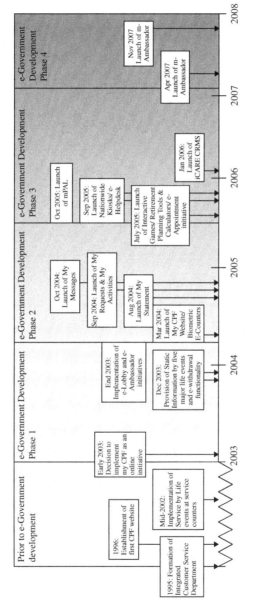

Figure 3.4:   Timeline of e-Government initiatives implemented by the CPF Board.

Table 3.5:   e-Government development phases at the CPE Board.

Phases	Pre-Implementation Phase (Before 2003)	e-Government Development Phase 1 (Early 2003–Early 2004)	e-Government Development Phase 2 (Early 2004–Mid-2005)	e-Government Development Phase 3 (Mid-2005–Early 2007)	e-Government Development Phase 4 (Early 2007–Present)
Strategic Objectives	"E-enablement" of existing schemes and services	Attaining customer centricity through re-organisation of information from the customer's perspective	Personalisation and customisation of e-services	Developing a suite of services and service delivery mechanisms that cater to its five customer segments	Providing open-ended services and delivering proactive services to digitally excluded customers
Key Initiatives Implemented	– Establishment of first CPF website – Implementation of "Service by Life Events" at Service Counters	– Re-organisation of information according to five major life events – Establishment of e-Lobby and e-Ambassador initiatives	– My Statements – My Requests – My Messages – My Activites – Biometric e-counters	– Retirement Planning Tools and Calculators – Interactive Games – e-Appointment – Nationwide Kiosks – e-Helpdesk – mPAL – iCare CRMS	– m-Ambassador – e-Concierge
Organisational Impact	• Increased Efficiency: Decreasing average service costs per CPF member • Increased Effectiveness: Increasing customer satisfaction, increasing customer reach				

and the stage models of e-Government maturity in the existing literature can be made. In general, although many different stage models of e-Government maturity (refer to Table 3.6) have been developed in the existing literature, five common stages of maturity may be identified across the various models (Siau and Long, 2005).

The first stage of e-Government maturity may be labeled "Web Presence" where simple and limited information is posted through the websites of public organisations. The second stage may be termed "Interaction" where basic search engines, email systems, and official form downloads are provided to allow basic two-way communication between citizens and the public organisation. The third stage may be labeled "Transaction" and involves allowing citizens to conduct complete service and financial transactions online. The fourth stage may be termed "Transformation" and involves horizontal integration between different public agencies and vertical integration across various levels of government. The final stage may be termed "e-Democracy", which is viewed a long term goal for e-Government that adheres to the spirit of deliberative democracy. In this stage, tools such as online voting, polling, and surveys are provided to improve public involvement and promote political participation (Siau and Long, 2005).

Comparing the process of e-Government development at the CPF Board with the stage models of e-Government maturity in the existing literature, two key differences may be identified. First, by mapping the stages of e-Government maturity (according to the existing stage models in the literature) onto the different phases of e-Government development that transpired at the CPF Board (refer to Table 3.7), it is evident that the stages of e-Government development can develop in parallel and does not necessarily follow a prescribed sequence. For example, because integration with various public organisations such as the Housing and Development Board (HDB) have existed in the form of data sharing agreements since the 1960s, the integration of data and services at the CPF Board preceded e-Government development. Consequently the e-Government

Table 3.6:   Various e-Government maturity stage models.

Model	Stages
Layne and Lee (2001) Four-Stage Model	• Catalogue: Delivers static or basic information • Transaction: Enables simple online transactions • Vertical Integration: Integrating government functions at different levels • Horizontal Integration: Integrating different functions from different agencies
Hiller and Belanger's Five-Stage (2001) Model	• One-Way Communication: Simple information dissemination • Two-Way Communication: Interaction between government and users • Service and Financial Transactions: G2C and G2B transactions • Vertical and Horizontal Integration: Similar to Layne and Lee (2001) • Political Participation: Promotion of political participation (e.g., online voting)
Baum and Di Maio's (2000) Four-Stage Model	• Web Presence: Provide basic information • Interaction: Ability to contact agencies • Transaction: Complete service and financial transactions • Transformation: Provide integrated, personalized service
UNPAN's (2003) Five-Stage Model	• Emerging Presence: Provide formal but limited static information • Enhanced presence: Provide dynamic, specialised information • Interactive Presence: Portal to connect users and Service Providers • Transactional Presence: Ability to conduct complete and secure transactions • Seamless or Fully Integrated Presence: One-stop portal to access a variety of services
Deloitte's (2001) Six-Stage Model	• Information Publishing: Provide increased access to information • Official Two-Way Transaction: Interaction between governments and users • Multi-Purpose Portals: Single portal to provide universal service across departments • Portal Personalization: Customised portals • Clustering of Common Services: Unified and seamless service across agencies • Full Integration and Enterprise Transaction: Sophisticated, unified, and personalised services for all customers

stage of Transformation (Siau and Long, 2005) was attained very early: integrated services were already available in the first CPF website established in 1996, prior to the development of a holistic e-Government framework at the CPF Board in 2003.

Second, we find that in the case of the CPF Board, the same stages of e-Government maturity can take on drastically different forms for the attainment of different strategic objectives. As an illustration, by posting electronic versions of their various transaction forms in the first CPF website launched in 1996, the CPF Board had attained the Transactions stage of maturity (Siau and Long, 2005) prior to the development of their holistic e-Government framework in 2003. But in the second phase of e-Government development, they developed personalized transactions to cater to the needs of individual CPF members. In the third phase of e-Government phase, they developed a holistic suite of transactions to cater to the needs of a broad spectrum of CPF members, and finally, in the fourth phase of e-Government development, they created open-ended transactions to enhance the flexibility of their e-services. The differences between the nature of transactions developed in each phase is in contrast with the monolithic definition of the various stages of e-Government maturity in the existing stage models, and demonstrate how variation is possible even within a single stage of e-Government maturity (Siau and Long, 2005).

The primary implication of these differences is that contrary to what the existing stage models appear to suggest, it is not the mere attainment of each stage, but rather the way in which each stage is enacted that results in true e-Government maturity. In other words, because e-Government development does not follow a prescribed sequence, and the manifestation of each stage is not homogenous across different contexts, the attainment of a stage can only be considered an extension to the range of e-services. It cannot be regarded as an enhancement or an indication of growing maturity, unless it is accompanied by a corresponding improvement in the efficiency and quality of the services of the public organisation.

Table 3.7:   Stages of E-Government development attained in each phase of e-Government development.

Phases	Pre-Implementation Phase (Before 2003)	e-Government Development Phase 1 (Early 2003–Early 2004)	e-Government Development Phase 2 (Early 2004–Mid-2005)	e-Government Development Phase 3 (Mid-2005–Early 2007)	e-Government Development Phase 4 (Early 2007–Present)
Strategic Objectives	"E-enablement" of existing schemes and services	Attaining customer centricity through re-organisation of information from the customer's perspective	Personalisation and customization of e-services	Developing a suite of services and service delivery mechanisms that catered to its five customer segments	Providing open-ended services and delivering proactive services to digitally excluded customers
Stages of e-Government Development Attained	– Web Presence – Interaction – Transaction – Transformation	– Web Presence – Interaction – Transaction – Transformation	– Web Presence – Interaction – Transaction – Transformation	– Web Presence – Interaction – Transaction –Transformation	– Web Presence – Interaction – Transaction – Transformation

REFERENCES

Baum, C. and A. Di Maio (2000). Gartner's four phases of e-government model. *Gartner Group Research Note.* Available at: http://aln.hha.dk/IFI/Hdi/2001/ITstrat/Download/Gartner_eGovernment.pdf (accessed October 5, 2003).

Deloitte and Touche (2001). The citizen as customer. *CMA Management,* 74(10), 58.

Hiller, J. and F. Belanger (2001). Privacy strategies for electronic government. *The Pricewaterhousecoopers Endowment for the Business of Government.* Available at: http://www.businessofgovernment.org/pdfs/HillerReport.pdf (accessed February 28, 2007).

Layne, K. and J. Lee (2001). Developing fully functional e-government: A four-stage model. *Government Information Quarterly,* 18(2), 122–136.

Siau, K. and Y. Long (2005). Synthesizing e-government stage models — a meta-synthesis based on meta-ethnography approach. *Industrial Management & Data Systems,* 105(4), 443–458.

United Nations and American Society for Public Administration (2003). *UN Global E-government Survey.* Available at: http://unpan1.un.org/intradoc/groups/public/documents/un/unpan016066.pdf (accessed September 7, 2006).

DISCUSSION QUESTIONS

1. (a) What does the existing literature on e-Government say about e-Government development?
   (b) How does *my cpf* model differ from the model found in existing literature?
2. What are some illustrations from *my cpf* case study to demonstrate that service transformation through e-Government development is iterative?
3. Based on *my cpf* case study, how were service and service delivery capabilities improved to enhance the benefits of e-Government development?

Case 4

CONSTRUCTING A PLATFORM FOR INFORMATION TECHNOLOGY VALUE CO-CREATION: LESSONS FROM THE ALLIANCE FOR CORPORATE EXCELLENCE PROGRAMME (ACE) OF SINGAPORE'S MINISTRY OF FINANCE

Barney Tan

University of Sydney

BACKGROUND

The Government of Singapore has, over the past 30 years, pursued a long-term vision of developing the country's competitiveness and national interests throufgh the transformative potential of information and communications (Infocomm) systems and technologies. Today, Singapore is internationally acclaimed as a demonstrated leader in the adoption, implementation, and use of Electronic Government (e-Government) strategies and systems to conceptualise, create, and deliver innovative IT-enabled processes and services. A strategic thrust in this vision has been the realisation of operational synergies across multiple governmental agencies. In line with this vision, Singapore's Ministry of Finance (MOF) spearheaded the formation of the ACE programme, a unique initiative to explore and capitalise on inter-agency synergies by consolidating and coordinating their backend business functions, creating a shared IT system, and standardised business processes.

The ACE initiative is rooted in the insights gained by Singapore's Ministry of Finance from a study conducted to determine how corporate services could best be delivered. The study revealed that many of the corporate activities, such as Human Resources (HR) and Finance, being performed across ministries was sufficiently similar to allow consolidation and outsourcing of these business processes. While this consolidation was performed across several departments in Singapore's various Ministries, each Ministry also contained Statutory Boards, autonomous agencies endowed with operational flexibility and independence to fulfill their functions.

Unlike the ministries, this autonomy afforded each Statutory Board the ability to adopt unique systems, policies and practices for its individual operations, including the provision of corporate services. As a result, any attempt at the consolidation of services across the diverse operating environments would be difficult. While acknowledging this complexity, MOF recognised that the Statutory Boards could still obtain significant benefits if they shared the underlying information system for the provision of common corporate services such as HR and finance. The Deputy Secretary (Performance) at MOF explained how, despite their distinct requirements, the Statutory Boards could find sufficient similarities in their operations to justify the adoption of a shared system, "Shared services for the Statutory Boards were not possible because everybody had adulterated their primary systems (as) everybody implements it in their own way. Every Statutory Board is configured to deal in a specific demeanor. So they don't have a common experience. But in theory, the backroom work of HR and finance are the same. But until you're able to have them on one system, you can't talk about shared services." MOF's shared systems approach advanced the idea that the Statutory Boards could enjoy economies of scale and a lower total cost of ownership if the systems underlying their corporate services of the Statutory Boards were operationalised using a common enterprise system. The design, development, and maintenance of the common system could be consolidated across the various agencies. Rather than each Statutory Board owning and managing its own systems, they would maintain their unique requirements, priorities and staff, but would share a common systems infrastructure.

A senior executive from MOF highlighted how this model would work, "This is an 'IT systems consolidation project,' not outsourcing of functions… there is some form of shared services from the support angle — system maintenance, production support, application maintenance — all are central services."

Several possible benefits spurred MOF to investigate the shared systems approach further. Cost savings might be realised for both the purchase of the system as well as its continual maintenance. Furthermore, a shared systems approach would reduce the existing complexity in the management of enterprise systems, allowing Statutory Boards to adopt best practices in their corporate provision and IT resource management.

Modernising systems for corporate services would also enable agencies to automate transactional activities in Finance and HR, and leverage on web-based self-services for employees. This was considered to be beneficial, particularly in the public service. With the rising standard of education, it was increasingly difficult for agencies to employ operators and data processing staff for transactional corporate activities. Coupled with the high IT literacy rate in Singapore, computerising transactional processes would significantly reduce the resources dedicated to administrative work, as well as enhance the delivery of services to IT-savvy government employees.

Underlying the shared system approach was MOF's belief that process harmonisation and standardisation across the Statutory Boards would result in operational benefits, as well as provide a strategic platform for further government innovation in the future. Harmonisation and standardisation meant that agencies would need to consolidate and rationalise their business processes with one another in order to derive the maximum benefits from the shared system.

However, the undertaking seemed daunting. MOF was to bring together multiple autonomous organisations to collaboratively design and implement a shared enterprise system, with harmonised business processes, involving significant and profound changes to their individual operating environments. Having such an initiative driven by MOF, considered an external party to Statutory Boards,

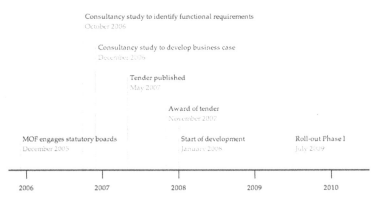

Figure 4.1:   Timeline of the ACE programme.

was itself an immediate challenge. Yet, at the end of 2005, MOF launched the ACE programme to engage multiple Statutory Boards with the idea of an integrated and shared system. The objectives of ACE were to create a collaborative arrangement among these Statutory Boards, investigate the feasibility of a shared system project, and oversee its deployment (Figure 4.1).

PHASE 1: STRUCTURING FOR INTER-ORGANISATIONAL COLLABORATION (2005–2006)

In the first phase of the implementation of the ACE programme, the objectives were to structure disparate Statutory Boards within a collaborative entity, creating a shared vision, philosophy, and platform; with the appropriate leadership, through which the programme would be enacted. As an external agency that would not eventually adopt the shared system, MOF found itself in a difficult position — it was championing the development of a system it would not later use, and so had to remain neutral to the policy and process decisions and changes that would be made for the system's functionality. The system needed to address the unique needs and missions of each agency, yet not those of MOF. For the ACE programme to work, it became clear to the MOF that it could not mandate the Statutory Boards' involvement in the programme. Instead, MOF realised that it was integral to elicit the willing participation and buy-in from the participating agencies.

The Deputy Secretary of MOF explained, "Traditionally, the easier way is for us to issue an (internal) edict — 'everybody needs to do this.' We deliberately chose not to do this. It's difficult to build (such a system) — it's even more difficult to sustain! Everybody will have complaints — 'I didn't build it. Somebody else told me I have to have this!' We would be doomed for failure." To accomplish this, MOF did not cast a wide net over the 60+ Statutory Boards within the Singapore public sector. Neither did it attempt to select Statutory Boards with shared cultures nor organisational backgrounds. Instead, it identified specific Statutory Boards that would be making significant systems upgrades on the same enterprise resource planning (ERP) software platform in the near future, with the belief that these organisations shared a common background, and would reap the most benefit from the programme in terms of both cost synergies and managing with the complexities of a changing enterprise system market. These Statutory Boards were essentially already using systems from Tier I ERP providers, namely SAP and PeopleSoft. MOF approached the various CEOs and invited them to participate in ACE.

Between the end of 2005 and middle of 2006, the ACE programme attracted seven candidate Statutory Boards where senior management had expressed interest in studying the feasibility of the shared systems project, driven primarily by their need to embark on significant, complex and expensive near-term system upgrades. Owing to the selection criteria, the ACE members were from diverse organisational backgrounds, with significant differences in their missions, existing systems and applications, processes, and organisation sizes (see Table 4.1).

There were initially mixed opinions on the practicality of the project. The diverse agencies were skeptical over several issues, including the cost of the system, its potential savings, and sacrifices that would need to be made to standardise the business processes across the organisations sufficiently, while maintaining operational efficiency and effectiveness. Bringing together the various CEOs of

Table 4.1:   The seven pioneering agencies of ACE programme.

Statutory Board	Parent Ministry	Size
People's Association (PA)	Ministry of Community Development, Youth and Sports	2,100
Inland Revenue Authority of Singapore (IRAS)	Ministry of Finance	1,500
National Heritage Board (NHB)	Ministry of Information, Communications and the Arts	363
Singapore Land Authority (SLA)	Ministry of Law	476
National Parks Board (NParks)	Ministry of National Development	765
Public Utilities Board (PUB)	Ministry of the Environment and Water Resources	3,014
Economic Development Board (EDB)	Ministry of Trade and Industry	537

the affected Statutory Boards, MOF worked to secure their collective buy-in on the idea of shared systems, and develop an appropriate plan for the project to move forward.

According to the CEO of the Singapore Land Authority (SLA) who shared how the willingness of organisations was important to achieve this, "you need people who have confidence in the idea of sharing systems. For people who have familiarity or prior experience, they need very little convincing, in terms of the security measures you can have, privacy with others must be satisfied, and so forth. But those who are not familiar — that would be one of the obstacles to overcome: to get their buy ins. But if you have enough converts, it would be less difficult."

The benefits of the shared system as a cost savings exercise alone were not sufficient. The senior management of each Statutory Board would need to support the philosophy of shared systems and common business processes, despite stemming from different organisations. The process of harmonising their HR and finance processes would involve significant sacrifices and changes to their organisations, as the Deputy Secretary from MOF expressed, "The harmonisation is a walk of faith. Before they started doing it, I'm sure they were thinking 'How are you going to accommodate me?' It's only through conversation where you can see their differences. We can share what's common and accept that we have unique parts. If we can share 80% of things, we can accept that there's a 20% difference. This is an experience not everyone goes through in their normal phase of work."

It was therefore necessary for the agencies to willingly come on board the programme with the right mindset for collaboration, regardless of the economic benefits of the programme. Each agency needed to understand and accept ownership over its role in the project, but this was not immediately forthcoming, expressed the CEO of SLA, "To make sure that the leadership of the organisation is represented — is there to hear, to listen, to be updated — is a major issue. Ownership of the problem and project must be at the highest level. It's very difficult, and you must really push through. And it can do good to the organisation! The project has to prove itself in the end. But at the back of everybody's mind is what he or she has to give up. They have things that they have to compromise. What are the things that they have to relearn, whether indeed the expected cost savings can be realised. So it is with faith that we go into this confidently."

With their partners supporting the vision and their roles, MOF developed a well-contained leadership structure for the ACE programme that ensured various agencies would have an equal and responsible seat at the table. The structure consisted of three distinct levels:

Programme Steering Committee (PSC): The PSC consisted of senior management officials of the ACE member organisations. The PSC would set the strategic vision of the project, secure necessary organisational resources, and mediate inter-agency differences in the design of the shared system.

Programme Management Committee (PMC): The PMC consisted primarily of Director-level representatives from the ACE member organisations. The PMC would be responsible for harmonising the requirements for the shared system, as well as the business processes underlying them.

Business Focus Groups (BFG): Multiple BFGs; centred on various groups of related processes and comprising of HR and Finance executives from the Statutory Boards, were formed. The role of the BFGs was to determine the common requirements for the system across the Statutory Boards, as well as identify the necessary, unique functionalities required by their organisations.

An experienced Programme Director was selected to manage the implementation process and ensure the feasibility of a shared system, and eventually, facilitate the development of the tender specifications for the system. The selection of a suitable Programme Director to bring about and manage the collaborative effort of the programme was a vital decision, as explained by the Deputy Secretary of MOF, "People say it's hindsight, but for me, it is foresight. It's by design. I appreciate the spirituality of it. I am careful that the Programme Director is the person that is able to bring it forward. If you can't bring about the camaraderie of give and take, it wouldn't work! If you can't be the mother hen that gets everyone to work harmoniously, it will fail. People will go back to their bosses and say it doesn't make sense and they will withdraw."

PHASE 2: HARMONISING DISPARATE BUSINESS REQUIREMENTS (2006–2007)

With a structure for collaboration and a Programme Director in place, the second phase saw the disparate agencies beginning the exercise of harmonising their business processes to study the feasibility of the shared system. The exercise itself acted as a shared experience which ACE's participating agencies could reconcile their commitment, roles, and positions in the project itself. This stage of harmonising their collaborative spirit was essential for the organisations to work together in the future. At this stage, effective and open communication processes, the equitable reconciliation of conflicting issues, the establishment of parameters and boundaries, and the dissemination of the project's vision played key roles in harmonising the ACE organisations with one other. More importantly, it provided the shared space for the organisations to begin a process of dialogue, in order for their collaboration to flourish.

Facilitated by the consulting firm Accenture, the agencies worked to identify the shared and unique Finance and HR processes of each agency. This was followed by an evaluation of the existing Tier I ERP systems available in the market (e.g., SAP and PeopleSoft) to determine if a system that satisfies the collective requirements of the agencies can be implemented at a reasonable cost. The Programme Director explained the magnitude of the study, "The harmonisation involved over 100 Statutory Board officers! Accenture looked at the As-Is processes with each individual agency, and tried to identify the common and non-common processes. We wanted to see if we could standardise the processes among ourselves first, and then do a gap-fit analysis to see if these processes could work with either SAP or PeopleSoft."

The PSC developed the acceptable boundaries in which the agencies would be willing to commit to the consolidated system. To lower system implementation costs, the PMC collectively adopted an 80–20 rule, aiming to achieve 80% standardisation across their processes, with 20% or less unique requirements. This would later be analysed with the existing market offerings of ERP vendors to determine if the harmonised requirements could be implemented.

The harmonisation of processes was conducted on two levels. On the first level, processes were categorised as common and non-common. When processes across agencies were identified as non-common, the team attempted to harmonise them by identifying a lead agency with the best process, and adopting it as a best practice. The Programme Director explained the rationale behind this, "Could we identify a lead agency? That would essentially be a best practice. The management philosophy was that if we couldn't achieve an 80–20 fit, we'd change our processes to follow the industry best practices. Why? This is so we could minimise the subsequent cost of system customisation."

The wholesale adoption of a non-common process from an identified lead agency's practice was a complex endeavour. The team needed to debate and agree upon which agency would meet their criteria for leading the best practice, as well as what changes were necessary for the process to enjoy wide-scale adoption by the others. In many cases, lead agencies would need to re-engineer their current processes for a better fit with the requirements of other agencies.

As a result, the members of the PMC were initially torn between striving for their individual corporate excellence and achieving harmonisation across their business processes. Issues of organisation size and technical capabilities played a major role in the discussions, as shared by the Director of Finance and Administration at International Enterprise Singapore (IES), a member of the PMC, "The frustration is that because you have other agencies who are behind in their IT development, you find that they are not so keen to push Accenture to the limit, as to what is technologically possible. You see, on a continuum, you have some agencies at one end (advanced technologically with automated processes), some at the middle, and some at the other end (using manual processes). For some functions, we are at the far end of it (technological advanced). So you find that those agencies at the other end tend to be satisfied if you were to move them to the middle of the continuum. But for agencies like us, who are at the other end, we find that then we are being pulled back!"

On the same note, some agencies would have to accept processes with more functionality and complexity than necessary, in order to meet the standardisation for the whole team. To illustrate, the Head of Finance from the Economic Development Board (EDB) shared an example of a troublesome leave application process, which differed significantly across Statutory Boards. In some agencies, the application for a half-day's leave was part of a single leave application process. In other agencies, full- and half-day applications were considered distinct processes due to the fact that they were currently utilising SAP's ERP system for HR. As a result, leave application in the latter process would require multiple approvals, causing significant changes to the way activities were carried out in the organisation, "We actually told the consultants that the harmonised approach doesn't suit us, because we cannot be moving backwards! It is a huge change impact if our people are already on a system that is so flexible and allows them to do so many things. On our current system, (leave) will be only one single application. So everybody is already used to it. When you are on a high benchmark for your current process, you see that as a minimum deliverable goal."

Getting agencies to harmonise their processes was a difficult task. Consultants from Accenture attempted to recommend best processes, but the Programme Director found that the best approach was to allow the team to determine the process on its own, even if it meant giving them additional time to complete it. In some cases, the PMC collaborated to develop and adopt completely new processes that were re-engineered for everyone, "Accenture drove the project very tightly, everything had to be on time. But I told Accenture — let them quarrel. When they debate, the energy level would be very high. There was a lot of discussion! In some cases, they would debate until they came up with a more improved practice! "

In situations where consensus could not be reached for a process, the team would classify it as a non-common process. The Programme Director shared an example, relating to variety of ways HR talent management was handled in different agencies, "For example, the way EDB does talent management is different from PUB. Could we get everyone to agree to follow a lead agency's processes? Some of the agencies would say that they can't. Those would have to become individual agency's specific requirements. For instance, NParks deals with daily-rated employees, so they would have to manage those individually. These would be unique processes."

At the end of the harmonisation process, a gap-fit analysis was conducted by Accenture to determine a suitable ERP system for adoption. The feasibility study found that there was an 84% fit with both SAP's and PeopleSoft's ERP systems offering, well within ACE's established target. To further secure the commitment from the seven agencies, a business case was developed to determine the cost savings ACE agencies would enjoy if all seven agencies participated in the system development. Again, organisation size and requirements became a factor in equitably allocating the costs of systems development. A senior executive from MOF shared the results: "At the end of the seven-year period, agencies could enjoy cost savings of around 30%... Of the seven agencies who participated in the study, (all of them) said, 'let's carry on'... We had to come out with some norm for sharing the costs because they are all not the same. It was quite a hard nut to crack. Those who were invited but didn't want to join in the first place, saw that the party was quite successful, and wanted to join now."

With the positive results, the members of the ACE programme proceeded to the development of the tender specifications. Four additional agencies expressed interest in joining the shared systems project (see Table 4.2). These agencies, bringing the total to 11, joined on the premise that they would have to accept the core processes and practices determined previously by the seven pioneering Statutory Boards.

PHASE 3: REFINING THE COLLABORATIVE ARRANGEMENT (2007–2008)

In the third phase of the implementation of the ACE programme, the key activities of the participating agencies were centred on the

Table 4.2:   Latter additions to the ACE programme.

Statutory Board	Parent Ministry	Size
Science Centre Board (SCB)	Ministry of Education	27
Intellectual Property Office of Singapore (IPOS)	Ministry of Law	170
Agri-Food & Veterinary Authority (AVA)	Ministry of National Development	789
International Enterprise Singapore (IES)	Ministry of Trade and Industry	450

evaluation and award of the tender, and collaborating with the consultants to finalise the project's specifications. As a result of the harmonisation initiatives of the previous phase, the BFGs were able to mobilise effectively as a unit to achieve its goals. In this phase, the equitable management of each party's individual agendas was necessary, as demonstrated by the cost-sharing approach that was developed for ACE members to apportion project costs. At the same time, rather than jostling for position among each other, the BFGs were mobilised in their efforts towards managing the Accenture project consultants. As the collaboration progressed, it was important for organisational resources and recognition to be provided by individual agencies to their participants. This served to revitalise the collaborative effort, and allow agencies to begin appreciating the joys of collaboration, such as increased networking and knowledge sharing through their newly-found collaboration partners.

The business case developed in Phase 2 helped the ACE participants understand each agency's operating environment from a cost perspective, including the IT manpower staff strength, and their current and potential IT costs, with and without the shared system. Members recognised that the organisations had significant differences, and as a result, needed to develop an appropriate cost-sharing method, as a Senior Executive at MOF shared, "If you look at the original seven agencies, you have a big difference. You have the PUB on the big end, and NHB on the small end. We can't have these agencies sharing equally — it doesn't make sense — especially because ERP licenses make up a (significant portion) of the (costs). Discussions went round and round until we could come up with a cost apportionment model — what is the most fair and equitable way to share the cost? The whole idea was to make the cost sharing fair to everyone, and by doing so, you can see there is true savings. If you apportion equally, the small agencies will never have a case!"

The 102 identified and harmonised common business processes were structured in a manner that they could be subscribed to by any of ACE's member agencies in meeting their own organisations' objectives and missions. Non-common processes were considered as "add-ons," providing the system with localised functionalities required by specific agencies. Each agency would be apportioned part of the implementation and annual operating costs depending on the number of common and add-on requirements they subscribed to. Under this price allocation model, ACE could flexibly distribute costs equitably across the agencies, while allowing more agencies to join the project at a later date. Newer agencies, however, were likely to incur a larger cost if they extended the system with additional "add-ons" for their individual requirements.

In May 2007, the tender was published and subsequently awarded in December 2007 to Accenture while Infocomm Development Authority (IDA) of Singapore was tasked to form a project management office to oversee the development of the system.

Representatives from the participating ACE agencies began working with Accenture and IDA to validate and finalise the system's 4,500 specific requirements. At this point of time, the ACE participants were beginning to suffer from a number of management issues they had not foreseen earlier. One crucial issue was capacity planning and resource allocation for the project. Many of the organisations did not have employees allocated to the ACE project on a full-time basis. Instead, the participants of the BFGs held dual roles — their involvement in ACE as well as their traditional portfolios. In smaller organisations, this problem was more pronounced.

A Director from the National Parks Board (NParks) shared the obstacles that arose, "We came onboard a train with 10 other agencies jostling inside a crowded space. We probably should have foreseen a bit of difficulty, in terms of capacity and resource planning. As reality sunk in, when we started the train, I was shocked! And I think my officers were also shocked of the commitment demanded of them. While we can say, at a high level, we can cope, but the reality is there are some who were struggling. We could barely meet the first part (of the project), and now they were in-line for the rollout! Usually I find that those are the smaller agencies. I think we underestimated the capacity issue, dramatically."

Staff turnovers during the 2006–2008 period meant that the participants in ACE committees were constantly changing. Agencies would first need to train new staff for participation in the BFGs committees, but at the same time, adhere to the deadlines set collectively by the ACE agencies. This problem was elaborated on by a Director from the National Heritage Board (NHB), "With new people, it's very hard — they don't know anything about the existing systems and you want them to comment on how the new system should work? It's a bit more tedious because we have to train them first. Deadlines can be shifted more (when we're working alone), but because we are dealing with everybody else, we can't. So now my staffs are grappling and there is no bargaining to push it back or delay a bit because I have 10 other agencies too. You can't just bring in anybody because you need someone who understands how our agency works."

At the same time, agencies were beginning to realise that each of them may not enjoy the level of the cost savings projected earlier in the programme, due to changes in the system requirements as well as the emergence of unforeseen costs. While cost savings remained substantial, the amount was not as significant as anticipated. Despite these issues, members of the PMC started noting several advantages arising from their participating in the ACE programme. Firstly, they recognised that members of the BFGs had begun collaborating with one another in various ways. There was an increased amount of knowledge sharing occurring within and across the agencies because of their joint involvement in ACE. The sharing allowed agencies to rely on one another's knowledge in how to deal with situations in their traditional portfolios.

Members of the BFGs had also begun working with one another to ensure their needs were heard by Accenture, whom they increasingly treated as an effective, but external, mediator. Accenture, as project consultants, attempted to keep to the project within its tight deadlines, which sometimes did not give the BFG members sufficient time to resolve their issues. However, as a Director from NParks noted, they were aware of this explicit role that Accenture played in order to rally together the collaborative effort, underscoring the importance of choosing a strong consulting partner, "The learning point is to choose a strong consultant that can really rally people together. I thought they really pulled everyone together quite well. Maybe why we didn't have conflicts with one another is that our differences were directed to Accenture. And we looked to Accenture to arbitrate, rather than to fight against us and leave us to arbitrate amongst ourselves."

The senior management of the various individual Statutory Boards at the PSC had also begun to appreciate the effort put into ACE by their individual employees. The same Director at NParks shared the programme's upcoming plans to recognise the immense work, "(MOF) was talking about a party where we could have all the people involved to receive a certificate of appreciation!"

CONCLUSION

The ACE shared systems project accentuates key management lessons in the effort to manage collaboration between multiple organisations in the public service environment. It is clear from the ACE experience that bringing organisations together and empowering them to collaborate is essential, but not sufficient to ensure success. Furthermore, unlike collaboration involving individuals, the leadership activities to develop the spirit of cooperation between the ACE organisations were distributed among different parties in different phases. It was only through this enacted leadership by different parties that the main challenges were overcome in each phase, while maintaining the inherent web of tensions that made the collaboration fruitful for each party involved. The challenge to leadership on such large projects is significant, and the risks are high. The ACE programme, a first of its kind in Singapore, highlights a new approach for projects in public sector integration, relying on enacted leadership rather than a single-party governed model. Enacted leadership serves to engage and involve all the parties in the effort — from uniting them with the will to succeed, to harmonising them with the grace to compromise and finally mobilising them in the shared spirit of collaboration.

DISCUSSION QUESTIONS

1. What does the ACE case study show about the nature of harmonising business processes across the government?
2. What are the challenges of harmonising business processes and how does the ACE case study reveal how these challenges can be overcome?
3. What role did Accenture play in the harmonisation of business process and how essential were they?
4. State the advantages of enacted leadership as compared to the single-party governed model used in the case of ACE.

Case 5

ACCOUNTING AND CORPORATE REGULATORY AUTHORITY'S BizFile SYSTEM

Calvin Chan
SIM University, Singapore

BACKGROUND OF ACCOUNTING AND CORPORATE REGULATORY AUTHORITY (ACRA)

Accounting and Corporate Regulatory Authority (ACRA) was set up as a new Statutory Board on 1 April 2004 through the merger of the Registry of Companies and Businesses (RCB) and the Public Accountants Board (PAB) with the mission to "provide a responsive and forward looking regulatory environment for companies, businesses and public accountants, conducive to enterprise and growth in Singapore." At the same time, the formation of ACRA allowed the Government to build up a central pool of specialists endowed with corporate regulation monitoring, and enforcement capabilities to complement changes in the corporate regulatory and governance framework.

In terms of its governance structure, ACRA is governed by a Board chaired by the Permanent Secretary of the Ministry of Finance and 13 other members hailing from the corporate arena, accountants, lawyers, academics, and the Accountant-General. On a day to day basis, its operations are managed by its CEO and Deputy CEO, together with nine Heads of Divisions/Units.

BizFile SYSTEM

The BizFile System is the flagship IT system of ACRA as it incorporates all the major transactional e-services as well as the backend enterprise database of ACRA. Primarily, the BizFile System supports the operational functions of ACRA in terms of the registration and renewal of business and company licenses as well as the selling of business and company information. Correspondingly, these operation falls under the purview of the Business Unit, Company Unit and the Information Resource Division in ACRA. Although other divisions in ACRA utilise the BizFile System in their daily operations, their utilization is mainly for administrative purposes. In terms of the underlying technology, the transactional aspect of BizFile System is built on a Government-wide centralised integrated IT platform known as PSi (Public Service Infrastructure), which was developed for the rapid implementation and delivery of government e-services.

The "Not So Good" Old Days

The BizFile System has its origin in the RCB branch of ACRA's genealogy. Prior to the BizFile System, all transactions (e.g., registration and renewal) had to be done through a manual process, which was typified by the filling of paper forms and long queues at the counters. Moreover, in the case of registering a company, multiple trips were often required before a company could be incorporated. For instance, one trip was needed to collect the necessary forms and to find out more about the regulatory requirements. Another trip was needed to submit the completed forms that include shareholders' particulars, the directors' information, the company's share capital and necessary documents such as the Memorandum and Articles, and to make the necessary payments. Assuming that the application was successful, one other trip was made to collect the certificate. Apart from the inconvenience experienced by the public from the multiple visits required, the manual filing process also resulted in inefficiency within the agency. It could sometimes lead to filing errors since the old system primarily involved over-the-counter manual filing.

Another matter was that in order to deal with the huge amount of data entry work, temporary data entry workers were recruited. However, this helped little in reducing data entry errors.

In addition, with the high level of transactions occurring on a regular basis, large amounts of money was collected, and checks and balances were performed daily. Therefore immediately finishing their work, the officers would consolidate their cash collections.

Early Attempts at e-Filing

Back in the late 1980s, ACRA was already keen on adopting an e-filing system likened to what BizFile is capable of doing and had actually piloted such a system. The Head of the Information Resource Division, who has been with ACRA for many years, provided more information on their early use of technology in the late 1980s, "We designed the electronic forms in-house, and the accountants and solicitor would go into the system and do e-filing. But the pickup rate wasn't good.... Since the take-up rate was no good, [partly] because [at] that time the technology [was] also not so advance, so [after a while,] we decided to terminate [it].... We said [to ourselves then], 'No, we better wait until the technology is matured, before we go ahead.'" Not intimidated by their 1987 experience, another attempt was made to realise the vision of an e-filing system in the early 1990s.

Push Towards e-Filing

By the late 1990s, the situation in ACRA had somewhat deteriorated. This was because the processing of company and business registrations was still done in the manual, paper-based manner. However, the number of companies and businesses being registered had been on the rise. At that time, one of the key alternatives explored was to make the services of ACRA available over the Internet via e-filing.

By 2000, ACRA was convinced about resuscitating their previous plan of an e-filing system and kick-started a range of activities in preparation for their next attempt at realising the long drawn ambition which they had been harbouring. As a start, a re-engineering exercise of the operations of both the Business Unit and Company Unit was conducted. Although external consultants were engaged,

ACRA officers were not exactly impressed by their recommenda-tions as it mainly reaffirmed what ACRA had been trying to do, with little value being generated.

In addition to the re-engineering process, a number of ACRA officers were sent on study trips to learn from other foreign govern-ments' experiences in e-filing system implementation. The Deputy CEO noted, "We had some study trips. [One] to [the Caribbean nation of] Anguilla and another to Australia to study how the filing systems were implemented."

The study trip to Anguilla was conducted by five officers between 9 and 19 June 2000. Clear objectives were laid down for the trip, which focused on the Anguilla's Commercial Online Registration Network (ACORN). In their report, it was recorded that, "The Government of Anguilla's ACORN system was launched on 16 November 1998. ACORN allowed licensed company managers and trust companies, in Anguilla, together with their approved overseas agents, to incorporate International Business Companies, Ordinary Companies, Limited Liability Companies, and Limited Partnerships under Anguilla's cor-porate and partnership legislation. In addition, users of the system could also transact all other registry activities electronically."

About a year later, before the tender for the development of the BizFile System was called, another team of five ACRA officers was sent to study a similar system in Australia. As documented in their report on this study trip, "Over a 3-day period from 11 to 13 July [2001], the team met with officials from the Australian Securities and Investments Commission (ASIC)... and representatives from the law firm... and the accounting firm.... In listening to both tech-nical staff who developed the system and the professional firms who were regular users of the system, we were given an insight into the enormous benefits of going online, as well as the possible pitfalls we might encounter in developing our own system."

Meanwhile, during this period from 2000 to 2001, the climate within the public sector in Singapore had also taken a turn towards greater emphasis on service orientation through the implementa-tion of e-Government solutions; in particular, the electronic delivery of public services. The commencement of the e-Government Action

Plan was announced by the Singapore Government in June 2000, with S$1.5 billion being set aside for the plan over a period of three years. Besides setting aside money to fund the development of e-services, a centralised integrated IT platform, known as Public Service Infrastructure (PSi), was also put in place to allow "for effective and efficient development and management of e-services" by the various government agencies.

During those days, ACRA was a constituent department of the Ministry of Finance. Therefore, most high profile projects had to be endorsed by the Ministry of Finance. Incidentally, the Ministry of Finance was also the ministry that spear-headed the e-Government Action Plan. The proposal to develop the BizFile System was endorsed by the Ministry of Finance and the system was developed on PSi, using funds from the S$1.5 billion set aside in the e-Government Action Plan. Within ACRA, the Information Resource Division was identified as the owner of the BizFile System and was primarily put in-charge of its implementation.

SYSTEM DEVELOPMENT

Setting up the Project Structure

After months of preparation, the tender to develop and maintain the BizFile System was called in January 2001. The tender was finally awarded to the Singapore Computer Systems Pte Ltd. (SCS) in June 2001 after about half a year of evaluation. Within a month of awarding the tender, the project Working Committee and seven accompanying Sub-Committees were also set up and for each sub-committee, relevant officers from different divisions were recruited so that various issues could be dealt with in sufficient depth. The project Steering Committee was set up by September 2001 and it was co-chaired by the CEOs of ACRA and SCS.

Tackling Technical Challenges

During the implementation, a number of technical challenges were encountered due to a lack of knowledge on the newly set up PSi.

With insufficient understanding of the capability of the underlying development platform, it was unsurprising that some re-design and re-working work was needed as implementation progressed. Given that the PSi was a centralised common infrastructure to serve the needs of the entire Singapore Government, it was impossible to cater to every unique and minute request of the BizFile System.

Throughout the entire implementation process, there were a number of occasions where "workarounds" had to be employed to overcome certain technical constrains while meeting the project timeline. Such "workarounds" continued to be the norm even until the User Acceptance Test (UAT) stage when anomalies were uncovered during testing.

Reviewing and Aligning Legislation

Apart from the technical aspects, another area where many resources were expanded was the review of the existing legal framework to complement the BizFile System. This task fell squarely into the portfolio of the Legislation Sub-Committee. In fact, the review of the existing legal framework commenced even before the formal Legislation Sub-Committee was put in place.

All these reviews of the law required the involvement of trained lawyers. Fortunately, there were quite a number of lawyers in ACRA. Apart from the CEO and Deputy CEO who were legally trained and had been called to the Legal Bar, a number of officers from the Policy and Planning Division were all lawyers seconded from the Legal Service.

Engaging Stakeholders

Throughout the implementation of the BizFile System, much effort was also expanded on the engagement of both external and internal stakeholders. The external stakeholders were all the professional firms, companies, and businesses that utilised ACRA services. Right from the start, the CEO recognised that the new BizFile System would have an indelible impact on this group of stakeholders and thus made explicit attempts to engage them. The CEO articulated, "What we recognised at the very beginning and tried to establish from the beginning is that this is going to be such a radical change for everyone, not just our staff, but all those people out there who have been doing business with us all these years in a certain manner. There was a necessity to buy them over."

Just before the BizFile System was launched, seminars were conducted for both members of the professional bodies as well as members of the public. Moreover, advance notice was also provided to inform these external stakeholders about the ensuing termination of counter services.

Besides the external stakeholders, efforts were also made by the senior management of ACRA to engage their staffs, who were the internal stakeholders. One measure adopted in managing internal stakeholders was the recruitment of contractual staff instead of regular staff to help ACRA in dealing with the hectic situation until the launch of the BizFile System.

Notwithstanding, the CEO shared that there were still fear among the regular staff about their job security, "For the [other regular] staffs, no matter what you tell them, the fear would still be there, because they didn't exactly know [what will happen]. They may have thought 'Yes, you don't need these contract people. But do you still need me? Am I still required?'"

In terms of the communication strategy, it was found that ACRA adopted a three pronged approach of (i) providing assurance and security, (ii) imbuing a willingness to embrace the impending change, and (iii) providing the means to make the change. This was aptly reflected by the CEO, "We gave them a promise that we would not terminate their services because of BizFile but they also had to promise us that they would accept that they may be required to do [a] different type of work."

Demonstrating Leadership

A number of officers in ACRA felt that an important constituent in the successful implementation of the BizFile System was the committed leadership demonstrated by their CEO. Being a totally new initiative which required legislature amendments, there were some quarters within the Government that were wary of attempting something that had not been tried and tested. The CEO related an incident where she was asked to reaffirm her readiness to take on the possible risk of something going wrong, "We had e-forms, so we were the first one where we actually prescribed a URL in the legislation as opposed to the actual [hard copy] forms. So some persuading had to done because it had not been done anywhere else [before]. But [as] it turned out, [they questioned us], 'You [are willing] take the risk of this happening?' I said it was a risk I was willing to take." While expressing her commitment to take on the possible risks of things going amiss, the CEO also showed her pragmatic willingness to accept the possibility of mistakes occurring in such a pioneering large-scale project. Furthermore, she also took on a highly hands-on approach, especially during the early stages of the project.

Providing Alternative Avenues

In designing the BizFile System, the decision was made to close all the counters and replace them with self-service kiosks. Users who were Internet savvy could also access the Internet to complete their desired transactions. Consideration was also given to users who were not Internet savvy and thus required assistance to do their e-filing. For those who could afford the fees, they could approach professional firms like accountants, lawyers, and chartered company secretaries to handle their transactions. For those who either could not afford or did not wish to engage the services of professional firms, a number of alternatives were set up.

At the self-service kiosks located at ACRA's lobby, a number of ACRA officers were appointed as Cyber-Guides to facilitate and guide public users to complete their e-filing via the BizFile System. However, these Cyber-Guides were only an interim measure as the eventual goal was to have total self-serviced e-filing. To address the concern of those who may be handicapped as a result of the closure of counter service and embarking on a fully e-filing mode, a Service Bureau was set up.

SYSTEM LAUNCH

Launching of Phase 1

After about half a year of developmental work, phase 1 of the BizFile System was launched on 15 January 2002. Essentially, phase 1 only composed of two e-services, i.e., online company name application and online incorporation of company. An officer opined that the largely uneventful launch was because there were only two e-services, "Because that first launch was a soft launch, it was simply [the two company] incorporation [related] modules, so there were just only [these] two modules out of the 200 over.... So it wasn't a big issue." When phase 1 was launched, self-help kiosks were made available at the public lobby of ACRA. Nonetheless, the counters continued to be opened and concessions were made to help those who still preferred to rely on paper forms to incorporate their companies.

By the time phase 1 of the BizFile System was launched, it was realised that the initial plan of rolling out the BizFile System over a few phases was going to be difficult. Both the Deputy CEO and an analyst from SCS explained the rationale behind the change of plans. The Deputy CEO explained, "But later we found that it's more complicated when it comes to phase 2. So we actually pushed this phase 2 to January 2003. [And] instead of putting it in 3 or 4 separate phases, we lumped it into 2 [phases]. [This was] because of data synchronisation and update problems... after each [new] launch, they had to update the system and migrate [the data] from the [old] system to the new system.... So if you're going to do it in phases, it was going to be the same problem again.... The more migration you have, the more likelihood for errors. So to prevent this [from happening,] we actually lumped everything into one phase eventually."

Launching of Phase 2

After much hard work and anticipation, phase 2 of the BizFile System was finally launched on 13 January 2003. However, the launch of phase 2 was unlike the uneventful experience of phase 1. On the day phase 2 was launched, all counter services offered by the

Business Unit and Company Unit were terminated and the only possible way of filing Business or Company related transactions with ACRA was through the BizFile System. This created a sudden surge in traffic through the system and resulted in extremely sluggish response time and this had even crashed the system. Besides the unstable system and perturbed customers, internally, several staff were also feeling uncomfortable and needed assurance.

In providing assurance and motivating the staff during these trying times, an officer recalled that she was really inspired when the senior management came out personally to help in dealing with the irate crowd, "When we're operational [with the] BizFile System, we're [stationed] outside [at] the kiosks. We [were] having quite [a] chaos because of the BizFile System…. So they [senior management] actually stepped out to help us in dealing with the public."

In addition, despite the pre-launch briefings and seminars, there were still quite a number of people who were unfamiliar with how the BizFile System worked and how to use it. An officer from the Business Unit shared, "[at the] beginning, some [of the] public didn't know how to use [BizFile]. So we [had to] guide them slowly."

Dealing with the Hiccups

It was unanimously agreed that the period during the phase 2 launch of the BizFile System was one of the most trying times for the agency. A hectic day of handling the public followed by long hours of working late into the nights to revive the BizFile System was the norm during those difficult days as all efforts were devoted to straightening out the technical glitches and getting the system up and running. During that period, a post-mortem meeting was held every evening together with the vendor and the PSi team to rectify the situation.

But what helped in building up the rapport between the vendor and ACRA was that the developers from SCS were stationed at the ACRA office throughout the development of the BizFile System, and even to this day, as there are still enhancements needed for the system.

After getting all the parties to work together, another key issue was to start prioritising all the outstanding issues so that the more urgent items would be addressed first. The Head of the Information Technology Division offered her views, "And then with [all] the various issues, I believe there must be some form of prioritisation to see what's more urgent.... But [at the] end of the day, I feel that it's really the commitment from the various parties [that's important]. Obviously there also had to be some 'pushing,' you know, to drive this. To make sure things were working, running, and people were running with it."

Progressing Towards Stabilisation

Since the time it was launched on 13 January 2003, the BizFile System has been making progress towards stabilisation. This progress towards stabilisation can be observed from the three areas of technical stabilisation, process stabilization, and e-service maturity.

In terms of technical stabilisation, this was manifested in a number of aspects such as the capability to sustain varying loads throughout the year, optimisation of system performance, and even the vendor level of knowledge on the platform.

On top of technical stabilisation, the supporting operational processes of the BizFile System were also improved as time went by. One good example was the development of the step-by-step brochures which guided the users through their e-filing process.

Another facet of process stabilisation was how the project management processes were improved so as to reduce the cost incurred in maintaining and upgrading the BizFile System. The CEO elucidated on how this was achieved, "I think you cannot deny that you had to incur these costs, so they were not avoidable. If you want the system to continue to improve, it's a cost you have to incur." Besides technical and process stabilisation, e-service maturity was also observed in the features and functions of the e-filing services itself. This was most visible from the feedback received, in terms of the numbers of compliments and complaints.

Current Status and Challenges Ahead

Although the BizFile System is stabilising and has attained a certain degree of achievement, ACRA is still pursuing further improvements to it. An important catalyst in pursuing improvements was having innovative ideas, and these were actively drawn from various avenues.

Along with these pursuits for continuous improvement comes a concern of cost as every enhancement will need to be paid for. Hence, two imminent challenges are the generation of more revenue, and the need to come up with creative working models for cost recovery.

But until such a new working model is established, the pressure rests on the shoulders of the Information Resource Division, which oversees the reselling of the business and companies information residing on the BizFile System. The Information Resource Division appears to be the only full-fledged revenue generating arm of ACRA since most of the other divisions perform largely regulatory functions. The Head of the Information Resource Division revealed, "my division is [the] so called revenue generating division. So our emphasis is [to] try to make money for ACRA."

DISCUSSION QUESTIONS

1. Why did ACRA decide to implement the BizFile System?
2. What were the system development concerns?
3. What were the challenges that ACRA faced during the launch of the BizFile System?
4. Who were the stakeholders of BizFile System?
5. Going forward, what are the future challenges and opportunities of the BizFile System?

Case 6

ACHIEVING AND ENHANCING E-GOVERNMENT INTEGRATION: LESSONS FROM THE LAND DATA HUB PROJECT OF THE SINGAPORE LAND AUTHORITY

Barney Tan

University of Sydney

Pan Shan Ling

National University of Singapore

ORGANISATIONAL BACKGROUND

The Singapore Land Authority (SLA) was formed in 2001, as a Statutory Board under the Singapore Ministry of Law. Serving as the national land registration authority, one of the responsibilities of SLA is the management and maintenance of the national land information system, LandNet. Today, there are 15 government agencies participating in LandNet to share and reference land data in their daily operations. Some of these daily operations include land use planning and infrastructure development. These agencies include the Ministry of Law, the Housing & Development Board (HDB), the Urban Redevelopment Authority (URA), the Land Transport Authority (LTA), the National Parks Board (NParks) and SLA. With LandNet, land data is now shared online in real-time. This facilitates quick and efficient decision-making, and strategic planning.

The practice of sharing land information among the government agencies goes all the way back to the 1980s. The Civil Service Computerisation Programme (CSCP) was launched at the end of

1981 to enhance the effectiveness and efficiency of public administration. In the Master Plan for the CSCP, the Data Administration Programme was officially launched in 1984 to better manage the vast data resources of the Civil Service by establishing rational national data policies, data standardisation and data sharing across the Civil Service. Under the programme, three data hubs were identified: the People Hub, the Establishment Hub, and the Land Hub. The People Management Committee, Establishment Management Committee, and Land Data Management Committee (LDMC) were set up to oversee the implementation and steer data administration of the three data hubs. The LDMC was established to spearhead land data sharing in the Civil Service. LDMC was later re-constituted as Land Systems Committee (LSC) in June 1985, chaired by Ministry of Law. Land Systems Support Unit (LSSU) was set up in September 1989 as the specialised technical support and co-ordination arm of LSC. The unit co-ordinates the on-going technical implementation and oversees the daily operation of the Land Hub.

Prior to the Data Administration Programme, agencies in Singapore that required land information had to search for and obtain them manually and individually from one another. To make matters worse, there were no Geographic Information Systems (GIS) at that point in time, and tracing papers were used and overlaid on top of each other. Mr. Chim Voon How, the present Chief Information Officer and former head of the Land Information Centre of the SLA brought up an interesting snippet of history, "… Because the more you stack (tracing paper), those at the bottom start to blur out because the tracing gets too thick."

However, with the CSCP in full swing, proprietary GIS systems were introduced into individual land-related government agencies. At this point, the Singapore government noticed that with the newly acquired IT resources, agencies had started to migrate from tracing paper to digitised maps. Ms. Kwong Yuk Wah, Manager of LSSU at the time, elaborated, "… When the civil service computerisation programme started in the early '80s, we realised that when we went through the computerisation of all the ministries, we have a lot of data resources. Hence, we must actually know how to use all the data resources."

However, due to the lack of integration, the disparate electronisation efforts of the various land-related agencies did not eliminate the problems of the duplication of data maintenance effort, inaccurate and inconsistent land data, and land data redundancy across the Singapore public sector. Consequently, the Singapore government realised that the functions of the public administration could be greatly improved if data were treated as a corporate resource and shared across the Civil Service through a centralised data hub. This led to the conceptualisation of Land Data Hub (LDH) project. The concept of LDH at that time was fairly simple; instead of letting every agency that manages land-related data handle, process, and modify their individual sets of data, a centralised hub that facilitated the sharing of common data among the various government agencies could be implemented.

The following sub-sections describe the process through which the integrated, inter-organisational e-Government that was LDH, was implemented and developed over time. In particular, as we noticed that LDH has gone through three distinct incarnations over the last 20 years, we present our case study in three chronological phases. The following figure (see Figure 6.1) provides an overview of the major milestones in the evolutionary lifecycle of LDH up to 2010.

Phase 6.1: Land Data Hub (1987–1997)

With the financial support of the Singapore government and the United Nations Development Programme (UNDP), a pilot project for LDH was initiated in 1987. The focus of the pilot project was non-technical, centered on the conceptualisation of data-sharing policies and data standards as opposed to the specific forms of Information Technology (IT) that would enable the implementation of LDH. Ms. Kwong Yuk Wah explained the purpose behind the pilot project, "… The pilot was not so much on the computer system, the pilot is mainly (related to) the policy. So we decided on what the data-sharing policy is, and what kind of data standard we should establish. It's more of an institutional kind of setup rather than the computer system."

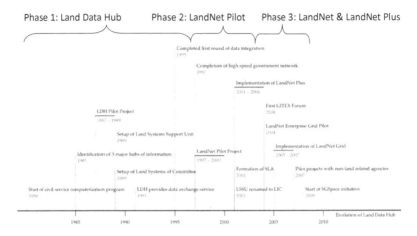

Figure 6.1:   The evolution of Land Data Hub system.

After the pilot project, the Ministry of Law was selected to over-see the implementation of the Land Data Hub. The decision was made as the government felt that it was more appropriate to place the project under the purview of a ministry. They believed that it was easier for a ministry to gain the mandate to enact the activities and changes that were required for the implementation of the inter-organisational system. Mr. Ng Siau Yong, the Director of the Geospatial Division at the SLA, described the rationale of the gov-ernment, "I believe that a top-down approach starting from the policy level is the way to go... for most ministries, the functions are more policy-oriented whereas the stat boards are more operations-oriented.... So I would say ministries, when they speak to other ministries in driving a certain government wide project, it would probably be more effective. At least they would decide at the Ministry level first, then at the policy level...."

Another reason why the Ministry of Law was chosen among the other ministries was that it was already responsible for three major land departments: the Survey Department, the Land Office, and the Registry of Title and Deeds. Each of these departments had a dis-tinct set of responsibilities relating to land information. An additional department, LSSU, was established under the Ministry of Law to manage the overall implementation of the Land Data Hub. A Land Systems Committee (LSC) was also established to discuss and oversee the policies and procedural changes required to facilitate land data administration and sharing.

In the initial setup, LSC was established for two purposes. First, its aim was to identify the agencies that could help in contributing land data to LDH. During this period, agencies that used large amounts of land data were identified on the basis that they had the data required to form an integrated base map for Singapore's overall land planning purposes. Among others, the agencies identified include the Urban Redevelopment Authority Board (URA), which is the national land use planning authority, the Housing Development Board (HDB), which manages public residential housing, Singapore Telecoms, which have map layers of the communications infrastructure, and the Public Utilities Board (PUB), which have the data related to drainage and sewerage, as well as the Ministry of Defence, which was managing the use of land for military purposes. Collectively, these agencies provided LSSU with enough information to create the overall base map within LDH that all agencies would reference.

Second, LSC played a critical role in establishing and making decisions about the data policies, enabling IT systems, and standards for data formats that LDH would require for the storage and exchange of land data. This ensured that there were concrete data policies and standards that provided guidelines for the other agencies, which in turn, would translate to the ease of data exchange when LDH was eventually implemented. The decisions of LSC with regards to system implementation and data standardisation were enacted by LSSU. Ms. Kwong Yuk Wah explained the roles played by LSC and LSSU in the implementation of LDH, "... LSC's role is really to discuss all the policies, all the standards... (and) the (role of) LSSU... is, after the setup of the policies, then (the LSSU would) go on to do the integration, implementation, setting of the standards, (and) basically do the integration."

After decisions concerning the policies, data formats and enabling of IT systems were made by LSC, LSSU commenced the implementation of LDH. During this period of time, the main priority of LSSU was to integrate the different forms of map data into a single map layer. This integration of data took almost five years and was divided into three forms of data: (1) mapping data, (2) graphing data, and (3) textual data. Ms. Kwong Yuk Wah described the challenges of data integration, "Textual data such as census data was a challenging prospect to integrate. We had to standardise the textual data formats based on what was decided by LSC. However, the data that was gathered from other agencies were in many different formats because before LSC has set any standards, agencies were free to decide on what formats suited their particular needs."

One of the reasons that contributes to this problem was the technical limitations of GIS technology at that time. There were no open standards for GIS as software vendors were all trying to lock customers in to their existing proprietary systems and data formats. This made data integration from the agencies tedious and time-consuming. Apart from deciding on the data formats for the base map, the data that came in from the various agencies had to be re-converted back into LDH's data format. Mr. Anupam Mukheriee, the Manager of Application Services at the SLA, offered his views, "… Each agency had its proprietary software. So the situation was: all of them were using different kinds (of software), some used ESRI, some used Intergraph, some used Autodesk… but we didn't have much choice then, as you know in GIS, there were products for specific applications. So the agencies were just using software that accomplished their own goals.…"

To deal with this problem, some in-house data conversion tools were created to make the process of data integration with the various agencies less time-consuming and tedious. Although there were no off-the-shelf products that provided such capabilities, LSSU was able to implement their own customised solutions to tackle the problem. The objective of data integration was to allow LDH to be a centralised source of data where the relevant agencies could retrieve the latest and most up-to-date version of the common map layers that they required for their operational and planning purposes. Aside from data integration, LSSU was also responsible for the distribution of the data. In the initial stage, data were distributed using magnetic tapes. This has evolved to the use of CD-ROMs for data exchange when the use of CDs became widespread.

However, due to technological constraints, individual agencies still had to keep their own data. LDH overcame this situation by implementing a control duplicate, which meant that although agencies had to keep their own base map that was sent from LDH, agencies were not allowed to modify the map in any way without the expressed approval of LSSU. All updates to the base map were made solely by LSSU and stored into LDH until the next scheduled release of the base map. Ms. Kwong Yuk Wah explained, "At that time, we didn't have broadband internet services that we have now. So agencies still had their own individual databases to store the map layers... the vision was always to provide an online overlay of map information, but that was not possible...."

To get agencies onboard in contributing to and retrieving data from LDH, the Ministry of Law decided at the time to sponsor the cost of running LDH, and provide the service of sharing the common map data for free to the participating agencies. Ms. Kwong Yuk Wah described the rationale behind the decision, "The decision was very clear that we didn't want funding (issues) to affect the progress of the project. So there was no discussion that the cost was to be shifted to the participating agencies."

As the costs of implementing and running LDH was borne by the Ministry of Law, it lowered the barriers of participation and allowed many agencies to participate and contribute data to LDH because most agencies saw the advantage of having a centralised source of data. Moreover, with established mechanisms for data exchange and the availability of more accurate and timely map information, it was not difficult to convince various agencies the importance of LDH's uniform data standards and policies. However, getting agencies to commit to the new data standards had its challenges as each government agency had to modify their systems to comply with the data standards that had been set by LSC. Fortunately, most agencies understood that the benefits far outweighed the costs. Ms. Kwong Yuk Wah explained, "... The demand for the data drives the supply. This means if agencies needed to exchange data from LDH, they would have to follow the standards that had been set by LSC... If the agencies did not follow the standards, they had to do their own data conversions when retrieving data from LDH...." This provided the motivation for agencies to move towards the standards and data formats established by LSC and accelerated the pace at which data integration and centralisation of map data was conducted across the Singapore public sector.

Phase 6.2: LandNet Pilot and LandNet Plus (1998–2004)

With the convenience of having a centralised source of common map data, the participating agencies began to expect more from LDH. For instance, there was a general drive towards greater efficiency across the Singapore public sector at the time, and government agencies had to find the means of improving the efficiency and effectiveness of their planning and operational activities. With the need for shorter planning cycles, there was an increased demand for timely data by various public agencies. Apart from having more timely data, agencies also wanted more flexibility when it came to retrieving data from LDH. A number of them were requesting the rights to retrieve map data as and when it was required, without having to make any specific request to LSSU. Mr. Chim Voon How described the situation at the time, "... As the planning cycles of the agencies got ramped up, there was a need for more timely information.... (Moreover,) agencies said that... every time they needed data from us, there's a service level of 3–5 days. So they asked if we can reduce (the time required). If (they) wanted the data now, can it be within a day or can (they) get the data and deal with the data (themselves)?"

At the same time, a high-speed, secured government intranet came into the picture, which inspired the notion to share land data electronically. The emergence of the enabling technology, coupled with the growing demands of the participating agencies provided the impetus for the second incarnation of LDH. This was because SLA soon realised that the current operational model was no longer adequate in fulfilling the needs of the various public agencies. It eventually led to the launch of a pilot project that was named "LandNet Pilot."

LandNet Pilot began in 1998 and involved three government agencies: the Ministry of Law, the URA and the LTA. These agencies were selected on the basis that they were the primary contributors and users of land data. Although the LandNet Pilot project was still helmed by LSSU, both URA and LTA played critical roles in enhancing the features and streamlining the requirements of the system. Mr. Tan Chia-Li, a Senior Planner at URA, elaborated on the roles of the collaborating agencies, "… We gave inputs to LSSU team on things such as setup, implementation of the system and its features, and setting up some of the standards…. Usually it's a two-way thing. Because LSSU proposes something, we test and give our feedback along the way…."

Despite the limited scale of the LandNet Pilot project, there were several challenges in implementation. First, the staff at LDH lacked the required knowledge and technical expertise to implement the LandNet concept, which was considered the first of its kind at the time. For instance, they struggled with building custom data conversion utilities and batch programmes to automate the sharing of data electronically. To deal with this issue, LDH staff trained under a number of GIS vendors and shared the knowledge gained extensively among themselves. Second, even with the high-speed government intranet, there were data transmission problems such as the bulk of data choking the network and firewalls blocking the data. Moreover, implementing the LandNet Pilot required substantial investments in infrastructure at the different agencies.

Faced with these challenges, the LDH team collectively brainstormed on ways to solve the problems, which provided invaluable insights for their future attempts at implementation. In addition, the three participating agencies actively tested new functions to provide insights for improvements. Most importantly, the LandNet Pilot project provided a glimpse of the benefits from sharing the data electronically. First, the reduction in manual processes led to manpower and time savings. The three agencies no longer need to export land data to CD-ROMs and send people down to deliver or collect CD-ROMs. Second, the conversion of the data became much more efficient. Each of the three agencies could download the land data, which was automatically converted on the fly into the required format. Third, data became timelier as custom batch programmes downloaded any changes every night. Finally, URA and LTA were able to gain the advantage of having the flexibility of contributing and retrieving data at their own convenience through the Singapore Government Network. Mr. Goh Chye Kiang, a Senior Systems Analyst of URA provided the following anecdote, "I think one of the main benefits of LandNet is the conversion of the data was done on the fly. When we download the data, when compared to the past whereby we get the data from a CD, and we had to do offline data conversion, it was a lot more straightforward."

The pilot project passed the User Acceptance Test of the three participating agencies. The available infrastructure that was created during the LandNet Pilot Project was carried over in the implementation of the escalated pilot project, known as LandNet Plus. However, the LDH team began to encounter a number of challenges during the implementation of LandNet Plus. One of the challenges the LDH team had to face was a change in ownership. In 2001, the Ministry of Law decided that there was a need for cost accounting to ensure that taxpayer money was prudently spent and accounted for. As a result, the decision was made to transfer the ownership of LDH from the Ministry to a new statutory board, known as the SLA, which would be formed by merging the Survey Department, Land Office, Registry of Title and Deeds, and LSSU.

A second challenge was that the high costs of establishing the requisite IT infrastructure. Mr. Anupam Mukherjee from SLA elaborated, "… We found that the cost was too high, because at every agency you had to setup a server, install additional software, and hardware. Furthermore, every agency had different GIS systems, which meant that a different GIS convertor was required."

The high costs meant that only a limited number of agencies could tap into this new online system for electronic data exchange (i.e., in particular, the two agencies — URA and LTA — that were recognised as the most significant contributors and users of land data). Although there was no means of tackling this problem directly, the SLA made extensive efforts in improving the data exchange for all the agencies, regardless of whether they were connected to the new online system (LandNet Plus), or still using, CD-ROM mode of data exchange through LDH. For instance, for the users of LandNet Plus, a version control system was created to tackle the problem of huge amounts of data choking up the network when agencies downloaded or uploaded data from LDH. Before the version control was implemented, agencies had to re-download all the map layers in order to get the latest version of the data, which was a long and time-consuming process. After the version control system was implemented, only changes to the map were downloaded and updated to the agencies' systems. This provided the agencies with a more efficient way of retrieving and contributing data to LDH. Mr. Anupam Mukherjee explained, "... We built automatic programmes to export the data from the agencies, take for example the LTA system, we would export the data in a nightly manner, and put the whole set of data into this LandNet agency server at LTA. Now in LTA agency server, another process would start and compare this dataset. Both sides would be compared and the system would automatically find out what has been deleted from the data, what has been changed, any road changes, whatever changes have been made and updated accordingly."

This implementation has significantly improved the performance of online data exchange as data could be retrieved and contributed more consistently without persistent network failures. For agencies that were not connected to the network, the CD-ROM exchange was also improved by allowing agencies to contribute in any format they had. Mr. Anupam Mukherjee provided this example, "LandNet started doing things automatically. When agencies come in with the CD, the operators will just load in the data, and LandNet would automatically convert it into Oracle Spatial Format."

This provided the agencies that were still on the CD-ROM mode of data exchange with more incentives to contribute data to LDH, and provided every participating agency with rich and relevant datasets that helped in their own land-related operations. Aside from improving the technical aspects of data exchange, a monthly agency administrator meeting was also established to allow for better communication between the agencies. Mr. Tan Chin Peng, a manager in the Landscaping/Aboriculture branch of NParks explained, "All members of LandNet will send their agency administrator to this meeting and through this meeting, we are aware of what are the current needs or data use of all the agencies. Furthermore, we are also able to find out data that is available, or what other new layers that are going to be shared out."

The monthly agency administrator meetings provided members with a clear picture of what forms of data were available for use in LDH, and the means to make requests for any additional map data that they might require for their operations. Agency members could also voice their opinions on places where they felt improvements could be made to LDH. SLA would then improve or develop the functionality based on the feedback from these administrator meetings. Overall, this phase provided members with better and more efficient means of data exchange, which was done to encourage agencies to contribute more data to LDH.

Despite the attractive potential benefits of an online mode of data exchange, the LandNet Plus project was not carried to fruition in the end as the costs of government-wide implementation was excessive. When a tender was called in 2001, the proposals received exceeded the budget by far, suggesting an estimated cost of $10 million to implement the system on a government-wide scale. Moreover, costly satellite servers had to be set up and maintained across many agency sites. The problem was that many agencies had different GIS systems with custom-built components. Consequently, plans to implement LandNet across the agencies were shelved. While the tender results did not sound a death knell for LandNet, further developments stagnated and a rollout across multiple agencies was deemed infeasible. The return on investment was hard to quantify and not everyone was sold on the idea of spending on IT infrastructure, especially when the implementation was projected in the region of $10 million. Fortunately, a new technology was about to emerge to breathe new life into LandNet.

Phase 6.3: LandNet (2004–2007)

In 2004, Mr. Jack Welsh, the Senior Vice President of Oracle's International Technology Group approached SLA with a newly developed technology not yet seen in the world. He wanted to conduct a proof of concept (POC) for the technology in the LandNet context. The technology was Enterprise Grid Technology. Enterprise Grid Technology effectively addressed the biggest concern which halted the progress of LandNet — the cost of implementation, by allowing LandNet to scale incrementally. For example, a new database server could be seamlessly added to the architecture when additional capacity was needed. To other parts of the system, all these database servers function as though it is one unified server. Furthermore, the POC sparked off further developments as Infocomm Development Authority of Singapore (IDA), Oracle, Autodesk, Sun, and SLA pooled their resources. In doing so, they created a small piece of software called the "LandNet agency agent" to handle and coordinate the updating of data to and from LandNet, replacing the need for participating agencies to make big ticket infrastructure investments such as satellite servers which could cost up to $150,000. The total cost to link up a new agency dropped to less than $10,000, lowering the barrier for any interested agency, thus paving the way for government-wide launch of LandNet. Mr. Anupam Mukherjee of SLA explained the fundamental impact of the introduction of Enterprise Grid Technology, "Enterprise Grid Technology helped the LandNet type of concept in a big way. We were able to increase the capacity by simply adding a new server into the architecture, giving us scalability to grow in an incremental manner. An agency agent was deployed on the members' side that allows for online data exchange between SLA and each agency at a low cost of just $10,000 per agency. This allowed more agencies to migrate from CD-ROM to online data exchange."

After the LandNet POC, it was determined that Enterprise Grid Technology was sufficient in meeting the objectives of improving data integration and sharing through an online mode of data exchange. Consequently, by 2007, the new, fully operational LandNet was launched with new web-based functionality that enabled participating agencies to overlay map information through their browsers without having to setup their own GIS systems. This provided agencies that have not previously participated in the LDH project with the means to test the capabilities of the new LandNet at a low cost, and encourage the adoption and use of geospatial information.

Yet, although the cost of implementing LandNet is substantially lowered with Enterprise Grid Technology, SLA was confronted with a fresh financial challenge as a result of a new directive from the Singapore Ministry of Finance (MOF). The new directive sought to ensure greater accountability in the use of public funds. Consequently, SLA made plans to introduce a pay-for-use model and actively gathered the support from participating agencies to share the costs of implementing and sustaining the LandNet project in lieu of public funding.

The policy change created a number of challenges to overcome. First, it meant that existing and potential participating agencies had to relook their bottom line and source for funding to participate in LandNet. Second, the pay-for-use model adds on to the ongoing challenge of securing the participation of different agencies. Previously, some agencies were already reluctant to share "sensitive" information. With the pay-for-use model, many of the agencies wondered why they were sharing their land data freely but yet, had to pay for access to land data. As a result, SLA had to overcome resistance to the pay-for-use model by convincing different agencies that cost-sharing was the way forward.

Mr. Asokan, the Senior Manager of Estates Geospatial Information (EGI) at the DSTA explained, "I would say that, because essentially with that policy, they (MOF) are only looking from one point of view. They don't look at it from the buyers' point of view. So the buyers now are required to find their own source of funding and justify for it. LandNet is viewed as that: the data is free and you are paying the cost for operating the system. That makes communications on our side tough because people would say 'I don't need to use the system. Do you need to use the system? Without using the system, can't you just use the data?"

However, SLA invested substantial effort in persuading the agencies that the cost-sharing approach was the only way to keep the LandNet project sustainable. In particular, SLA had numerous dialogues with not only top management, but with middle management of the participating agencies as well, to explain that the average cost would be lower if every agency chipped in. SLA also understood that participating agencies had to seek the budget to pay for LandNet and was very accommodating in that it agreed to continue supplying the agencies with the data they needed until their budgets were approved. Consequently, even though there was some resistance to the cost-sharing model in the beginning, many of the participating agencies began to see that the value of participation indeed outweighed the cost of sharing the running costs of the LandNet. Mr. Tan Chia Li of URA explained, "... Right from the start we were aware that there's this charging that is coming, and we also have interest in (being involved in) the operations of LandNet. Otherwise, we would have to go and incur more resources to get information from various agencies. So right from the start we were (already committed), and little selling was needed (to convince us) to be involved in the project."

The way the cost-sharing model was implemented was also a critical factor in securing the continuing commitment of the various government agencies. Mr. Ng Siau Yong explained, "We thought ok, based on past behaviour, we approximated that when it was free, the usage was of a certain amount. Now that agencies needed to pay, we thought the usage would be cut by about half. But it turned out to be less than half. And that is no good. So then we slowly adjusted, now is more on (a) subscription (basis) so (the emphasis) is not so much on pay-per-use anymore."

In response, SLA quickly modified the cost-sharing model to be more equitable. "Heavy" data users had to pay higher fees while "lighter" users paid less. This modification provided greater incentives for agencies to use and contribute data to LDH/LandNet and ensured that agencies continued to have access to the most up-to-date data.

Besides playing an important role in motivating agencies to migrate towards the online mode of data exchange, technology also gave rise to improved data quality as it enabled SLA to provide member agencies with a higher level of service quality with data now available on a real-time basis. However, in order to encourage an even greater extent of data sharing and to get new agencies onboard, it was believed that the simple, operational use of geospatial data would not suffice. Mr. Ng Siau Yong of SLA explained, "… My view is that the usefulness of data depends on how people use it. If people don't use it effectively, then your data is useless. We started promoting the use of spatial data, because when you start getting people interested in different uses of spatial data, it can be more effectively used to produce economic benefits."

Hence, during the POC, SLA launched several initiatives to change the conventional perception of LDH as being "just a data repository" to an invaluable inter-organisational information system that enabled value-adding collaboration. One of these initiatives was the launch of the quarterly Geospatial Information and Technology Exchange (GITEX) forums. The objective of this forum was to allow various government agencies to interact and present how they have successfully used geospatial information to improve their planning and operational effectiveness. Aside from how agencies use information, they may also present on various geospatial tools that may be used to improve their analysis of the data retrieved from the LDH. Mr. Asokan from DSTA provided an interesting example: "Our presentation was about the use of open source geospatial tools. With the availability of data due to the rollout of LandNet, agencies had the opportunity to exploit this data for their own internal needs apart from just using LandNet. They can also download the data and use open source tools to do their own internal analysis and so on. So our presentation touches on the various open source tools that we ourselves are using internally."

Moreover, private sector organisations were also invited to these forums to showcase what new GIS technology was available, which kept SLA and its members informed about the latest technological developments in the GIS landscape. Overall, the GITEX forums served to increase the communication between SLA, the participating government agencies and the private sector, and provided a conducive environment for the various agencies to collectively innovate in various ways which the geospatial information can be used.

Apart from the GITEX forums, SLA was also aggressively targeting traditionally non-land related agencies to participate in LandNet. These agencies stem from different clusters such as healthcare and education. SLA encouraged participation by creating pilot projects or providing a conceptual showcase of what LandNet could provide. Mr. Lim Ming Khai, the Head of Geospatial Operations & Development of SLA gave an example of a pilot project conducted with Ministry of Health (MOH), "We approached MOH and said that we could place all their survey information on digital map and let them see graphically the density of the patients and the locations of the hospitals, GPs and clinics in relation to one another. It is very interesting to look at the maps as you have the distance perspective and the geographical perspective, which gives new insights as compared to traditional tables and graphs."

This form of collective innovation through novel ways of using the available data was something that was not achieved in the previous incarnations of LDH, and has led to the development of similar pilot projects with a number of other non-land related agencies. With each successful case, agencies begin to see further possibilities of applying geospatial data in their operations, and through dialogue with SLA, agencies are able to explore how they can collaborate with SLA to co-produce additional relevant information or applications to support their areas of need.

CONCLUSION: MOVING FORWARD WITH SG-SPACE (2007–PRESENT)

From 2007, the story of LandNet continues to unfold. As LandNet possesses immense, untapped potential for the participating agencies in the innovative leverage of geospatial data, SLA is currently exploring ways to link up with the data exchanges or "hubs" of other non-land related agencies to form a more powerful entity: SG-SPACE (see Figure 6.2). SG-SPACE is a type of National Spatial Data Infrastructure (NSDI) that has been implemented in a number of developed nations, such as the United States and Australia. Mr. Ng Siau Yong explained, "… We noticed that many countries are moving towards NSDI. So we assessed ourselves and said 'yes!'… (actually,) we had already started many years ago. Land Data Hub is a small version of a NSDI. We already have the clearinghouse, we have the service, LandNet. What we perhaps lack is a comprehensive (set of) policies, standards, (as well as) the capabilities. LDH consisted of mainly land-related agencies. The new agencies that were not part of LDH did not have a means of comprehensively sharing their data…."

Through SG-SPACE, LDH would be linked to other data hubs such as the People Hub managed by Ministry of Home Affairs (MHA) and the Business Hub managed by Accounting and Corporate Regulatory Authority (ACRA). The ultimate aim is to provide richer and more useful information in the geospatial format, and help the local agencies develop their capabilities in exploiting geo-spatial data. Clearly, SLA can expect new challenges on top of the perennial challenges of inter-agency collaboration: these include technical, data management, and communication challenges.

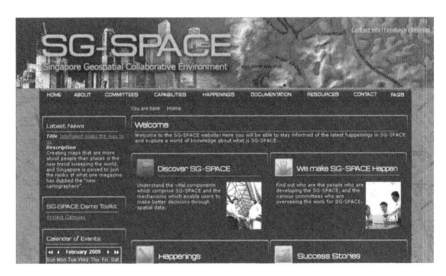

Figure 6.2:   SG-SPACE.

In particular, technical challenges may stem from the hybrid model of data management adopted by SG-SPACE, which utilises both centralised and decentralised models. Moreover, as SG-SPACE enables the sharing of live data, it means that the underlying technology has to be able to support this. With regards to data management, SG-SPACE will face increasing complexity in data classification and ensuring data confidentiality as more agencies become involved. This is because each agency will possess data of differing sensitivities and classifications. For example, the information that a participating agency obtains from third parties is not shared, and there is also a need to establish proper classification rules to determine what pieces of fundamental and critical data have to remain available at all times.

With the integration of the different data hubs, effective communications between agencies become even more crucial. However, communication challenges may arise as data access policies across the different hubs need to be unified and the details of data exchange have to be worked out. Yet, despite the challenges, there is ground for optimism. Inter-agency committees at various levels have been established. A high-level steering committee was assembled to provide the guiding principles as well as resolving inter-agency issues related to data sharing and harmonising of data policies. A coordinating committee that reports directly to the steering committee was also set up to handle the operational level issues.

Further down, there are also technical committees that handle implementation issues such as the creation of data standards. A committee was also created to promote and create awareness of spatial information. With the committees performing specialised functions at the various levels, cross-agency communications can help to identify and cater to the needs of every stakeholder group to obtain participant buy-in. SLA itself has also taken pains to safeguard the confidentiality and privacy of data. For example, with SG-SPACE, only aggregate data concerning people are displayed. This demonstrates that SLA recognises the concerns of the participating agencies, and by addressing these concerns, the SLA is able to gain buy-in from the participating agencies. The increasing commitment and buy-in from agencies can be seen from the way they are stepping forward to take up responsibility and ownership over certain layers of information. NParks and BCA for instance, have taken the lead in contributing and managing the data from diverse sources for the tree layer and building data layers of SG-SPACE respectively. In this, the SG-SPACE initiative will provide more value sharing opportunities among agencies and will allow government agencies to become more effective in leveraging geospatial technology.

DISCUSSION QUESTIONS

1. What does the SLA case study reveal about the nature of e-Government integration?
2. What are the challenges of e-Government integration and how does the SLA case study suggest that these challenges can be overcome?

Case 7

NS PORTAL: TRANSFORMING THE PUBLIC SERVICES OF THE MINISTRY OF DEFENCE OF SINGAPORE

Barney Tan

University of Sydney

BACKGROUND

On 14 March 1967, the National Service (Amendment) Act was passed in the Singapore Parliament that required all Singaporean males above 16 years and 6 months of age to render full-time National Service (NS) for a period of two to two-and-a-half years. After this period of full-time training, the enlistees; termed "NSFs," transition to the role of citizen-soldiers termed "Operationally Ready National Servicemen" (NSmen) until the age of 40. More than 40 years on, there are currently more than 300,000 NSmen in active service, forming the backbone of the national defense capabilities of Singapore. The Government Ministry tasked with overseeing the defense, manpower and technological capabilities of the Singapore military is the Ministry of Defence (MINDEF). Established in 1966, the Ministry is responsible for the recruitment, training, and administrative needs of the servicemen.

As a serviceman transitions through his NS lifecycle, taking on the roles of a pre-enlistee, a NSF, and a NSman in succession, he will require the administrative services provided by the various agencies of MINDEF. These services may include registration for NS, notification of overseas travel, the booking of dates for the annual Individual Physical Proficiency Tests (IPPT) and application for deferment from NS. Yet, with hundreds of different transactions provided by over

Table 7.1:   Services provided by the various MINDEF agencies.

Service areas	Transactions available
Registration for NS	• Submission of registration application • Updating personal particulars • Enquiry/Change of medical examination date • Enquiry on NS registration and deferment status • Confirm status of registration or deferment • Enquiry of date of enlistment
Career/Scholarship with MINDEF	• Application for positions within MINDEF • Application for MINDEF Scholarship
NS Pay Matters	• Updating of banking particulars • Request for pay slips and other financial statements • Verification of payment and tax relief details • Submission of make-up pay claim
Overseas Notification	• Notification of overseas trip • Amendment of pre-reported trip • Cancellation of pre-reported trip • Application for exit permit • Renewal/Extension of exit permit • Eligibility enquiry of exit permit • Status enquiry of exit permit • Update return date of exit permit • Cancellation of exit permit • Updating of overseas address • Registration with Singapore Embassy
Full-time NS Liability	• Application for NSF resumption • Enquiry on status of application of resumption
Equipment Needs	• Request for military equipment • Exchange of military equipment • Return of military equipment
Annual IPPT	• Book date for annual IPPT • Submission of annual IPPT results • Scheduling of Remedial Training
Provide Feedback	• Submission of feedback form

60 different agencies (see Table 7.1 for a non-exhaustive list of the transactions provided by the various agencies of MINDEF), coordinating the administrative processes that underlie the needs of the servicemen was complex, paperwork-intensive, and tedious.

PUBLIC SERVICE DELIVERY BEFORE E-GOVERNMENT

Prior to electronic government (e-Government) implementation, the administration of the various transactions of MINDEF was characterised by repetitive, manual work processes, with each agency or unit responsible for its administrative procedures. Colonel Tung Yui Fai, the former Head of the NS Affairs Department elaborated on the nature of public service delivery prior to the e-Government implementation, "Prior to the MIW portal (MINDEF's first e-Government portal), NS transactions were decentralised to the units that the NSmen belonged to. Transactions were done primarily via snail (postal) mail, faxes and phone. NSmen often lament the long time taken to conduct simple administrative transactions; like booking for IPPT, updating personal particular, submitting claims for makeup pay, and in or out processing during in-camp trainings...."

As an illustration, every pre-enlistee liable for NS had to submit the required registration forms and documents physically during NS registration. The forms would be handed over to the counter staff for data entry; a tedious, error-prone process that takes around five minutes to complete per form. After registration, the enlistees would be informed by post of the dates that they would have to go to the Central Manpower Base (CMPB) for a medical examination, and if they were unable to make it for the appointment pre-scheduled by the CMPB, they would call or visit the agency to schedule another appointment. A NSman who enlisted in 1997 recalled his experience with the public services provided by MINDEF, "Previously, the validity of our (the servicemen's) passports was for only a year, so we had to renew our passports frequently. And every time before we travelled overseas, we had to make a trip to the CMPB, submit our passport and the renewal form, wait a couple of hours, just for them to give us a chop (signifying approval of extension) on the passport that would tell you that your passport has been renewed."

In addition, there was minimal integration and data-sharing among the different entities within MINDEF, even if their operations were relevant to each other or if they required the same data from the servicemen. Every agency or unit had their own information system and if a serviceman wished to transact with more than one entity within MINDEF, he would have to join different queues for each entity that his needs are pertained to. Ms. Sherlyn Foo, a member of the former Systems and Computer Organisation (SCO) department of MINDEF described the lack of integration among different entities within MINDEF at the time, "You will often see the servicemen filling out certain information repeatedly. If, for example, you want to conduct a certain transaction with MINDEF, here you fill in all your personal particulars. But if you go to another counter that belongs to another department, you have to fill in the same thing all over again. The integration was definitely much lesser then...."

The diversity and sheer volume of transactions handled by various agencies within MINDEF, the labor-intensive, manual operations of the agencies, and the lack of data integration resulted in a deep-seated inefficiency within the organisation that was overcome only by the ample resources of MINDEF. An army of counter staff and data entry clerks were required to sustain the operations of MINDEF and the top management quickly realised that while the massive resource commitment could alleviate the problem of inefficiency in the short term, it is not a viable long-term solution. Mr. Chan Yeng Kit, the former Director of Manpower at MINDEF and Permanent Secretary of the Ministry of Information, Communications and the Arts described the realisation of MINDEF's top management, "... We were looking at global changes, environmental changes and what MINDEF as an organisation would need to do to respond. The conclusion was that we needed a large-scale change management programme... changing of mindsets, changing of the way we approach administration in defense, and the way we approach the whole concept of defense in the first place... All of us know how much inefficiency there is in the military. Things are very well-oiled sometimes because we pour in a lot of people, a lot of resources and it works! But the concern was that unless the ministry can reinvent itself, the SAF (Singapore Armed Forces) is going to be left behind. We are going to be seen as out of touch...."

DEFENSE TOWN: INITIAL EXPERIMENTATIONS WITH INTERNET TECHNOLOGIES

Guided by the Civil Service Computerisation Programme (CSCP) of the Singapore government, the focus of Information and Communications Technology (ICT) use in MINDEF in the early 1990s was on computerisation and process automation through the development of information systems such as the Integrated Manpower Information System (iMIS). Ms. Ng Yuk Tong, a former member of SCO provided description of the functionalities of the iMIS system, "It (iMIS) is actually a collection of applications on the mainframe. Different application will handle a different part of HR (Human Resource) Management. For example, there will be one that handles all the record maintenance so when there is a posting or a promotion, somebody will use the application to update the record... there are also applications for promotion, ranking and report generation...."

It was not until the advent of Internet technologies in the mid-1990s that the notion of using ICTs for the provision of information and services first arose. MINDEF launched its first corporate website in June 1996 and at the time, the website consisted of only static informational pages organised along departmental lines as the primary concern of MINDEF then was to ensure the availability and adequacy of accurate corporate information. Within a year however, electronic transactions were made available on the websites of individual departments, agencies and units within MINDEF, although at the time, the utility of the electronic transactions left much to be desired. Mr. Chan Yeng Kit candidly recounted the nature of the earliest electronic transactions provided by the CMPB, "When we first started some of these things (electronic transactions), CMPB said that they have enabled transactions on their website. You can download the form, print it out... but you still had to mail it in! After some time, they allowed online transactions (via electronic forms) on their website... but if documentary proof was required, you still have to mail it in. So you have the electronic channel (electronic transaction forms) and you have the postal channel (submitting documents by post)... when you start asking questions you realise how silly your own processes are...."

In addition to the inadequacies of the earliest electronic transactions, the development of the electronic services (e-services) were uncoordinated and decentralised as they were initiated and managed by the individual departments, agencies, and units within MINDEF. By the end of 1998, there were approximately 18 different online transactions housed in different websites and more than 13 telephone hotlines that were dealing with different categories of services. This function-based, organisation-centric structure of public services made it difficult for servicemen to obtain the services they require because they had to know the MINDEF entity that their needs pertained to and go to the right web address, or dial the right hotline number in order to perform a transaction or make a simple enquiry.

The first concerted effort towards the integration of MINDEF's e-services was driven by the development of eCitizen, a Singapore's government initiative aimed at providing an integrated public service portal for its citizens. Spearheaded by the Public Service for the 21st Century (PS21) committee, eCitizen was conceptualised as an ecosystem of 15 electronic "towns" catering to the various needs of Singapore citizens. Due to the central role of MINDEF in area of national defense, MINDEF was invited to make their e-services available in "Defense Town"; a section of eCitizen focused on the defense and security of Singapore, and the initiative to integrate their existing e-services was launched under the stewardship of the Management Development and Services Organisation (MDSO) of MINDEF. Phase I of the Defense Town project was launched in April 1999 and lasted for around five months. By the end of the phase, detailed information about MINDEF's services and all 18 electronic transactions were made available on Defense Town under the umbrella of the eCitizen portal.

Despite the successful integration of their existing e-services, MINDEF's management noted that the backend processing of the submitted electronic forms remained a labourious, manual process. Thus, while the customer interface had been re-organised in the form of a web directory with links to the 18 electronic transactions available, the problems of the lack of integration and data sharing among the various internal departments remained unresolved. To look into the problem, a study team that comprised of members from the MDSO, the Public Affairs department, and the SCO of MINDEF was established to review the existing business processes of the organisation. The result was an extensive Business Process Improvement (BPI) study that sought to streamline the operations and business process of MINDEF. Ms. Sherlyn Foo elaborated on the nature of the BPI study, "Besides implementing additional applications, we went through an extensive BPI study where we identified the problem areas. We asked ourselves... besides enabling form downloads, can we make the interface more interactive? Are there data that need to be passed from one (entity) to another that we can share among the different applications?"

The BPI study led to Phase II of the Defense Town project. Launched in September 1999 at a cost of US$2.28 million, the aim of Phase II was to develop Defense Town into a fully integrated online service centre. The primary focus of the phase was on developing 18 new electronic transactions and integrating the electronic transactions with the relevant backend databases of MINDEF. Through this integration, manual, backend processing is no longer required after an electronic form has been submitted. In addition, the benefits gained from the integrated online service centre include: (1) Marked improvements in service cycle time as surface mail is replaced by electronic mail and acknowledgements, (2) reduction in the generation and mailing of paperwork, (3) diversion of labour resources to more meaningful job functions, (4) error reduction through the incorporation of computation and business rule checks into the system, and (5) marked increase in convenience for users who can now access MINDEF's e-services 24/7 and would no longer need to visit the relevant department or agency physically.

MIW: MINDEF'S INTEGRATED E-GOVERNMENT PORTAL

The Birth of the MIW Portal

Although the Defense Town project hinted at the momentous potential of the Internet for improving public services and revolutionalising business processes, the potential was largely unfulfilled as its development; driven by various entities within MINDEF in isolation, lacked strategic coherence. In addition, the success of Defense Town was curtailed by a low rate of adoption among the NSmen population. A NSman who was in active service during the Defense Town phase provided a possible explanation for the low rate of adoption, "I don't think they (MINDEF) promoted Defense Town much… I didn't know about it until I was at eCitizen looking up some information related to (housing)… I guess it is not very intuitive to go to eCitizen; a general citizen portal, to look for MINDEF e-services… and I have to say, the user interface of eCitizen then was very 'unfriendly'…."

In April 2000, against a backdrop of rapid, global advances in ICT, a committee comprising of key representatives from various departments within MINDEF was established by Mr. Peter Ho; former Permanent Secretary of Defense Development at MINDEF and the former Head of the Singapore Civil Service. The committee, which met fortnightly, was established for the purpose of examining the organisational implications of the technology-induced upheaval in the external environment. The findings of the committee, coupled with the successful experience of running Defense Town quickly convinced the top management of MINDEF that the Internet was a promising solution to the chronic inefficiency and bureaucratic mindset that was pervasive within the organisation at the time.

Consequently, the plans for a revolutionary strategic initiative; termed MINDEF.com, was quickly laid. Mr. Peter Ho provides an elaboration of the MINDEF.com initiative, "I felt that we were not leveraging enough on what was a new platform for communications: The Internet… It's (using the Internet) not just about delivering information, it's also about interacting and transacting… there are many things that we can do… so I coined the term MINDEF.com… and the reason why I chose MINDEF.com rather than MINDEF.gov or MINDEF.org was just to emphasise that we were breaking out of the traditional model of doing things, the old bureaucratic way. We're going to try a model that is much more practiced in the private sector…."

A proposal was quickly drawn up by a project team led by Mr. Chan Yeng Kit for the creation of an internet portal. However, the MINDEF management was very clear on their stand that the MINDEF.

com project was not merely a technology driven project, but a change management exercise aimed at effecting sweeping changes to the rigid bureaucracy of the entire organisation. Mr. Alphonsus Pang, Director of the MINDEF Corporate Development and Services Division (MCDSD), elaborated on the organisational mindset change necessitated by the implementation of MINDEF.com, "The reason for MINDEF.com was that... he (Mr. Peter Ho) wanted a mindset change. This mindset change is something much deeper and strategic than any of us could have imagined as an outcome... the idea was to rethink current processes and change it.... I think Mr. Peter Ho's encouragement was to ask us to think customer-centric.... You want to improve processes and make things more efficient, but often, the motivation behind it is organisation-centric. It takes a lot of effort, especially in the beginning to go into the shoes or a person receiving (the services)... to see how things are like from their point of view...."

More importantly, the management of MINDEF realised that the project would not only affect the communications and transactional capabilities of MINDEF, but could also have direct implications on the overarching defense capabilities of the Singapore military. The portal could be used to support the development of strong bonds among servicemen through the development of virtual communities. Consequently, the MINDEF.com project was envisioned as an opportunity and a platform for promoting the commitment of the servicemen to NS as well. Mr. Chan Yeng Kit elaborated on the vision of the top management, "I think it is a fairly well-known fact from the wars that have been fought that... what give people the most courage on the battlefield is not patriotism or the glory of winning the war... It is because your buddy is out there: you are looking out for him and he is looking out for you.... After the two to two-and-a-half years of (full-time) national service, the bonding is very strong at the units... but once they leave, they are scattered.... Even though they might meet for two weeks every year after that, by then, the bonding and esprit de corps are very different.... So the thinking was: 'Is there a way that we can electronically allow them to maintain this community; provide an electronic platform... so that the sense of belonging and esprit de corps could be maintained....'"

The MINDEF.com initiative was eventually launched with two formal objectives. First, MINDEF.com would help to improve the services of MINDEF and foster stronger bonds among servicemen through three strategic thrusts: (1) Creating a MINDEF internet portal that is the preferred mode of access for all MINDEF/SAF services, (2) exploring and establishing new channels of communication between MINDEF and NSmen, and (3) helping to build strong virtual communities among the servicemen, particularly the NSmen. Second, MINDEF.com would be a change management exercise that would help reposition MINDEF in the new economy. This would be achieved through four strategic thrusts: (1) "Dot.com" the Ministry, (2) changing existing mindsets, (3) re-engineering business processes for alignment with new strategic objectives, and (4) convergence of MINDEF's public services. A portal development roadmap created by the organisation is depicted in Figure 7.1.

Implementing the MIW Portal

In implementing the Internet portal, the decision was quickly made to outsource the development of the portal to an external vendor under a "Build, Operate and Own" (BOO) model. Under this

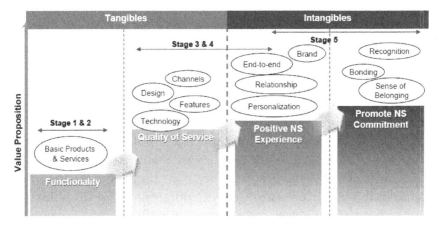

Figure 7.1: A portal development roadmap charting the planned stages of development.

model, MINDEF will provide the e-services to be made available on the portal. The external vendor, on the other hand, will be responsible for building the portal, managing the content, ensuring the portal's availability, and generally overseeing the operations of the portal. Mr. Peter Ho explained the rationale behind outsourcing the development of the portal to an external vendor, "… At the time, we had SCO in MINDEF, which had a very proud tradition of setting up the computerisation programme for developing the management information systems for MINDEF…. But I said no, I didn't want the SCO to do it… technology is the least of their problems… the real challenge was to keep on getting more and more people to use this portal… (but) they can't do that, they are not marketing people."

In addition to the marketing expertise of the external vendor, outsourcing the development of the portal to the private sector gives rise to a number of advantages. First, due to the experience and the technical expertise of the external vendor, the management felt that the development cycle for the portal could be considerably shortened. Second, the management believed that if they could create a public perception that the portal was privately run, it would attract more users to the website and make servicemen more receptive towards the portal. Third, the management envisioned a seamless integration of the public services of MINDEF with the commercial offerings of the private sector to provide greater convenience to the servicemen.

Consequently, a portal run by a private organisation would offer MINDEF a lot more flexibility and speed in development. Mr. Tan Ah Tuan, Deputy Director of the Infocomm Infrastructure Programme Centre, elaborates, "… They (the external vendors) are able to run it like a business. They can tie up with other private companies and bring services to the portal. For example, when you go for an overseas trip, you inform MINDEF through an overseas notification. At the end of the process, there's a link that says: 'Do you want to buy travel insurance: packages? There's a preferential rate for you.' You can do that on a privately run portal. If you have a .gov.sg (suffix on the web address), you will have to call for tender to decide which company you lists on your website. Otherwise, people may ask 'why is the government favouring this insurance company over the other one? So there is this flexibility to tie up with other commercial services…'"

The decision was also made to amalgamate the telephone hot-lines of the various departments within MINDEF to establish a common hotline number operated by a centralised call centre, and bundle the development of the call centre with the development of Internet portal in the same outsourcing contract. The reason for the decision was twofold. First, the top management of MINDEF believed that a private call centre operator would provide better service to the servicemen as civil servants tend to be less immersed in the service excellence mindset of the new economy. Second, the management of MINDEF saw the bundling of the call centre with the Internet portal as a mechanism for incentivising the portal operator. Mr Chan Yeng Kit explained, "We know that call centres cost a lot more (to operate) than Internet servers. The best way to incentivize him (the vendor) to improve the portal and make it really user friendly and seamless is if he runs both at the same time… (In that way,) the increased number of customers arising from the call centre and the website become additional cost savings for the vendor. Of course the vendor will have certain SLAs (service level agreements) and service standards that he has to meet as far as the call centre is concerned. But we felt that there was synergy, so we put both together and got the same operator to do it."

With the decisions to outsource the development of the portal and the centralised call centre to an external vendor, a closed tender was called and five Information Technology (IT) vendors were invited to submit their proposals for the portal. The management of MINDEF eventually decided to award the contract to Green Dot Internet Services (GDIS), a subsidiary of Green Dot Capital and a member of the Singapore Technologies (ST) group. Under the five year contract, GDIS would build and operate a centralised call centre and the MIW (My Internet World) portal, an Internet portal that provided information, interaction platforms, e-services, lifestyle content, products, and services for servicemen and their families around the clock.

Mr. Chan Yeng Kit commented on the reason for the decision to award the contract to GDIS, "We decided on ST (of which GDIS was a part of) for a mix of reasons. One reason was that on the whole, their proposal based on cost, as well as ideas was probably, or is the best. The other reason is we sincerely believe that this would be a strategic tool for MINDEF, and if it's going to be a strategic tool or one of the key pillars, we would want to ensure that this is not compromised from the security point of view.... Just as MINDEF relied on ST to service and maintain their aircrafts, we treated ST as a strategic vendor... (A third reason was that) they were prepared to be flexible as well...."

ENSURING THE AVAILABILITY OF INFORMATION AND BASIC SERVICES (APRIL 2001–OCTOBER 2001)

The management of MINDEF drove the development of the portal with a relentless sense of urgency. The MIW portal (see Figure 7.2) was eventually built from scratch within eight months and was launched to great fanfare on 1st April 2001. At the time of its launch, the focus of e-Government development was on making available all related information and the existing e-services of the various MINDEF agencies. To this end, the individual MINDEF departments and agencies were strongly encouraged to make their services available on the portal whenever possible, as the existing e-services available on Defense Town were made available on the new MIW portal as well (see Table 7.2).

Although the primary objective of the first phase was not technically demanding, the initial phase of portal development was characterised by a tentative, trial-and-error approach to systems development due to the relative inexperience of both MINDEF and GDIS at the time.

The development of the portal was also hampered by problems of communications and coordination, which were further exacerbated by the short development timeframe allocated for the implementation of the project. Dr. Francis Yeoh, the Chief Executive Officer of GDIS at the time of MIW portal's launch, provided the following

Figure 7.2:   MIW portal.

anecdote, "My team of engineers was collating applications that were developed independently at different times! We had to coordinate the backend mechanics and come up with user interface simultaneously. We were pulling shifts to work 24-hour days and we were working on the software right up to the night before the official opening, when we should have, ideally, finished it weeks before for extensive trouble-shooting."

In addition to the technical challenges of portal implementation, there was also a sense of apprehension among internal MINDEF departments and agencies about the Public–Private Partnership (PPP) approach to portal development as the approach entailed a detailed examination of their existing business processes. Mr. Tan Ah Tuan described the reason for the apprehension that resulted in some extent of resistance among internal MINDEF stakeholders to the implementation of the MIW portal, "I think that

Table 7.2:   Services offered on the MIW portal and call centre at launch.

Services	Description
Portal Services	
Email	Each user was given a free lifetime web-based e-mail account with 5 MB of storage.
Unified Messaging System	Eases the management of multiple communication channels by converging voicemail, e-mail, and fax messages into a single e-mail inbox. Users could receive their voicemails and fax as e-mail attachments.
Online Discussion Forums	Users were able to participate in public electronic discussion forums or create discussion forums for their own areas of interest that are accessible to all.
Chat rooms	Users were able to access the public chat rooms and interact with other online users in real time.
Personalisation Tools	Users were able to select the preferred colour schema and customise the miw.com.sg website to show frequently accessed links. By June 2001, MINDEF e-services were re-organised according to user profiles to ensure that the more relevant services are shown first.
Call Centre Services	
MINDEF eServices Center (eSC)	eSC is a one-stop, 24-hour call centre that integrates all services currently offered under the various MINDEF hotlines. eSC can be accessed via telephone or fax at 1-800-eMINDEF (1-800-3646333). The automated phone system allows callers to access services relevant to them by identifying the user group they belong to. Users can choose to speak directly to Customer Service Operators anytime should they wish to.
MINDEF E-Services	
e-Personnel Services	Electronic transactions for registration for NS, enquiry on date of enlistment for NS, overseas notification, exit permit application, job application for SAF/ MINDEF, scholarship application of SAF/MINDEF, request for medical report.

(*Continued*)

Table 7.2:   (*Continued*).

Services	Description
e-Finance Services	Electronic transactions such as changing of bank account and enquiry on payment status.
e-Training Services	Electronic transactions such as booking of IPPT date and accessing e-Training records.
e-Logistics Services	Electronic transactions for Tri-service e-Mart (an application that manages the replacement of personal equipment and expendable items), e-cookhouse (an application that connects the indenting of meal rations with accounting and payment processes).

different people had their doubts about going for the PPP approach. There are people who will, of course, find it inconvenient that they have to work with other people to look at their processes. They may have to open up their internal processes for external parties to examine.... And a very natural question (that arises) would be: 'Are you efficient in your processes? Can you do better than what you are doing?' So now people are being measured and challenged in their performance."

To overcome the resistance of various internal stakeholders to the implementation of the MIW portal, the MINDEF.com's steering committee; consisting of influential representatives of the various internal stakeholders, was established to provide direction, allocate resources, and make key decisions for the project. Based on the directives and decisions of the steering committee, a working committee, in conjunction with the project management team, would bring the vision of the steering committee to fruition by coordinating the internal stakeholders and the external developers in project implementation.

Mr. Peter Ho described the role the MINDEF.com steering committee played in overcoming the resistance of internal stakeholders to the implementation of the MIW portal, "In the early meetings (of the MINDEF.com steering committee), every meeting is like a long story of why all of this is necessary. Then of course, sooner or later, some of them will begin to get persuaded... they see this as exciting because this is a vision of the future that is possible and yet, within reach. It's not incremental, it's a leapfrog from where we were to an exciting new possibility…. In the world outside MINDEF, it is already happening! So they see the distinct possibility that we could do it, and do it well…."

Yet, despite the concerted implementation efforts of the internal MINDEF organisations and GDIS, the initial MIW portal was not well-received by the servicemen population; complaints flooded in about the poor navigability, the lack of aesthetic appeal, and poor organisation of the website content. Consequently, the site posted less than 20,000 visitors a month; a mere fraction of the entire servicemen population (estimated at 360,000). The lukewarm reception towards the MIW portal provided the impetus for a major revamp of the portal just six months after its initial launch, and ushered in the next phase of MINDEF's e-Government journey.

IMPROVING THE QUALITY OF SERVICES (NOVEMBER 2001–APRIL 2004)

Having attained the goal of making available the information and services of the various internal MINDEF organisations on the MIW portal, the objective of the next phase of e-Government development was on improving the quality of the services provided. Accordingly, the portal development team pursued three key strategies to the attainment of this end. First, following a series of usability studies conducted by GDIS, a complete revamp of the user interface was performed to improve the usability, utility, and attractiveness of the MIW portal.

In addition, the lifestyle content on the portal was re-organised in the form of an online magazine, with a greater variety of articles, online resources and special promotions pertaining to topics such as military, finance, career, travel, family, health, and leisure. Mr. Jon Hoo, a Senior Marketing Manager with GDIS, provided a description of the revamped MIW portal that was launched in November 2001, "All our articles and special promotions are tailored made for the Nsmen…. Think of MIW as an online cross between a lifestyle magazine, a military-interest site, and a human interest community publication dedicated to the National Service experience."

Second, accessibility to MINDEF's public services was enhanced with the development of new access platforms such as Wireless Access Protocol (WAP), Short Message Service, (SMS) and Palm Query Application (PQA)1, hence resulting in greater flexibility and convenience to suit the lifestyle needs of the individual user. To illustrate, an active serviceman described how the use of SMS technology for overseas notification provided him with a wider array of access options to the services provided by MINDEF, "When I go overseas, three out of four times I would forget to notify MINDEF in advance. But now I can use the SMS at the airport… it is sometimes quite hard to get Internet access there (at the airport) but I will usually still have my (mobile) phone with me… so notifying MINDEF is not a problem".

Third, a continuous stream of new applications and e-services were introduced on the MIW portal by the portal development team, extending both the variety and richness of the services offered. A non-exhaustive list of the key applications developed or revamped during this phase is presented in Table 7.3. Colonel Bernard Toh, the Director of Public Affairs at MINDEF, elaborated on the commitment of MINDEF towards continuous innovation and service excellence, "MINDEF has made a commitment to offer all its services and transactions that can be performed electronically, online. With the availability of the MIW portal, the pace for delivering services online has stepped up considerably… (We have) seen quite a transformation in how we communicate with our key "customers" — the NSmen. We have opened up many more channels for interaction, which gives the NSmen greater convenience and flexibility in fulfilling their national service obligations. We will continue to innovate and experiment with new technologies and methods to maintain effectiveness and service excellence."

The primary challenge associated with the objective of improving the quality of public services through the use of emergent technologies; such as WAP, PQA and SMS, and the development of groundbreaking applications lies in the level of uncertainty involved. During this phase of e-Government development, a proliferation of new

Table 7.3: Services added or revamped between November 2001 and April 2004.

Services	Description
MIW PDA Apps	An application that allows servicemen on-the-move to perform transactions via their internet-enabled personal digital assistants (PDAs). Users have to download PQA and "hot-sync" to his PDA. Once that is done, the user can use the application to connect to MIW and carry out transactions.
MIW e-LIFE	A personal health organiser application available on the Internet portal and downloadable for the PDA that enables a user to monitor his health and fitness level.
MIW Help Online	MIW Help Online consist of three real-time help services; MIW Text Online, MIW Talk Online and MIW Help Callback. Using Voice Over IP (VOIP) technology, these services allow customer service officers at the eSC to render help to users using a dial-up Internet connection without requiring that the user terminate his connection to call the eSC.
e-MUP Batch Submission	e-MUP Batch Submission is an application that allows the employers of NSmen to submit their makeup pay claims in a batch. The previous e-MUP application requires the employer to enter the NSmen's salary information individually and manually.
E-Delphi Feedback	An online feedback application that introduces interactivity to the process of obtaining feedback. Based on the Delphi methodology, this application is particularly useful in facilitating the convergence of views and seeking suggestions on new services.
Natural Language Help	A search application that allows a user to query MIW by typing in his question in any form. Instead of searching by keywords, the system processes the question phrased in natural language and presents a logical and accurate answer.
Patriot eBonus	An application that supports the Patriot membership scheme. Users become Patriot members by downloading a Patriot icon from the MIW portal to their mobile phones or PDAs. The user can flash the icon to the participating merchants to obtain membership benefits.

(*Continued*)

Table 7.3:   (*Continued*).

Services	Description
Enhanced IPPT Booking system	Enhancement to the existing IPPT booking system to cater to remedial training and reminders (via electronic mail or SMS). Also allows NSmen to check past results and attendance.
e-Self-update	An application that facilitates the self-updating of personal particulars for all users.
MINDEF Payment Services	An electronic payment application that allows servicemen to pay for magazine subscriptions, SAF card replacement fees, and fines via eNETS or credit card.
e-PREP	An application that allows NSFs to take up online preparatory and refresher courses while in service.
BMTC Posting Order	An electronic posting system that informs NSFs of their new posting after basic military training.

technologies; such as wireless communication protocols, mobile data services and application development platforms, were rapidly emerging in the general IT environment. Yet, due to the rate at which new technologies emerging and the sheer number of alternative technologies available, internal stakeholders at MINDEF were often apprehensive about experimenting with, or advocating the use of a particular technology, even if they have identified a potential avenue for leveraging the technology to improve the quality of their services.

To overcome the apprehension towards experimenting with new technologies, the management of MINDEF was highly supportive, encouraging, and tolerant of failure. Resources in terms of funding and manpower were made readily available, and the portal development team and the internal MINDEF organisations that were willing to experiment were encouraged to develop their new ideas whenever possible.

In addition, system development failure is never cast in a negative light by the management of MINDEF, but is instead perceived as a stepping stone towards the attainment of future successes. Mr. Peter Ho cited the example of the development of WAP applications to illustrate the mindset of MINDEF's top management towards technological experimentation, "I told them (the portal development team and internal MINDEF stakeholders) 'If you want to experiment, I will support you.' So we allowed them to even try things like... WAP (Wireless Access Protocol). We knew when the idea was raised that it (WAP technology) is not going to last, because it's very slow.[9] But there were enough techies out there who wanted to try. So we said, 'You go and try. I will give you some money to go and try.' We allowed them to experiment with technologies because if you don't experiment, you will never be ready to make the next leap when the real killer app (application) comes about."

The three strategies adopted by MINDEF to achieve the organisational objective of improving the quality of the services provided at the MIW portal and the eSC proved to be highly effective as the volume of transactions handled by the two service platforms tripled to over 350,000 transactions per month (approximately 300,000 transactions per month on the MIW portal and 50,000 per month through the eSC) by April 2004. In addition, a customer satisfaction survey that was conducted between October 2003 and February 2004 revealed that servicemen were generally satisfied with the quality of MINDEF's public services, with 75.24% and 89.54% of the customers surveyed indicating that they were satisfied with the services of the Internet portal and the eSC respectively (see Appendix A). Encouraged by the success achieved, MINDEF was ready to set their sights beyond the operational objective of improving service quality as they embarked on the next phase of their e-Government journey.

PROVIDING A POSITIVE NATIONAL SERVICE EXPERIENCE (MAY 2004–APRIL 2006)

The objective of the first phase of e-Government development at MINDEF was to ensure that the information and services provided by

---

[9] Other criticisms of WAP technology during this period include intermittent connections (service provider dependent), constrained user interface capabilities and a lack of openness (e.g., many service providers controlled the device browser to ensure that the first page accessed by the user was their own wireless portal).

the various internal MINDEF organisations were available on the MIW portal and the eSC. In the second phase of e-Government development, the organisational objective of MINDEF went beyond simply ensuring the availability of information and services to improving the quality of their services by enhancing the aesthetic appeal, content organisation, accessibility, as well as the variety and utility of their public services. With an array of quality services in place on both the MIW portal and the eSC, MINDEF was ready to look beyond the operational aspects of e-Government implementation and focus on the strategic objectives of portal implementation originally envisioned by the top management. Mr. Desmond Loo, the Operations Manager at the MCDSD elaborated on the strategic objective of MINDEF in the third phase of e-Government development, "The focus of the third phase is to provide (the servicemen with) a positive experience. By positive experience we meant that they can do what they need to do without any hassles... When a NSman goes for his in-camps or his IPPT, he has to deal with all these administrative matters. We try to provide them with that positive experience upfront by addressing administrative matters without hassle, so that when they go for (military) training, they have no concerns or worries weighing on their minds. That was the key for us...."

Towards the attainment of this strategic objective, a number of new features (Table 7.4) were implemented on the MIW portal that were aligned to four strategic thrusts. First, MINDEF sought to restructure their services from a customer-centric perspective by integrating relevant information and services on the portal to provide a stronger end-to-end service experience for their users. As an illustration, the My NS Booklet system was implemented on the MIW portal that extracts data from a number of discrete systems. The system then organises the data categorically and presents the information drawn from the disparate sources to the NSmen from a single, integrated perspective, hence resulting in greater convenience for the servicemen.

A NSman who had been in active service since 2000 elaborated on the benefits of the My NS Booklet system, "Previously, if I wanted to check my in-camp training records, IPPT results, or my make-up

Table 7.4:   Services added or revamped between May 2004 and April 2006.

Services	Description
My MIW	A customisable page that with quick links to a host of services such as eSelf-Update, My Call Up, My Unit and My NS Booklet, which servicemen can use to administer and track their NS transactions.
My Call Up	Previously, MINDEF call-up notifications were sent through surface mail. With My Call Up, NSmen receive notification of their call-ups via email or SMS. They can check and acknowledge the notification via My MIW or call a hotline number to listen to a recorded message through an Interactive Voice Response System.
My Unit	Provides access to in-camp training programmes and administrative briefing instructions. Serves as an interaction platform for servicemen and officers within the same military unit.
Automated In/ Out Processing System (AIOPS)	System that allows NSmen to sign in or out of in-camp training using their NRICs.[10] Automates and simplifies the administrative procedures associated with in-camp training.
My NS Booklet	An online system that records the NS activities of an NSman. Integrates and presents information such as an NSman's in-camp training records, IPPT results, make-up pay history, SAF e-mart transactions and exit permit applications.
MIW Shopzone	A one-stop shopping site with products selected specially for NSmen. Special promotional prices and delivery services are also made available for users.
MIW Game Centre	Developed in conjunction with Oberon Media, the MIW Game Centre allows users to download a free trial of an online game for up to an hour of free play, or to purchase the game for unlimited play.

(*Continued*)

---

[10]National Registration Identity Cards (NRICs): The official identity document of Singapore Citizens that is imprinted with the thumbprint of the citizen.

Table 7.4:   (*Continued*).

Services	Description
MIW@Jobstreet. com	Developed in conjunction with Jobstreet.com, MIW@ Jobstreet.com caters to pre-enlistees looking for short-term employment before NS, or NSFs looking for a job after their NS.
MIW Auction Services	Developed in conjunction with eBay, the MIW Auction Services provides users an avenue to buy and sell items of interest to NSmen.
FitSync	A mobile fitness management programme that aims to help NSmen keep fit and stay fit. The application guides an NSman to set clear fitness goals, choose an appropriate fitness plan, and track his progress conveniently with his handheld device or on the web portal.
MIW Online Insurance Service	When NSmen submit their overseas travel notification to MINDEF on the MIW portal, the system automatically calculates the travel insurance premium and extends the insurance plans offered by the American Insurance Group (AIG) at special discounted rates to the NSmen.

pay claims, I have to go to different sections of the website.... With the NS Booklet, everything is organized for you... There are tabs for you to click on and you can retrieve the information you want easily."

Second, GDIS developed a personalised page called My MIW, which provided the means for individual servicemen to tailor their service experience according to their unique needs when they log onto the MIW portal. Servicemen can customise My MIW to display their email messages, MINDEF notifications, as well as other information and services that are frequently accessed within the personalised webpage. In addition, they can use My MIW to view their service history, and create or modify their personal information, create a more efficient, interactive, and convenient platform for administering and tracking their transactions with the MIW portal.

Third, MINDEF sought to foster the creation and maintenance of social relationships among servicemen through the cultivation of virtual communities hosted on the MIW portal. As an illustration, GDIS launched an online application called My Unit that allows NSmen to access upcoming training programmes and pre-training administrative briefing instructions from their commanding officers through the MIW portal prior to in-camp training. In addition, electronic discussion forums are created within My Unit for NSmen to discuss training matters, share their experiences and maintain social ties with other servicemen in the same unit after in-camp training has concluded.

An active NSman elaborated on the utility of the My Unit application, "I can meet up (online) with the others going for the same in-camp (training) and we can talk about what to bring, when we can book out and things like that.... We can also ask the more experienced NSmen what they did for the previous in-camp (training)... My Unit also helps me to keep in touch with my buddies in my unit, because usually after in-camp (training), it is quite difficult... it takes a lot of commitment... to stay in touch...."

Fourth, MINDEF attempted to increase the "stickiness" of the MIW portal through a comprehensive rebranding initiative that introduced stronger commercial and lifestyle elements to their website. For example, as part of the rebranding exercise, GDIS launched (1) MIW ShopZone; an e-mall which offers a wide range of items that are of interest to the demographic group represented by the NSmen, (2) MIW Games Centre; an online repository that features the latest online games, (3) an online job search directory developed in conjunction with JobStreet.com that provides targeted job searches based on the profile of the servicemen, and (4) an online auction service developed in conjunction with eBay. Through the rebranding initiative, the management of MINDEF hoped that servicemen would benefit from the synergistic mix of public services and private sector offerings that in turn, results in a service experience that transcends the conventional form of public service delivery.

In the enactment of the four strategic thrusts in the third phase of e-Government development, MINDEF was faced with two key challenges. First, the provision of seamless end-to-end services demanded close collaboration, data sharing and coordination among various internal MINDEF organisations. As the processes of the internal stakeholders were traditionally isolated and independent from one another, the management of MINDEF encountered strong resistance in their efforts to effect the operational, normative, and cultural changes necessary for the integration of services.

To overcome this challenge, a comprehensive change management exercise; spearheaded by the National Service Affairs Department (NSAD) and endorsed by the Chief of Army and the top management of MINDEF, was initiated with the aim of streamlining the operations and business processes of the various internal MINDEF organisations for integrated public service delivery. The NSAD first ensured that consensus is reached among the various internal MINDEF organisations concerning the importance of customer-centricity. Next, the transformation effort was characterised by iterative cycles of business process re-engineering. By involving key representatives from various internal MINDEF organisations, the relevant business processes were collectively examined from a customer-centric perspective, and consensus was established with regards to which process to add, remove or modify, with the eventual aim of achieving seamless integration between the information and services of different internal MINDEF organisations.

Second, despite the efforts of MINDEF in emphasising the lifestyle and commercial elements of the portal, remained a lingering perception — that the portal was nevertheless, a government website. In particular, this perception limits openness and creates some extent of unease among the users of the interaction channels on the MIW portal, which in turn, represent considerable hindrances to the relationship-building and rebranding efforts of the organisation. An NSman who had been in active service since 2000 described the general public perception of the MIW portal, "You (the user) can see the banner advertisements and the lifestyle content on the website… but you (the user) are still aware that the website belongs to MINDEF…. Of course, sometimes there are some interesting discussions going on in the forum. But the fact that the portal belongs to the government limits the discussion of the more 'controversial' issues… and it's usually the juicy, controversial issues that attract the most attention.... We (Nsmen) would rather go to the Hardwarezone[11] forum to discuss those things...."

While the management of MINDEF acknowledges that it is an ongoing challenge to change the public perception of the MIW portal, they have adopted measures to play down the government-related aspects of the portal. For example, although the provision of MINDEF-related information and e-services is one of the primary objectives of the portal, GDIS was given free rein to promote and play up the lifestyle elements of the portal. Consequently, the content on the home page of the portal is dominated by lifestyle and commercial content while MINDEF-related information and e-services are relegated to quick links on either sides of the home page. In addition, GDIS was handed the responsibility for moderating user-generated content on various interaction channels such as the chat rooms and the electronic discussion forums, and as far as possible, moderation and censorship were minimised to encourage open and uninhibited interaction within the virtual communities.

The third phase of e-Government development began in May 2004 and lasted for almost two years. Through the four strategic thrusts enacted as part of the phase, MINDEF had transformed itself into a responsive, agile organisation with a customer-centric service delivery approach that integrates public services with the offerings of the private sector. By April 2006, the volume of transactions handled by the MIW portal had doubled to an average of more than 600,000 a month while the volume of transactions handled by the call centre increased only marginally to around 60,000 a month. In addition, a customer satisfaction survey found that the percentage of customers who were satisfied with the quality of the e-services on the MIW Portal and the services provided by the eSC had risen to 92.02% and 98.27% respectively (see Appendix A). While these statistics attest to sustained improvement in terms of the efficiency

---

[11]An e-Commerce website (owned by a private company) that hosts the largest and most vibrant virtual community in Singapore.

and effectiveness of MINDEF's public services, MINDEF's five-year contract with GDIS was up for renewal by April 2006, and the events that transpired would usher in a new chapter in the organisation's e-Government journey.

THE NS PORTAL: A UNIFIED PORTAL FOR THE NS COMMUNITY OF SINGAPORE

The Need for a New NS Portal: Integration with the Ministry of Home Affairs

The tenets of the e-Government Action Plan II[12] (eGAP II) launched in 2003 had a profound influence on the direction of MINDEF's e-Government journey. The global events of the period (such as the global fight against terrorism) had created a heightened awareness in MINDEF for the need to collaborate with the Ministry of Home Affairs[13] (MHA) of Singapore to ensure the security and defend the country. This awareness, in tandem with the Singapore government's push for a "networked government" (encapsulated within eGAP II) led to a series of intense discussions between the two ministries on the potential areas of collaboration. By mid–2005, a joint decision was made to collaborate on the development of an integrated portal and call centre (Figure 7.3) for the servicemen population of both ministries. Through the integrated portal and call centre, the ministries would benefit from economies of scale due to a lower base contract price and the larger pooled servicemen base. The ministries would also enjoy stronger bargaining power with the private

---

[12] The use of ICT in public organisations is governed by the Government Infocomm Plans of the Singapore government. These strategic ICT plans establish the key thrusts and strategies that provide guidelines on the use of ICT to transform the public sector. eGAP II was the third Government Infocomm Plan of the Singapore Government.

[13] The Ministry of Home Affairs (MHA) is the government ministry responsible for public safety, civil defense, and immigration in Singapore. MHA consists of seven major organisations that include the Singapore Police Force (SPP) and the Singapore Civil Defense Force (SCDF). Interestingly the MHA also has its own intake of National Servicemen.

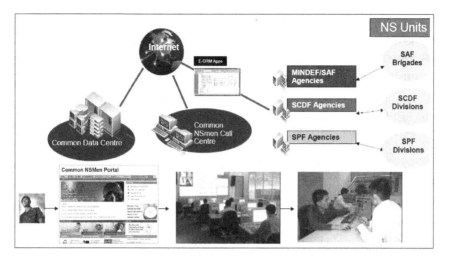

Figure 7.3: Overview of the integrated NS portal.

businesses seeking to leverage the portal by bundling their commercial offerings with the public services of the integrated portal. In addition, the integrated portal and call centre would allow both ministries to co-own business assets, risks and opportunities with a common external vendor and establish a stringent, consistent standard for the public services of both organisations.

The portal development experience gained to date grounded MINDEF in the knowledge of the possibilities, risks, and benefits associated with e-Government development. Armed with the knowledge of what they can and want to achieve, and driven by the decision to collaborate with MHA on the development of an integrated NS portal and call centre, MINDEF; spearheaded by the Defence Science and Technology Agency[14] (DSTA), made the decision to not pursue the contractual option of continuing with GDIS for the next

---

[14]The Defense Science and Technology Agency (DSTA) is a statutory board established for the purpose of implementing defense technology plans, managing defense research and development, acquiring defense material and developing defense infrastructure for MINDEF. In the implementation of the NS portal, DSTA played the role of a technical advisor, serving as an intermediary between the internal MINDEF organisations and the external vendor.

five years and call for an open tender for the development of the integrated portal and call centre instead. Mr. Chau Chee Chiang, the Chief Information Officer of the DSTA, described the rationale behind the decision to call for an open tender, "When we started out in year 2000, we knew exactly what we wanted to achieve... but we can't pin out the exact requirements (in terms of specifications) that we want. In this case, we needed a partner that is willing to give and take; that is, be able to negotiate.... We felt that by calling an open tender with such an abstract requirement may not make sense. At the end of five years... the question then was: 'Hey, should we renew, continue to do it with this guy (GDIS)?' Or should we, now that we know what we want... we can write down exactly what we want to do... shouldn't we be fair to citizens, to our tax payers, and get something value for money (by calling for an open tender)?"

Four IT firms, including the incumbent GDIS, submitted their proposals for the open tender. To facilitate a systematic evaluation of the proposals, MINDEF used the Analytic Hierarchy Process to form an objective judgment. First, the criteria for vendor selection and the weighting of the various decisional attributes were established by MINDEF with the help of DSTA. Next, two envelopes were prepared by each vendor: the first envelope contained the business proposal while the second envelope contained the proposed costs of portal development. In evaluation, the first envelopes were opened first and the proposals were assigned a benefit score based on the pre-determined vendor criteria. The benefit scores for each of the proposals were confirmed and endorsed. Finally, the second envelopes were opened and the assigned benefit scores were divided by the proposed costs of each vendor to derive a cost benefit ratio, and the contract was eventually awarded to the vendor with the highest cost benefit ratio.

The IT vendor that was awarded the contract for developing the new integrated portal was NCS; a wholly-owned subsidiary of the SingTel Group of Singapore. Mr. Chau Chee Chiang explained the primary reason behind the awarding of the contract to NCS, "NCS had the highest cost benefit ratio ... their proposed costs was 35% lower than what we were currently paying... so on the day the tender closed, we had already saved 35%.... Clearly, they saw a compelling enough business case to fork out their own money for the project...."

With greater knowledge and experience in vendor management and portal development, MINDEF instituted a unique contract pricing scheme (see Figure 7.4) to measure and regulate the performance of NCS. There are two key components under this scheme: "Pay-to-Operate" and "Pay- to-Perform." During the transitional period; defined as the first two years of the contract, the performance of NCS would be primarily evaluated on the basis of "Pay-to-Operate" Key Performance Indicators (KPIs) that were related to operational efficiency and meeting service level agreements. For each subsequent year of the contract, the importance of "Pay-to-Perform" KPIs in performance evaluation would increase, as NCS is expected to increasingly focus its activities and attention on performance-oriented tasks such as service transformation, innovation, customer growth, interagency collaboration, and knowledge management. According to the agreement between MINDEF and NCS, 70% of the contract price will be based on "Pay-to-Operate" KPIs while 30% will be allocated for "Pay-to-Perform" KPIs in the first year. The 70:30 ratios will be gradually reversed to 30:70 by the fifth year.

Mr. Chau Chee Chiang elaborated on the rationale behind the unique contract pricing scheme: "The assumption was that the new

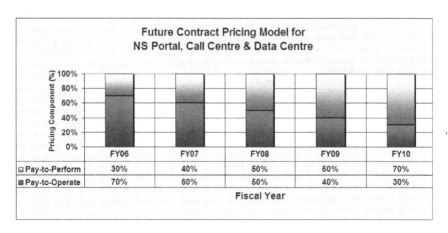

Figure 7.4: NS portal contract pricing scheme.

vendors are unlikely to even get the basic things right, or rather, it will take him a lot of effort to just get the basic things right (initially)… But as they continue to do this (basic operations), they'll be able to reach a point where they can do it with both eyes closed…. So in the fifth year, even if you can do the same things that you have done in year one, I'm not going to pay you $70 out of $100. I will pay you only $30! You will have to work very hard for the remaining $70 of the contract, by meeting the targets set in the ('Pay-to-Perform') KPIs."

THE FIRST YEAR OF THE NS PORTAL: THE CHALLENGES OF MIGRATION (MAY 2006–APRIL 2007)

The migration from the MIW portal to the NS portal (see Figure 7.5) was carried out in two stages. The first stage, which took place on 14 April 2006 (Good Friday), involved the migration of static and non-transactional websites; such as the MINDEF corporate website. The second stage and the launch of the NS portal and integrated call centre (NS eSC) took place on 1 May 2006 (Labour Day) and involved the migration of the main Internet portal. Public holidays

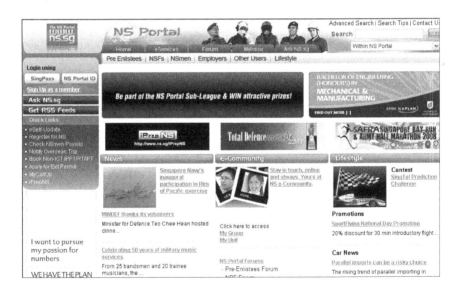

Figure 7.5:   The NS portal.

were chosen for the dates of both stages due to the low web traffic on public holidays. The migration exercise was conducted with the precision of a military operation, and barring a few technical glitches that were quickly resolved; the process unfolded smoothly and was largely incident-free. The real challenges of the large-scale migration however, only became apparent in the months that followed.

The first challenge of portal migration relates to the issue of brand confusion. The URL of the previous portal (http://www.miw.com.sg) was owned by GDIS and the previous vendor maintained that they had the right to continue operating a commercial website on the URL even after the migration of the MINDEF portal. MINDEF's attempts to buy the URL from GDIS were rebuffed as both parties were unable to arrive at an agreement on the value of the URL. Consequently, a men's lifestyle portal that featured "informative and entertaining lifestyle content relevant to the lifestyle needs of modern men" was launched and operated on the old URL for a period of time, even after the integrated NS portal had been launched. This resulted in some confusion among the servicemen population. An active NSman recalled the confusion he experienced, "I don't use the portal regularly and for some reason, I didn't know that the portal had moved.... I was shocked when I went to miw.com.sg... the website looked different... where were all the e-services?"

MINDEF invested extensive resources and effort in trying to overcome this challenge. When the intentions of GDIS became apparent, DSTA; commissioned by MINDEF, conducted a comprehensive study of the servicemen population. The findings of the study revealed that the servicemen population's awareness of the MIW brand was limited and its co-existence with the NS Portal would not threaten the viability of the new portal. Nevertheless, MINDEF sought to establish a stronger brand for the new portal. The URL for the new portal (http://www.ns.sg) was carefully formulated to be easier to remember and more relevant to NS as compared to the old URL. In addition, promotional and publicity tools; such as bus advertisements, online banner advertisements and email flyers, for the NS portal were heavily utilised. The use of these tools persists to date.

The second challenge of portal migration relates to the relative inexperience of NCS in running a full-fledged e-Government portal with such a vast customer base. This translated to technical problems with security assurance, capacity planning, usability, and website performance. As an illustration, a serviceman recalled his experience with the NS portal when it was first launched, "I remembered when the NS portal was first launched, the website was SLOW.... Every page took really long to load and after a while I just gave up. The appearance of the website was also very different. I had to learn how to use many of the website's features all over again... it was frustrating because somehow the previous interface was better...."

A third related challenge concerns the inevitable "starting over" of the cultivation of virtual communities. While the virtual communities in the previous portal had, to some extent, achieved self-sustaining critical mass over the course of five years, MINDEF was unable to effectively migrate the communities onto the new portal, and extensive efforts had to be invested in cultivating new virtual communities and restoring the level of interactions and activities. A NSman provided a description of the new virtual communities hosted on the NS portal, "A lot of the (members of the previous communities) did not move over (to the NS portal)... the discussion forums were dead and less interesting. I don't participate in the discussion forums anymore... up to this point in time, I still think that the previous communities were better... they were more active...."

Acknowledging the inexperience new vendor and the need to rebuild communities were inevitable consequences of portal migration, MINDEF was patient and allowed NCS time to establish the new portal. Nevertheless, a customer satisfaction survey conducted between May 2006 and July 2006 found that the percentage of customers who were satisfied with the quality of the e-services on the NS Portal and the services provided by the new NSmen call centre had tumbled to 88.12% and 88.89% respectively (see Appendix A). NCS however, was able to restore operational excellence by reinstating and improving on most of the features of the previous portal within a year. By the start of the new financial year, NCS was ready to pick up the development of the e-Government portal from where the MIW portal left off.

PROMOTING NS COMMITMENT (APRIL 2007–PRESENT)

With the teething issues of portal migration resolved, NCS was ready to bring the quality of the public services of both MINDEF and MHA to the next level. Accordingly, the focus of e-Government development had shifted beyond providing a positive NS experience to the overarching strategic vision of promoting NS commitment among Singapore's NS community. To this end, NCS designed and deployed a number of new features on the NS portal (see Table 7.5) in accordance with a two- pronged strategy.

First, NCS was seeking to enhance the relationship and community building capabilities of the NS portal further by developing website features that facilitate the creation of social bonds and a sense of belonging. To illustrate the point, NCS revamped MINDEF's My Unit application to include useful and interactive features that were conducive to the formation of social ties. The servicemen were also granted the autonomy to form their own interest groups through the My Group and My Alumni applications. In addition, controlled blogs developed by five resident bloggers hired by NCS were launched on the Lifestyle section of the NS portal.

Mr. Gerald Ang, the Marketing Manager of the NS Portal, elaborated on the rationale of creating the blogs on the portal and the importance of community building, "the purpose of blogs is to create opinion leaders in the community. The blogs do not necessary have to be just about NS life, it can also be about their personal life or whatever they (NSmen) are interested in…. It creates an additional channel, an informal channel for NS men to share, to vent, or just to talk and socialise on the Internet space…. Essentially if your portal doesn't have a community, it is a dead website…. Every innovation on the Internet has to be driven from the bottom-up…. If innovation comes from the corporate level but it's not accepted by the users, you'll be wasting time, money and effort… the community aspect is very crucial. We (learn) from the people on the ground what they like and dislike, and ultimately give them something that they can use and benefit from…."

Second, NCS was looking to enhance the variety and richness of the applications on the mobile channel through the launch of the

Table 7.5:   Services added, revamped or in planning since May 2006.

Services	Description
Services Added or Revamped	
Revamped My Unit	New features added to the My Unit application includes: (1) My Buddy Link-up; a feature that allows NSmen to search for their buddies to keep in contact with, (2) Our Photo Gallery; a feature that allows NSmen to view pictures taken during their NS training, (3) Our Reflections; a feature that allows NSmen to share their NS experiences, (4) Our Calendar; an online organizer that allows NSmen to view their upcoming NS activities, and (5) Discussion Forums that allows NSmen to discuss and share ideas with each other.
My Group and My Alumni	Applications that allow NSmen from different units to create their own interest groups based on common interests or graduation from the same school. All features that are available in "MyUnit" are also available on My Group and My Alumni.
e-Time Capsule	A digital repository that allows NSmen to contribute NS-related pictures and/or short stories recalling the experiences, camaraderie and bonds forged during their NS days. The eTime Capsule was symbolically sealed on September 2007.
Blogs	Five resident bloggers were hired by NCS to create blogs on the Lifestyle section of the NS portal. The bloggers include a NSF, an NSman, an entrepreneur, a love coach, and a polytechnic student about to enter NS.
Mobile eServices Hub (MeSH)	A one-stop mobile service platform suite offering government e-services and value-added lifestyle promotions and contents. Bundled applications include: (1) a suite of NS mobile services, (2) a personal messaging inbox, (3) downloadable mobile vouchers, (4) a history channel dedicated to the history of Singapore, and (5) location-based services for participating merchants.

(Continued)

Table 7.5:   (*Continued*).

Services	Description
Personalized Applications	Personalised applications; such as a personal calendar, to-do-lists and transaction history, are available to servicemen upon login.
Services Being Planned	
Mobile Virtual Concierge (JENE)	Using an avatar-based (virtual interactive character) user interface, the application based on the mobile platform is used to send a service request comprising of the location data of the mobile device to a hub server. The hub server responds by pushing one or more mobile service offers to the mobile device based on the location data.
Mobile Lifestyle Service	Mobile services that facilitate ticketing and mobile payments.

Mobile eServices Hub (MeSH); a sophisticated bundle of mobile applications that consist of a comprehensive suite of mobile e-services, a messaging system, lifestyle content, and location-based services. In addition, there are plans to develop the mobile platform further with the development of the Mobile Virtual Concierge and the Mobile Lifestyle Service applications in the pipeline. Mr. Ng See Sing, General Manager of Portal City (the e-Government portal arm of NCS), explained the importance of developing the mobile service platform, "We are exploring mobility; how to make more of the services mobile.... We are trying to move the older SMS-based applications to the more intuitive (to use) Java-based platforms.... It's the same concept as the Internet portal, we bundle services with lifestyle (content) like LBS (Location-Based Services) capability and merchant offerings.... People don't use e-services everyday... they will forget the URL... but if we have something (lifestyle content) that is sticky... we hope that in time to come, they will remember us because they will use lifestyle content more often than e-services...."

Although MINDEF and NCS have a clear understanding of what they hope to achieve with their strategy, there are formidable challenges in the paths of each of these initiatives. In their relationship and community building efforts, NCS realised quickly that it was a delicate balance between the needs of the servicemen and MINDEF. On one hand, fostering social bonds has to involve open, uninhibited interactions among community members. To create a sense of belonging, ownership of the interaction platforms also has to be ceded to the community as an organic, self-organising virtual community is bound to resist censorship and control. Yet, on the other hand, MINDEF has the image of an authoritative governmental organisation to uphold.

Mr. Gerald Ang elaborated on the dilemma faced by NCS in balancing the needs of the two stakeholders and the measures adopted to resolve achieve the balance, "I think the main aim is not to cheapen the image of the NSmen or the ethical values we want to put across.... Censorship is crucial but it has to be done in a very diplomatic way. We try to give some leeway to people posting in the (discussion) forum. If you go look at it (the discussion forum), there are a lot of complaints... but we do not touch (moderate) that. Because if we were to censor and moderate heavily, then we will basically be shooting ourselves in the foot and we will be deterring people... at the same time, we're constantly trying to engage MINDEF to see how we can put on more things on the portal."

In their efforts to exploit the mobile platform more extensively, the challenges facing NCS is primarily technical. Specifically, due to the relative limitations of mobile technology as compared to computer and Internet technologies, there were considerable difficulties in migrating the rich, computing resource intensive applications and e-services developed for the NS portal onto the mobile platform. Mr. Loh Mun Kong, the Project Director of the Business Solutions Group at NCS, provided a summary of some of the technical challenges encountered, "it is the way the e-services are done (on the Internet). It's pretty complex. On a computer, the screen is big... not a big issue. But when you move that to a mobile phone, you don't expect the user to flip pages after pages of information. On top of that, mobile data transmission means that the user has to pay (for data transmission)... and not every application is able to go onto the mobile (platform)... we also have to cater to different type of phones like 2.5G and 3G... for example, some (phones) can display maps, some (phones) cannot display maps, we have to cater to all these." To overcome the technical challenges of exploiting the mobile platform, NCS had to strike a balance between the difficulty of migrating the service or application onto the mobile platform and the benefits associated with migration. In general, only e-services or applications that are heavily used by the servicemen are migrated onto the mobile platform. NCS also had to rely on their ingenuity and technical expertise in resolving the technical challenges. Mr. Loh Mun Kong elaborated further on the technical solutions to the challenges faced, "We actually stripped down the application. We did not change the application but we tagged the application with WML (Wireless Markup Language) tags, and made it open to the mobile platform. The difference between the Internet version and the mobile version is that the Internet version has more things, which if they want, we can direct them to.... Luckily, we had a platform that we can build on. BEA (a middleware used to connect software applications to databases) comes with this thing called a mobility server that we can actually add onto the entire platform. So we use the same BEA tools for this...."

Effective resolution of the latest challenges, in tandem with an aggressive marketing campaign featuring advertisements in major media channels, seminars, road shows, contests and promotions, turned the NS Portal into an overwhelming success within two years of its inception. By September 2007, there were approximately 300,000 registered users of the NS portal generating over 700,000 electronic transactions a month. In addition, according to a customer satisfaction survey conducted between August and September 2007, 97.47% and 92.66% of the users surveyed indicated that they were satisfied with the services provided on the Internet portal and the NS eSC respectively (see Appendix A).

CONCLUSION

Looking back, MINDEF's e-Government journey was long, arduous, and fraught with obstacles and challenges. Yet, the fundamental way in which e-Government development transformed the organisation;

by revolutionalising the mode of public service delivery, changing the service mindset and culture, and keeping MINDEF relevant in the new economy, provides justification for the vision, conviction, and commitment of the MINDEF management. While new challenges will inevitably arise, the service system of MINDEF honed by the experience of the past eight years, and the relentless organisational drive towards service excellence are causes for optimism and confidence.

APPENDIX A

Customer Satisfaction Ratings for NS Portal and Call Centre (2003–2007)

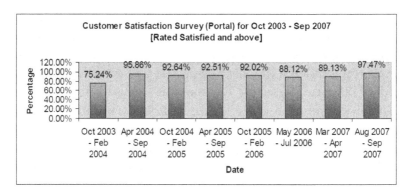

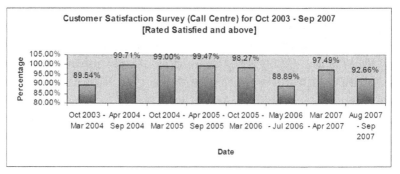

DISCUSSION QUESTIONS

1. What were the different phases of e-Government development at MINDEF? How did each phase of e-Government development transform the public services of MINDEF?

2. In developing the Integrated MINDEF portal, what were the challenges encountered in each phase of development? How were these challenges overcome by MINDEF?

3. What are the advantages and disadvantages of the PPP model of e-Government development?

4. What are the lessons that can be learnt from MINDEF's experience with the PPP model of e-Government development?

Case 8

CAPABILITY DEPLOYMENT IN CRISIS RESPONSE TO ASIAN TSUNAMI DISASTER

Gary Pan

Singapore Management University

BACKGROUND

On 26 December 2004, an earthquake occurred under the Indian Ocean, 250 km northwest of the Indonesian island of Sumatra. According to the U.S. geological survey, the magnitude of the earthquake measured 9.0 on the Richter scale and the immense energy released from the earthquake triggered a series of tsunamis traveling at more than 600 km/h. The tsunami devastated the coastline of 13 countries, leaving more than 280,000 people dead and millions homeless. Soon after the disaster, the United Nations and the international community responded quickly with crisis relief operations for the nations affected. Unfortunately, these relief efforts soon ran into difficulty. One major challenge was how to ensure rapid distribution of aid supplies to the tsunami victims. In response to this challenge, the United Nations proposed a regional coordination centre in Singapore to coordinate all relief activities in the region. Singapore was considered the ideal candidate to coordinate the relief activities, due to its proximity to a number of tsunami-hit countries, her well-developed communications and logistics networks, and her status as a medical hub in the region.

THE TSUNAMI CRISIS COORDINATION CENTRE

The Singapore government responded by setting up a contact centre immediately to manage enquiries from victims' families and friends. Psychologists from the Ministry of Community Development, Youth and Sports were on hand to provide counseling. On 1 January 2005, the government organised a meeting with several public sector agencies to discuss the setting up of a Tsunami Crisis Coordination Center (TCCC). One manager who attended the meeting commented on the topics discussed during the meeting, "TCCC's location was one of the key issues raised during the meeting. Two sites were nominated. One was at Paya Lebar Airbase. The other was at the Singapore Expo. However, the site decision could not be made without the United Nations's involvement. In the end, the Singapore Expo was selected at the meeting as the temporary site to establish the regional coordination centre."

A crisis management task force was set up, including senior Singapore Armed Forces officers and key decision makers from other public sector agencies such as the Security Agency (pseudonym). The task force's responsibilities included the development of a strategy to coordinate the crisis relief activities. From the earlier SARS[15] experience, the Singapore government was fully aware of the important role played by IT in crisis situations. It therefore decided that the development of IT to enhance TCCC's coordination of crisis relief activities was a priority. This would involve establishing an IT infrastructure to store and disseminate information. Security Agency was assigned the task of developing the IT infrastructure and applications. Besides the SARS crisis, Security Agency was involved in a number of collaborative projects with other government agencies and industry partners. Security Agency employs a team-based working environment and has a job rotation policy to facilitate knowledge transfer among its employees. Security Agency is an advocate of knowledge sharing which allows its engineers to share their experiences with their colleagues. This knowledge transfer forms part of organisational learning and is achieved through sharing official documents and conducting formal presentations.

---

[15]Severe acute respiratory syndrome (SARS) is a highly contagious, serious, and potentially life-threatening form of pneumonia.

Singapore selected Security Agency to develop the Crisis Management system due to its experience in developing IT in combating SARS in 2003 and the expertise gained from its technological collaboration with other organisations. According to a manager at Security Agency, "After the SARS crisis, we conducted debriefing sessions to evaluate the key factors of managing crisis and documented the lessons learnt. In terms of the involvement in the Defense Technology Ecosystem, we participated extensively in several collaboration projects, and leveraged our partner organisations' expertise. Such collaborations are important in helping to bring our IT expertise to the next level."

DEVELOPING AN IT INFRASTRUCTURE: A TECHNOLOGICAL PLATFORM TO INTERCONNECT IT RESOURCES

On 5 January 2005, the IT infrastructure team began setting up TCCC's networks and servers in the Singapore Expo. The team leader commented, "The overall team performance was highly commendable. Several meetings were conducted within the last few days to decide the locations of partitions and cabling solutions. The team completed the designs of the network and server logic in less than two hours. We managed to complete the tasks within a short time because we were able to re-use the standard designs and components adopted in prior projects (i.e., SARS)."

The central servers were kept at Security Agency since the organisation was temporarily used as an IT infrastructure and command centre before the official location was announced. It was decided that the network setup would be carried out simultaneously at Security Agency and the Singapore Expo. Table 8.1 shows the sequence of events:

Security Agency proceeded with purchase of equipment (e.g., network, server hardware, and work stations), and the suppliers were able to deliver the equipment to both sites within four hours. One of the Applications and System Development team members commented as follows: "We had to search for additional space to store the server racks. We also had to seek help from the Administrative

Table 8.1:   Activities related to the setting up of the
TCCC IT infrastructure.

5 January 2005	
0130 hrs	Network infrastructure at Security Agency
0400 hrs	TCCC active directory
0700 hrs	TCCC email service
0930 hrs	Floor marking at Singapore Expo
1200 hrs	TCCC web portal

Support Group to install additional electrical housings after their office working hours."

At 2 pm, the Singapore Armed Forces received confirmation from the United Nations and selected Paya Lebar Airbase as the venue for TCCC. The installation work at the Singapore Expo was abandoned and all activities transferred to Paya Lebar Airbase. On 7 January 2005, the IT infrastructure team started work at Paya Lebar Airbase and managed to complete the installation within 24 hours. The team leader explained how this was possible in such a short time, "One of the key reasons was the experienced system security consultant we hired to advise us on security-related issues such as scanning, hardening and testing of the network security. It certainly saved us a lot of time." Table 8.2 summarises the install-ation of the IT infrastructure on 7 and 8 January 2005.

Table 8.2:   Installation of IT Infrastructure on 7 and 8 January 2005.

7 January 2005	
1600	Infrastructure set up at Paya Lebar Airbase
1800	Received PC to prepare client image
2300	Deployment of client image at Paya Lebar Airbase
8 January 2005	
0700	Active directory at Paya Lebar Airbase
0800	Domain name server and dynamic host configuration protocol services at Paya Lebar Airbase

The TCCC IT infrastructure includes internet, electronic mail, directory name service, other directory services, and dynamic host configuration protocol. Ancillary services include telephony, video conferencing, streaming media, wireless connections, and high performance, computing. The IT infrastructure allowed storage, dissemination and exchange of crisis information, and provided network resilience and backup servers. For example, an on-site IT consultant was engaged to maintain essential services such as electronic mail and the web servers. The substantial network bandwidth, the high level of performance, and the functionality of desktop systems and servers were crucial in enabling TCCC users to exchange data and collaborate effectively.

DEVELOPING A CRISIS MANAGEMENT SYSTEM: COORDINATING THE DISTRIBUTION OF AID SUPPLIES

A major IT application adopted by TCCC was a web-based crisis management system, which was able to monitor the availability and demand for aid supplies and assess how supplies could best be distributed. The crisis management system could also track the deployment of relief personnel in tsunami-hit countries. The Applications and System Development team leader commented on the crisis management system design and development processes, "Our team had to develop a prototype very quickly to gather feedback from our main users: the Singapore Armed Forces' G4 Army and 6th Division. Interestingly, we found a website by the name of *Strong Angel 2* that not only gave us an idea of the type of system that we needed to build but also provided us with photographs and freeware like *Groove*, a collaboration tool."

A member of the Applications and System Development team also commented, "It was a 'talk, plan, ask, and do' day on 8 January 2005. We traveled to TCCC to gain a deeper understanding of the system requirements. We gathered information regarding Singapore Armed Forces' work procedures which helped us to identify the features to be incorporated within the crisis management system. In addition, our design also considered the public's needs. For example, the call-ins that enquired about the status and locality of aid supplies. Questions were raised to ensure we were on the right track and the Singapore Armed Forces was generally satisfied with our design."

The Crisis Management System development activities involved setting up hardware, graphics, geographic information systems and databases. The development team adopted Oracle Weblogic Server (Java infrastructure platform enterprise edition) to manage interactions between heterogeneous services such as Microsoft.Net, and messaging services. According to the Applications and System Development team leader, "We chose BEA because all of us were familiar and trained in using the web logic software tool. Two team members who were familiar with Adobe Photoshop formed the Graphics sub-team. The geographic information systems sub-team comprised staff from another division. We consulted staff that had the right knowledge since it was important to seek as many sources of assistance as possible."

The development team had to modify military systems to one that was suitable for more flexible ad hoc activities. One of the development team members explained why the change in mindset was important, "In military operations, the systems adopted usually require a high level of precision as they are designed to serve a particular mission. For Crisis Management System, it had no fixed format (e.g., variable data field length and lack of drop-down boxes) because it was difficult to predict the *ad hoc* nature of relief activities that the system might need to support."

The Crisis Management System was developed within two days. Even though the design was similar to the one used in the content management system adopted during the SARS outbreak, the development team still had to overcome several obstacles. The development team leader highlighted some of the problems, "Before we launched the system, we faced several constraints. For example, we had to borrow two servers that were in the process of performing reliability tests in other projects. In addition, the geographic information systems sub-team also had to borrow a server from one of its vendors. We also spent a substantial amount of time on system testing and troubleshooting to ensure the reliability of the new system before actual implementation."

User training was conducted to familiarise Singapore Armed Forces' officers in using the Crisis Management System. One of its key features was an automated querying function. This allowed a user to carry out his or her search easily, especially when it was only necessary to submit a query string to the search engine. One of the Singapore Armed Forces users explained why it was easy to adopt the Crisis Management System, "in terms of the workflow and interfaces (e.g., intelligence, operations and logistics), the Crisis Management System was similar to our Command Control System we operated since the early 1990s. Those training sessions only helped to normalise the migration to the new web-based system."

After the launch of Crisis Management System, some Singapore Armed Forces users raised some practical issues and a number of features were modified. For example, one of the development team members mentioned, "We were informed by one of the operations centres that some information were not updated and had to be modified. This was due to a coordination problem because no one was situated at the center to facilitate the update process. Also, there was an issue of having an unresponsive email server. Two of the software engineers rushed to the scene to assess the problems and discuss possible solutions with the users. Throughout the entire troubleshooting period, the development team leader was kept informed of the discussions via electronic mail and instant messaging. A few software engineers were activated at 6 p.m. after receiving three different crisis management system change requests within four hours. The software engineers worked very fast. They knew exactly what to change and the alterations were completed by 7:30 p.m. on the same day."

On 11 January 2005, approximately 20 non-governmental organisations began their operations at the TCCC. These included international relief agencies such as the International Committee of the Red Cross and local organisations, including the Singapore Red Cross Society, Mercy Relief, and the National Volunteers and Philanthropic Council.

Throughout the entire period, the Singapore Armed Forces' 6th Division officers supported the non-governmental organisations such as the Singapore Red Cross by receiving phone calls from donors, entering spreadsheet data, performing visual matching of supply and demand for aid supplies, and packaging and shipping the supplies. Examples of the aid supplies sent by the Singapore Red Cross to the affected victims in Meulaboh, Indonesia, include medical supplies, water, batteries, emergency packs, face masks, blankets, field tents, and two trucks. A typical "family pack," equivalent to one day's ration, contained two 1.5 liter bottles of drinking water, a six-pack carton of soya bean milk, and hard tack biscuits for adults and cream biscuits for children.

During the response process, the Singapore Armed Forces set up a number of operational centers to coordinate the relief activity. The Crisis Management System provided a common IT platform for Singapore Armed Forces and the non-governmental organisations to communicate and collaborate. The Crisis Management System architecture consisted data models and databases that served all participants within the TCCC environment. It did not comprise "islands of databases," but instead provided a common, shared, distributed, accurate and consistent data resource.

The operational centres included the Ops Centre, the Plan Centre, the Situation Centre, and the Call Centre. With the use of a centralised database, the Ops Centre enabled monitoring of worldwide information on the tsunami crisis and updates on the aid supply situation. For example, frequent contact was maintained between the Singapore government and the Indonesian authorities, in order to assess the situation on the ground. Despite the communication, it was learnt at one point that the airports in the northern area of Sumatra, Medan, and Aceh were overcrowded and unable to cater to the influx of people and relief supplies. The coordination concern highlighted the importance of organizing delivery of aid supplies based on updated information at TCCC. The availability of up-to-date information made the loading and distribution of aid supplies much easier. In addition, the Plan Centre efficiently matched supply and demand, improved the packaging of relief supplies and scheduled transportation. The Situation Centre obtained situational updates on the ground and communicated these to the relief personnel. For example, the close relationship between the Singapore Armed Forces and the Indonesia army played a key role in allowing officers at the Situation Centre to update the situation on the ground in Indonesia. As a Singapore Armed Forces officer commented, "We are accustomed to working with the Indonesian authorities. We are familiar with their system and we have no problem communicating with them."

The Call Centre mainly handled requests for aid and offers of donations from the public. To facilitate the TCCC operations, every workstation was provided with Windows XP, Microsoft Office and Internet Explorer, anti-virus software and electronic mail. During peak periods, more than 100 staff were working in the TCCC on 24-hour rotation. The Crisis Management System was crucial in achieving the necessary level of coordination and information exchange within the TCCC.

The support for TCCC continued into early February 2005. The relief activities began to wind down, with many non-governmental organisations leaving TCCC. Overall, TCCC had handled almost 2,000 tonnes of aid supplies. When asked about the key factors that contributed to the successful collaboration between the Singapore Armed Forces and Security Agency, the Applications and System Development team leader concluded: "It had to be the strong support and resources committed by our leaders. Besides, there was a strong sense of ownership in each working team. Even though there was more than one group performing the task, there was always one owner for each task. Such an arrangement helped to eliminate any confusion and conflict among the groups."

DISCUSSION QUESTIONS

1. What were the steps taken to develop an IT infrastructure for TCCC?
2. What were the steps taken to develop a Crisis Management System for TCCC?
3. What were some of the obstacles faced while developing the IT Infrastructure and Crisis Management System, and how were they handled?

Case 9

FACILITATING FEATURE-FUNCTION STAKEHOLDER FIT IN ENTERPRISE SYSTEM IMPLEMENTATION: LESSONS FROM REPUBLIC POLYTECHNIC

S. Sathish

National University of Singapore

BACKGROUND

Republic Polytechnic's mission is "To be an institute of excellence in problem-based learning..." and their five core values are stated in Table 9.1 below.

When Republic Polytechnic (RP) began operations in July 2003, it comprised of six educational departments, which later expanded to nine educational departments (refer to Table 9.2 below).

RP has developed exchange programmes with the University of Maastricht of Holland and links with the University of Newcastle in Australia. Companies such as Apple, Cisco Systems (USA) Pte. Ltd, Fujitsu Asia Pte. Ltd, HP Singapore (Sales) Pte. Ltd, Microsoft Singapore Pte. Ltd, Oracle Corporation Singapore Pte. Ltd, Singapore Computer Systems Ltd, and Sun Microsystems have training programmes with RP, while companies such as IBM Singapore Pte. Ltd. and NEC Singapore Pte. Ltd. signed Memorandums of Understanding (MOU) with RP as part of strategic collaborations to develop and deploy security-related technologies.

Since its inception, RP has received numerous accolades. RP started work towards ISO certification in December 2002 and in November 2003, RP was awarded certification for ISO 9001 (Quality),

Table 9.1:   Core values in Republic Polytechnic.

Core value	Definition
Excellence	Continuous learning and innovation are crucial
Teamwork	We are a team
Ethics	Integrity is never compromised
Initiative	We will be pro-active and progressive
Customer-oriented	Customers are the focus of everything we do

Table 9.2:   Educational departments in republic polytechnic.

Schools	Centres of education
School of Information and Communications Technology (SIT)	Centre for Culture and Communication (CCC)
School of Applied Science	Centre for Educational Development
School of Engineering	Centre for Innovation and Enterprise
School of Technology for the Arts (STA)	Centre for Professional Development
	Centre for Science and Mathematics

ISO 14001 (Environment) and OHSAS 18001 (Occupational, Safety/Health).

RP was the first polytechnic in Singapore to receive all three awards within its first year of operations. Then, on 19 November 2003, RP received the People Developer Standard (PDS) from the Singapore People Excellence Award Council.

LAYING THE FOUNDATION FOR AN E-LEARNING SYSTEM

RP's main focus was their Problem-Based Learning (PBL) education methodology. According to this pedagogy, students worked on a single module each day, and up to five modules a week, and were given one problem each day. Students worked in teams of five to solve the problem, with some guidance from academic staff (i.e., facilitators), and they presented their solutions at the end of the day. In addition to their solution, students were graded based on the effort they put in (e.g., through peer reviews), lessons they learnt (e.g., as noted in their online journals), daily quizzes, tests (four per semester) and final exams. The main architect of this pedagogy was the Director of the Office of Academic Affairs (D-OAA). As a top management staff noted, "There were some givens and those givens were given to us by [the D-OAA] according to his vision. Above those givens, it's really about trying to flesh out what it is that we would do."

While opinions were mixed on whether the educational pedagogy drove RP's technological direction or *vice versa*, it was clear that another key foundation stone of RP was their IT strategy. As part of this strategy, RP relied heavily on outsourcing, and they worked with about seven external parties and had about 20 external IS staff seconded to RP. RP also boasted an in-house Office of Information Services (OIS) with only one Director (D-OIS) and two IS staff. This afforded RP great flexibility in switching IS staff based on immediate needs. Moreover, IT skills were passed on to other staff to make them more self-sufficient. The key driving force behind their technological strategy was the Deputy Principal of RP. As one IT staff noted, "We actually have a very strong backer, which is the 'number two' man here, our Deputy Principal."

A core component of this IT strategy was to have a paperless campus, which made processes faster, more efficient, and cheaper. This enabled RP to achieve an operating cost of about S$10,000 per student in 2003 which was S$1,000 — S$2,000 cheaper that other polytechnics. RP also developed a completely wireless campus thus making everything and everyone fully mobile, as all staff and students had wireless notebooks. RP freely supplied notebooks to their staff while financial packages were worked out to make notebooks more affordable for students. A top management staff shared the following example to show the benefit of using laptops in a fully mobile environment, "We used to go into the AutoCAD lab and ask students to draw something in three to eight hours.... You mean AutoCAD is learnt in eight hours and after that, you don't have a chance to use it for the next five to seven days?.... So we decided to push all our AutoCAD software applications out to every staff and student. So if you pay 100 concurrent licenses, 100 students can concurrently use it both inside and outside the AutoCAD lab."

With these two strategic pillars in place, top management sought to maximise the advantages inherent in being mobile and using laptops to facilitate their unique educational pedagogy. This led to the decision to implement an enterprise-wide e-learning management system. This system would not only facilitate a standardised educational pedagogy across all educational departments in RP but would also fully utilise the notebooks beyond merely downloading documents and visiting websites.

IDENTIFYING AN APPROPRIATE VENDOR AND PACKAGE

In line with their outsourcing policy, RP invited various local and international vendors to present their enterprise-wide packaged Learning Management Systems. While the D-OAA oversaw this process, other top management staff, internal IS staff and academic staff also sat in on the presentations. Feedback was then elicited from everyone. Top management staff discussed whether the package was in-line with RP's strategic direction and the needs of their respective educational departments, while internal IS staff conducted detailed technical evaluations of the packages to assess their fit with other internal systems. While several facilitators offered input on the educational pedagogy, they were largely new to the educational philosophy so their input was limited to the general features of the packages. As a result, although RP was concurrently fleshing out the details of their educational pedagogy, they knew enough to realise that there were no packages that perfectly fit their unique needs. As a top management staff elaborated, "We couldn't really find a Learning Management System that really jumped at us and said, 'Look, this is a really good pedagogical process. Why don't we adopt this?' It was more like, 'We're not sure what we want to do but we definitely know we don't want to do that.' So I think we came fairly early to the conclusion that there wasn't anything out there that really gelled with our philosophy of education even though that philosophy hadn't quite been worked [out] yet."

RP thus sought a vendor and package, that were flexible enough to accommodate heavy customisation to suit their unique needs. Several vendors felt that heavy customisation was not possible or was strongly discouraged. Several top management staff felt that this was unacceptable, as they did not see why the organisation had to change to suit a package. In addition, there was skepticism about the level of personalised support that could be obtained, especially from overseas-based vendors. RP staff were worried that their physical distance could result in longer development time. Furthermore, there were worries that large vendors had to accommodate numerous customers and thus, any changes that RP requested would have to get majority support or be queued behind a long list of other requests. RP eventually selected Wizlearn Pte. Ltd's Academic Version 7 package.

POST-PURCHASE TAILORING TO ENSURE FIT

The post-purchase tailoring of the package, organization, and stakeholder needs lasted approximately six months. OIS was in-charge of facilitating technical backend requirements, and incorporating the package with other RP systems, while OAA retained control over the functionality of the new system, which was known as Learning Environment Online (LEO). A LEO manager was appointed by OAA and he oversaw the implementation and maintenance of the package, as well as the relationship between RP and the vendor. While the LEO manager had some prior experience with academic and IT issues pertaining to e-learning platforms, he was unfamiliar with RP's unique educational pedagogy. Thus, he frequently liaised with the D-OAA to learn what this pedagogy entailed. In addition, the LEO manager queried several staff to get insights into what transpired before his arrival, and to better understand RP's motivation and direction.

To meet RP's heavy customisation needs, an IS team from the vendor was seconded full-time to RP. These external IS staff was responsible for customising and managing the system. To give them greater independence, the vendor gave the team leader a high degree of autonomy to make decisions. Moreover, the team leader had intimate knowledge of the package because he had been involved in the development of it. Together, the external IS staff and LEO manager formed the LEO development team, and the external staff liaised primarily with the LEO manager. This was preferred by the vendors as it minimised the need to liaise with, and report to, too many different groups.

During this period, the LEO manager sought the input of various top management staff and key facilitators to ascertain the requirements of different modules and departments. The LEO manager also initially gathered input from a sample of facilitators about general system features, as they were still unfamiliar with the educational pedagogy. Then, as the facilitators' understanding grew, their involvement increased. For example, towards the latter part of this period, an end-user team was set up with representatives from each educational department and they liaised between the development team and their respective departments. As a top management staff explained, "[this was done] so that there is some awareness going on and they can see things taking shape. They would not come to the first day of term and see the interface for the first time. That would be a disaster."

Subsequently, the bulk of this phase involved discussion between the LEO manager and external IS staff. The LEO manager consolidated and prioritized the requests that he received to devise a list of what needed to be done. He then tried to push through as many changes as possible. At the same time, the external IS staff did what was required to customise the package while trying to resist unnecessary changes that created unnecessary work or invited more risk, by proposing that they follow the built-in best practices in the package. In the process, they developed a close working relationship and common understanding through their daily communication and the fact that they shared the same office, which was located just outside the D-OAA's office.

Finally, the system was ready to be rolled out in June 2003, a few weeks before the start of the first school term in July 2003. While the system had a better fit with RP and their staff's needs, it was not exactly what they initially envisioned. As a top management staff elaborated, "I think actually, the number of procedures was a bit more than necessary because we were inheriting a fixed database structure, a fixed page structure, within which we tried to add features and perhaps one or two pages, and one or two data tables. So the resulting structure was different from what might have come out if we had to build the system from scratch. But of course, it's much faster to start with an existing system."

EDUCATING RP STAFF

The initial rollout plan called for zero training. It was felt that the system was fairly intuitive and facilitators could pick it up themselves. Moreover, the development team felt that gathering 50 people and spending the whole day telling them which buttons to click was not effective, especially since not all staff needed to know how to use all the features of LEO. However, some basic training was inevitably required to give facilitators an overview of the core features of LEO, especially since most facilitators had no prior exposure to LEO and there were only a few weeks before the semester began.

Basic training about the system was provided to facilitators from all educational departments. They could play with the system and simulate how they would use the system. A large part of the training also focused on educating facilitators about the underlying organisational strategies and educational pedagogy underscored the system. However, several facilitators questioned the effectiveness of these training sessions, as they felt that the sessions were too brief.

Instead, many facilitators relied on peer learning to learn how to use the system and understand the motivation behind it. They asked each other questions and shared what they knew with their peers, particularly those teaching the same module or in the same department. Likewise, facilitators directly approached the development team for clarifications. One facilitator described the ease with which they communicated with the development team: "You can just send any questions to the help LEO [email] and they will reply back to you. And most of the time... we just take the notebook, walk upstairs and ask the developer how does this work, and he will just show you. And then, you will just come down and share amongst your peers."

In addition, various facilitators relied on hands-on experimentation with the system and self-education to learn what they needed to know to do their personal tasks. To facilitate this, the development team provided supplementary online resources. This included a FAQ that incorporated screen shots and screen movies to serve as a quick reference guide of the steps to be followed every day. Other facilitators relied on both peer learning and self-learning, because as one staff noted, "The best way to learn the software is to learn to use it while you're using it but make sure you've got colleagues there to answer your questions and help you while you're using it."

As for RP's first batch of students, there were no manuals or special training to teach them how to use LEO. They only underwent a basic general IT training course on how to use IT in RP and what LEO entailed. Facilitators then guided students in using the core features of LEO during their first few lessons. This was considered sufficient as LEO was deemed fairly straightforward and students only used a small subset of its features.

MAINTAINING THE SYSTEM

Making Improvements to LEO

RP was a dynamic institute that was constantly evolving, and such was the case as well for LEO. Firstly, the development team looked to add features that had been suggested during the tailoring stage but subsequently placed on the backburner due to various reasons, such as the lack of urgency. They also sought to add features that had been omitted during the tailoring stage. For example, RP implemented online tests via LEO for their students. It became a challenge to provide such tests via the online LEO system and yet at the same time block general Internet access and online communication using internet messaging or email to prevent cheating. Challenges also arose due to issues such as a lack of consistency among student laptops.

In addition, the development team was open to ideas on how to further enhance LEO and the way it was used. Ideas for change primarily came from three sources. The top management offered suggestions based on LEO's fit with organisational strategy and educational pedagogy, which was evolving as well. In doing so, the top management sometimes adopted a consultative approach and sought feedback before suggesting changes. At other times, due to the perceived seriousness of misalignment, the change came as a directive rather than a request and the development team had no choice but to follow. For example, facilitators could initially view students' daily quiz scores as part of their holistic assessment but the D-OAA found that the daily quiz score and the daily grade was overly correlated. He hastily consulted several other top management staff and with little warning to facilitators, told the development staff to block facilitators' access to the daily quiz until after they submitted the daily grade. However, such instances were rare; although the top management felt that such decisive action was sometimes unavoidable when something urgent had to be fixed, it left several facilitators upset. By and large though, they were upset with the way the change took place rather than the content of the change, as they trusted that top management was acting for the interest of RP. As a staff stated, "[we were not consulted prior to the change] for the quiz. It tends to be very one directional from the top. What happened was that they sent us an email that said that we couldn't see our students' quiz scores and one hour later, we couldn't see the students' quiz scores anymore... I found that there was not much feedback."

Another source of suggestion for change was the facilitators who offered input based on what worked and what did not, as they used the system on a daily basis, and based on what was required to support the educational content and needs of their respective modules and departments, or even the entire RP. In several cases, the facilitator would even discuss the idea with his peers or immediate superiors to garner their support before making the suggestion. Finally, the third source of suggestions for change was the development team itself, which learnt and understood the changes affecting the organisation and the package. It offered feedback to rectify bugs or flaws in the system and made the system align better with organisational and different individuals' needs.

One main formal channel for suggestions was the Staff Suggestion Scheme (SSS) online system, which ran independently of LEO. Staff were able to make formal suggestions about anything in RP, including LEO, via the SSS. To encourage staff to make suggestions, they were paid a token amount of S\$2 for every suggestion made via SSS. At the same time, staff members were told that the number of suggestions they made would be reflected in their annual staff appraisal, and that they had to make a minimum of five suggestions via SSS annually. Several modules even set up their own web portals to consolidate feedback. In addition, there were staff sharing sessions organised by each department in RP twice a year, and all RP staff were invited to attend these sessions. Sometimes, OIS or the development team even set up *ad hoc* teams comprising of staff from different departments to assess various features in LEO. Moreover, staff could informally contact the development team with their suggestions, such as via Internet Messenger or email. One staff member explained the rationale for offering multiple channels of feedback, "We're not stopping any of them because the important thing is to get feedback. If you try to limit to only one channel, then by the time I feedback, I'll forget what I wanted to feedback. So that defeats the whole purpose."

As for students, they had a formal suggestion scheme portal in LEO where they could offer feedback on anything in RP, including LEO. Each educational department also had web portals independent of LEO to gather feedback from their own students. After taking the daily quiz, students were also prompted with a page that sought their feedback on issues such as LEO. OIS even held face-to-face sessions with randomly selected students to gather feedback on the systems in RP. Alternatively, students too could directly give feedback to the IT Helpdesk or any staff personally or via email or internet messenger. However, despite these avenues, students rarely made suggestions about LEO, as their main concern appeared to be about the curriculum or backend system issues, such as the speed and stability of the network.

Formal feedback was first sent to the Deputy Principal who then routed it to the relevant parties. This was a practice that the Deputy

Principal followed in his previous job, as he felt that it was important for him to keep abreast of what the people in the school were thinking, and this provided him with reliable first-hand information. Although some may feel that such routing created an unnecessary bottleneck, RP staff generally felt that this offered multiple benefits. It brought the matter to the top management's attention and when the Deputy Principal forwarded it, it gave the suggestion greater credibility. As one staff described, "I think there's an added advantage of going through the staff suggestion scheme. The more important reason is because the person who vet through it is the VP. In that sense, he's aware of some of the things that are ongoing. If you directly email OIS, they may think, 'Who are you to say something?' But if there's something from upper management, it would probably be easier."

Subsequently, upon receiving the feedback, the LEO manager had the autonomy to decide on whether to follow-up or reject a change initiative, although to ensure that this authority was not abused, checks were put into place, such as the LEO manager would sometimes be asked to justify his reasons to the Deputy Principal or D-OAA. As for the external IS staff, they were tasked with implementing the changes as directed by the LEO manager, and could do so without having to consult the vendor office. External IS staff though, were not allowed to make changes to LEO by themselves even if they received direct feedback, so as to ensure that the LEO manager was the sole point of accountability.

The LEO manager considered various issues before deciding which changes to implement and in what order. While it was acknowledged that it was not feasible to speak to everyone, he tried to consolidate input from diverse relevant stakeholders. For example, he considered feedback from the D-OAA, who wanted to ensure that they had a sound academic system. He also took into account the technical considerations of the internal IS staff on how the system fit into RP IT infrastructure. He was receptive to input from the external IS staff on the features and limitations of the package and its upgrades. Finally, he even sought feedback from facilitators to better comprehend educational issues. A top management staff member explained the rationale for such a convoluted approach, "You can't issue a decree to say that, 'We'll do this' and get the best for an organisation. You have to do a lot of consultation. You have to win over the programme chairs, module chairs who set the questions, directors who are in charge, and negotiate with the IT department on what's available."

The LEO manager also assessed whether the proposed changes reinforced or countered RP's academic policy and strategic direction, and he would reject suggestions that went against RP policy. In addition, since this was an enterprise-wide system, the LEO manager assessed whether the proposed changes affected the consistency of the system across RP. Thus, if the suggestion was for something unique to only a particular subset of RP, then it would not be implemented. Instead, the person who suggested it would be advised to develop a workaround or change the way they worked.

Subsequently, the LEO manager assessed the urgency of the proposed change and would try to resolve the more urgent ones first. He also considered the scope of the change. Thus, for changes that were more complicated and required to a lot of code changes, they would most likely leave it until the semester break when they could make the changes with minimal disruption. While most of RP were unaware of the details behind the LEO manager's decision-making process, a number of them revealed that they were more interested in the final decision rather than the mechanics behind it.

Sometimes, the development team arranged face-to-face meetings with the person who made the suggestion to clarify issues about it, or even to make the change in their presence. In most cases, the development continued to follow their original stance of customising the package. However, at times, changes were made to the educational process in RP instead.

For example, due to a limitation in the package, it was unable to handle certain mathematical notations so the affected modules had to change the way they assessed students. Alternatively (particularly if a suggestion was rejected), the users would work in conjunction with the development team and OIS to adopt available technological workarounds. For example, when RP blocked Firefox and only used Internet Explorer, several staff downloaded a plug-in so that Firefox could function like Internet Explorer and still be used.

Sometimes, staff would even develop their own add-ons that tapped onto the LEO system. Such add-ons could benefit themselves, their immediate module and department, or even RP as a whole. In such cases, they would develop the add-ons themselves with some guidance from and monitoring by the development team to ensure that the add-on did not run counter to LEO and that the add-on could only view the data in LEO but not manipulate it. As of mid-2004, RP had developed about 144 of some 175 applications in-house.

Once a change was implemented, the person who suggested it was typically notified. However, for minor changes, other users would not be explicitly notified. Rather, they would be left to discover the changes on their own or through word of mouth. For moderate changes, a simple email would be sent to all affected users to notify them of the changes. For more complex changes, these emails would contain detailed instructions, typically in the form of PowerPoint slides with step-by-step guides, on how to cope with the change. Users were expected to learn how to cope with the help of these guides. These guides were also concurrently uploaded to a common website for future reference by all relevant staff. Finally, for major changes, such as adding totally new features, training would be provided for affected users. From there, users were invited to submit their feedback on the changes. Feedback though, was not explicitly advertised. Rather, in line with RP's open culture and flat hierarchy, anyone was able to directly send comments about the changes to the development team.

LEARNING TO USE LEO

Stakeholders of LEO required education on how to use LEO in two situations. Firstly, when changes were made as described above. Secondly, for people who were new to RP. As noted previously, one key mode of education was training. For existing staff, training was typically reserved for those affected by major changes in LEO or the way it was used. For new staff, they typically went through a short introduction to RP's systems, with particular emphasis on the core features of LEO. The bulk of their training centered on RP's educational pedagogy, giving them a firm understanding of how things worked in RP and why. While such training was often conducted by administrative staff or the development team as required, other facilitators would sometimes be roped in as well to help teach new staff how to use LEO. As for students, they too were given some basic introduction to LEO as part of their general introduction to RP during their Freshmen Orientation Programme.

For Staff members, peer learning was relied upon to a large extent. Typically, staff would ask help from their peers who were sharing the same office, especially those handling the same module. The impression was that these peers were not only more experienced and thus better equipped to give advice, but their close proximity also made querying them easier. Exchanging information was made easier as staff could easily interact with one another using email, VoIP or Internet Messenger even if their colleagues were not physically present to answer their queries face-to-face. To enhance such peer-to-peer interaction, a buddy system was put into place where each new facilitator was assigned a senior facilitator as a mentor or buddy who could help them to settle in and teach them about what LEO entailed. One new facilitator provided this opinion of his senior peers, "They've been really helpful. That's one of the things I like about working here at RP. I guess it's because RP hires people who have a passion to teach… and who are able to work with others. They are more than willing to help others who are in difficulty so [although] I was relatively new around here, it was easy and relatively painless to get whatever help I required."

Several facilitators opted to get help directly from the development team since contact information for members of this team was readily available so they could send queries via email or Internet Messenger, or even hold face-to-face meetings. This was preferred, as they felt that the development team was the best source of knowledge about the system and what it entailed. Other staff though felt that such reliance on the development team should be minimised. In their opinion, if everyone in RP started going directly to the development team for help, the team would be overburdened and unable to perform their duties.

Another group of facilitators that benefited from peer learning were those who were promoted to more senior positions that required more extensive use of LEO. Sometimes, these new module chairs or problem crafters could ask peers holding similar roles in their departments for advice on how to use the advanced features in LEO. At other times, they may even approach staff holding positions at a similar level in other departments. Staff built contacts with these peers from attending a common foundation programme when they first joined RP, or by working on collaborative efforts such as temporarily teaching in a different department or joining *ad hoc* teams to evaluate LEO. As one staff explained, "For example, there's not many module chairs here. If I'm lost over something, I could ask the other people who had a stint doing module chair. But sometimes, after the stint is over, the system changed. If I ask them, they say, 'Hey, in my time, these things were not like that.' So I think a good way would be to approach another module chair from some other departments."

Another mode of education was self-learning, as staff often learnt from their experiences while experimenting with the system in their spare time or on-the-job when they urgently needed to get something done. To enhance such self-education, the development team maintained and expanded the online section of Frequently Asked Questions (FAQ) that they first put into place after rolling out the system. This FAQ described how to use the various features of LEO. Not everyone frequented this FAQ, because they found it too cumbersome and contained too much information. They either had trouble immediately locating what they wanted to know or the language used was too technical. Finally, staff was forced to learn about LEO on their own due to peer pressure. As a top management staff elaborated, "There is psychological pressure on those who don't know how to use the IS. They are forced to pick it up, as otherwise others will see them as 'lousy'. Also, without this knowledge, they are unable to get their job done… IT is not just about the technology. At times, it is also about playing psychological games."

As for students, they relied heavily on peer learning too. They learnt how to use LEO from senior students, who were better positioned to share their experiences. Several students even formed informal collaborative support groups so they could help one another not just with their lessons but also with issues like using LEO. Furthermore, a number of staff members felt that one of the core objectives of having such an IT-centric institute was to instill in students the knowledge of how to use IS effectively, and thus students should be encouraged to learn how to use LEO on their own without any spoon-feeding from staff.

WORKING WITH AN EXTERNAL VENDOR

One ongoing challenge throughout the implementation of LEO was the fostering of a close working relationship between RP and the external vendor. This working relationship essentially comprised of two parts: the relationship with the external vendor's main office staff and with the external IS staff from the vendor who were seconded full-time to RP.

The main concern was the challenge of integrating the external IS staff seconded to RP with internal staff to foster a more conducive work environment and an "RP Family." A strong believer and proponent of fostering such a relationship was the Deputy Principal. He firmly believed that it did not make sense for anyone working full-time in RP to be treated as outsiders. As the Deputy Principal elaborated, "I kept telling my colleagues, my philosophy is, 'Does it really matter who pays your payroll?' Our strategy is to try and convert this group of people. 'Yes, you're employed by Company A but you're here eight to nine hours a day. You never go back to your own office because if you do, the guy does not even, have a table for you. So you should feel more at home with us than with your own company.'"

Consequently, external IS staff was given the same benefits as internal staff, including laptops, access to information, RP email addresses, and RP staff IDs. They were also invited to participate in

RP's sports and family days, and wore the same outfits as RP staff. Essentially, RP made no overt effort to segregate the identification of internal and external staff. In general, such measures caused the external IS staff to feel as if they truly were RP employees. As such, they were expected to be more proactive in their thinking rather than merely following instructions. They were also expected to share the same responsibilities as internal staff and contribute ideas towards improving LEO for the good of RP.

Despite these efforts, there remained inherent difference between internal and external staff, such as in terms of staff rewards and incentives. The external team still drew its pay from their parent company and RP sought to peg their pay based on results and deliverables rather than time spent in RP. In contrast, RP were the ones paid their internal staff directly and offered them other forms of incentives, such as planned career paths, titles, promotions, and greater responsibilities.

RP also faced a challenge in changing the mindset of these external IS staff to move them beyond working strictly based on their contract or service level agreements and instead go the extra mile to contribute to RP. As a top management staff stated, "For me, I feel that once I'm in partnership with you, I always like to believe that you will do your best. So you cannot say, 'Oh, my contract says I can only say 100 words a day, therefore it's a 101st word so I cannot say anymore.' No, I expect you to contribute the 101st word and 120th word and 180th word."

While the parent vendor company approved such efforts as they felt that it helped to foster a closer bond with customers, RP's efforts did make it more challenging for the vendor to maintain their own close relationship with the seconded team. A vendor representative would make regular trips to RP to have lunch with the team and see how they were doing. Sometimes, the vendor would also rotate staff, and bring seconded staff back to the main office and send new staff to RP, with the approval of RP. Consequently, while they were more willing to contribute to RP, a number of the external IS staff still kept in mind that they were outsiders. As one external IS staff revealed, "Of course, we all know we are not a RP staff because one day, we would be transferred back to the office. So for us, we just do our best to provide our best service for our customer."

MOVING FORWARD

As RP moved forward with LEO, a number of changes took place. Due to the vendor's rotation policy, none of the original external IS staff were left in RP. They had all been replaced by new staff. Concurrently, a new LEO manager was appointed. The role of the LEO manager was also clearly defined and he would focus primarily on academic quality and the implementation of academic policies while control of the external IS staff and LEO development were transferred to OIS. The LEO manager and D-OIS would thus work in consultation with one another before making changes to LEO. Among other things, this was meant to serve as a check and balance as the LEO manager handled policy while the D-OIS handled LEO and its data. This would also help to more tightly formalize the working relationship between the LEO manager and external IS staff, which though suitable initially, was no longer ideal after a few years of maintaining the system.

The emphasis in maintaining LEO also shifted. Whereas the focus was initially on the application, subsequently, attention moved towards the infrastructure to support it. As the staff and student population grew, the load on the system increased, which often caused the servers to temporarily crash at the start of each new semester. The solution was to split students' data into two servers. Other challenges included security issues, such as limiting access to student data to relevant staff. RP also wanted to better integrate LEO into their Student Administration and Finance Systems, so they outsourced these projects to the same vendor that developed LEO.

Finally, the vendor planned to introduce a new .NET version of its package. RP was thus facing the quandary of whether to upgrade their existing ASP version to this new .NET version or simply retain their current ASP version. Retaining the existing version could prove troublesome in the long run as the package had been become a patchwork of features that needed to be streamlined. However, adopting the new version was challenging too, as due to the heavy customisation over the years, the LEO system became unrecognisable from the vendor's original package.

Overall, RP staff was happy with LEO and considered it a success. They felt that it was easy to use, suited their needs, and was uniform and organised. Even so, RP was not resting on its laurels, as it continuously strived to improve the way they did things in RP and enhance the features of LEO.

DISCUSSION QUESTIONS

1. Identify the main phases during the implementation of LEO in RP, and the key activities in each phase.
2. What were the different identity orientations in RP? RP's aim was to develop a collective identity. Evaluate the effectiveness of the steps taken by RP to achieve this aim. In your opinion, was a collective identity necessary to facilitate FFS fit while implementing LEO?
3. How is external staff different from internal staff? In your opinion, should external staff be treated similarly or differently from internal staff? Evaluate the effectiveness of the way in which external staff was treated in RP to facilitate FFS fit while implementing LEO.

Case 10
LTA'S ONE.MOTORING PORTAL

Calvin Chan

SIM University, Singapore

Mahdieh Taher

National University of Singapore

BACKGROUND

The Land Transport Authority of Singapore (LTA) was officially established on 1 September 1995 through the merger of four public sector entities; namely the Registry of Vehicles, the Mass Rapid Transit Corporation, the Roads & Transportation Division of the Public Works Department and the Land Transport Division of the former Ministry of Communications (now renamed as the Ministry of Transport). It is currently a statutory board under the Ministry of Transport and is tasked to spearhead land transport development in the island state of Singapore. It oversees the long-term land transportation planning in Singapore and it also looks after the transportation needs of all road users, including those who drive and those who take public transport. The ultimate goal of LTA is to ensure "a smooth and seamless journey for all." LTA aims to deliver a land transport network that is integrated, efficient, cost-effective, and sustainable to meet the nation's needs. It also targets to plan, develop, and manage Singapore's land transport system to support a quality environment while making optimal use of the transport measures and safeguarding the well-being of the traveling public. The other objective of LTA is to develop and implement policies to encourage commuters to choose the most appropriate transportation mode.

Ensuring "a smooth and seamless journey for all" is certainly no mean feat, given the large customer base served by LTA. According

Mode of Transportation Taken in Singapore

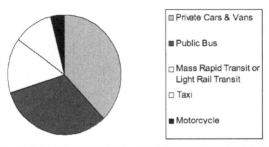

Modes of Transpport	Percentage (%)
Private Cards & Vans	38
Public Bus	32
Mass Rapid Transit or Light Rail Transit	15
Taxi	11
Motorcycle	4

Figure 10.1:   Mode of transportation taken in Singapore.

to the statistics from a survey conducted between 14 February and 27 July 2004, 8.2 million trips were made on the roads of Singapore daily. Moreover, there were 727,395 vehicles on the roads of Singapore in 2004, and this figure was projected to further increase (see Figure 10.1).

This attitude towards customer orientation is reflected by the IT Group of LTA. Moreover, when looking back at the history of LTA, the Group Director for Innovation and Infocomm Technology (GDIIT) expressed that it has always exuded a culture of innovativeness, "LTA has a culture of being bold enough to be the first in doing certain things. An example is the ERP (i.e., Electronic Road Pricing) system. It went through piloting and learning. It has a culture which enable us to say 'Even though no one has done it before. But, if it made sense for us to do it, we should do it.'" As a testament to the excellence that LTA has achieved, LTA was admitted to the coveted Singapore Quality Class (SQC), which recognises organisations with highly commendable performance.

GENESIS OF ONE.MOTORING

In their pursuit to meet the ever rising expectation of road users, LTA launched the ONE.MOTORING Portal in October 2000. The ONE.MOTORING Portal was conceptualised as a flagship one-stop motoring portal that provide the public with a comprehensive range of information and services pertaining to buying, owning and driving a vehicle in Singapore.

The idea of ONE.MOTORING Portal first came about in 1999. At that point, LTA received about 900,000 telephone enquiries, 500,000 letters, and 500,000 walk-in visits at the counters a year. Although a possible solution was to increase the number of staff serving the public, this was deemed not to be sufficiently cost-effective as the overall operating cost would invariably increase. Furthermore, LTA was also faced with a limitation in the floor space needed to accommodate the walk-in public, let alone housing additional staff. There was also a rising expectation for better customer service from the public. At about the same time, there was also a campaign within the Civil Service pushing for excellent public service in the 21st century.[16]

In order to rise to the challenges, one of the managers that oversees customer service operations in LTA began to ponder for a solution. Through a spark of inspiration ignited by the increasing popularity of the Internet at that time, the manager was motivated to put up a proposal to leverage upon the Internet in educating the public on the various processes related to vehicle licensing and ownership. In so doing, he was hopeful that it would reduce the number of public queries related to such issues.

Enthused by this spark of brilliance, he got in touch with the IT Group in LTA to explore the feasibility of his inspirational idea. Subsequently, the GDIIT (Director) heard about this idea and her past experience and instincts immediately alerted her to the far-reaching potential of the idea. Instead of merely having a static webpage offering informational content to the public, she envisioned a large-scale flagship portal for the LTA where the public

---

[16] This campaign is known as Public Service for the 21st Century (PS21) Movement.

could visit for static informational content as well as to fulfill their desired transaction directly online. Buoyed by her enthusiasm towards this vision, many in LTA subsequently bought into this novel vision of what would become the ONE.MOTORING Portal.[17] As the deliberation of the ONE.MOTORING Portal concept progressed, the vision of the portal not only became clearer, but it also simultaneously grew more sophisticated. Recognising that the public often needed to transact with private companies while fulfilling their motoring needs with the LTA,[18] the vision of the ONE.MOTORING Portal was subsequently enlarged to also incorporate other motoring related information and services offered by the private sector.

By 2000, the concept for the ONE.MOTORING Portal was formalised and a paper was submitted to the senior management of LTA. It was subsequently routed to LTA's board of directors and even to the parent Ministry of LTA, i.e., the Ministry of Transport, for approval. At that point in time, the roles and responsibilities of LTA and the industry players were already clearly demarcated in the paper that was submitted. In just a single sitting, the paper was approved by the board of directors.

Upon receiving the approval, the implementation of the ONE.MOTORING Portal was spread over multiple phases. Once the approval was obtained, a tender was called to develop Phase 1 of the ONE.MOTORING Portal. During this first phase, the portal only consisted of static informational content. Direct enquiry functions were introduced in Phase 2. Only in Phase 3 were the more complex online services added. A noteworthy distinction in implementing the ONE.MOTORING Portal was the consideration of views and feedback from the public in deciding what content and services were to be included into the portal.

---

[17] This vision was considered to be novel back in 1999. The term "e-Government" wasn't even formalised at that time and the transactional services on the Internet were largely e-commerce related websites developed by the private sector.

[18] For example, when a new car is bought, not only will the new owner apply for a new car license, but also will need to purchase motor insurance from private sector insurance firms.

HAVING ONE.MOTORING AS A DOT.COM

As opposed to most conventional government agency websites, one intriguing feature of the ONE.MOTORING Portal was the URL. Differing from most government websites in Singapore, which were registered with the tag "gov.sg," the URL of the ONE.MOTORING Portal was registered as "www.onemotoring.com.sg" right from the very beginning. Two primary rationales were suggested for doing so.

Firstly, the direction for having the ONE.MOTORING Portal as a dot.com was based on a customer-centric perspective. As noted earlier, the public often needed to transact with private companies while fulfilling their motoring needs with the LTA. Therefore, to offer greater value and convenience to the public, the plan was for the ONE.MOTORING Portal to become a one-stop portal where all motoring related needs can be serviced, regardless of whether the required service was provided by a public agency or a private firm.

The second rationale was based on a desire to advance the motor industry, which was noted to be "not the most IT savvy industry" in Singapore. In general, the motoring industry in Singapore was still largely brick-and-mortar based. Since LTA was going to develop the ONE.MOTORING Portal, they took the opportunity to get the motor industry to participate in this initiative with the hope of jump-starting the industry to be more IT savvy. As such, LTA understood that it will be important not to simply have the portal as a government website and thus proceeded to register the URL as a dot.com.

Understanding they were venturing into uncharted waters, LTA proceeded cautiously and adopted a more evolutionary approach instead of jumping immediately into the full swing of things. For a start, only regulatory content and services were uploaded onto the portal. Private sector information was only included much later and even this was achieved mainly through hyperlinks to the websites of the private sector companies, such as "motor dealers, finance companies and insurance companies."

Besides the evolutionary approach undertaken in developing the content, the manner in which the outsourcing of the ONE. MOTORING Portal unfolded was also of evolutionary style. While the outsourcing ultimately took the form of a Public–Private Partnership, the first phase of implementation was achieved through a regular IT outsourcing initiative. This was not unlike the manner which most typical government IT projects in Singapore were developed. Under such an outsourcing model, the planning and business development of the portal were overseen by the LTA, while the vendor focused solely on the technical development and maintenance of the portal. Such a model lasted until the implementation of Phase 2 of the ONE. MOTORING Portal.

At the time when Phase 2 of the portal was being planned, users of the portal had grown so accustomed to using it that some of them had begun to request for more sophisticated services to be included. One of the requests was some who asked for the information on the portal to be made accessible through mobile devices so that motorists driving on the roads can access them "on-the-fly." There were also other requests for "some kind of lifestyle" content, such as advice on vehicle maintenance and driving tips. In addition, at around the same time, the Government also initiated an "Economy Drive" to steer all government agencies towards lowering their operating costs. As a result, LTA found itself to be in a "Catch-22" situation where on the one hand it aspired to meet the mounting requests of the public, while on the other hand, it also had to join the Government's drive in reducing cost.

Believing that this challenge could be surmounted, the GDIIT spurred the ONE.MOTORING Portal project team on in their search for a solution. She persuaded them to be more "business minded" and to "put away the old mind set" in their pursuit. After a few sessions of brainstorming, someone suggested that they could rope in a private sector operator for the ONE.MOTORING Portal. Being "bottom-line driven," it was thought that the private sector operator would be able to propose innovative ways which could simultaneously meet the demands of the public while keeping costs low. From then onwards, the notion of progressing into a Public–Private Partnership model began to take root in LTA. They began to look for a business partner to help them manage the ONE. MOTORING Portal, instead of just having an IT vendor to develop and maintain the portal. A Project Manager elaborated on the qualities that they were looking for in the prospective partner, "We were looking for business partner who was not only competent in managing both the hardware infrastructure and security, but also at the same time, aware of what customers needed and how to meet these needs in the best way possible."

WORKING OUT A PARTNERSHIP MODEL

Once there was a consensus within LTA to adopt a Public–Private Partnership model, the next task on hand was to figure out a workable partnership model. As the concept of Public–Private Partnership was still not widespread in Singapore at that time, LTA proceeded by trying to learn from other partnership models existing either locally or internationally. When they discovered that the Ministry of Defense (MINDEF) had a MIW Portal[19] operating under a Public–Private Partnership model, they immediately made arrangement to meet both MINDEF and their business partner, Green Dot Internet Services Pte Ltd (GDIS). LTA also sought the inputs of other IT solution vendors to gauge their level of interest to participate in a Public–Private Partnership as well as to tap on their ideas in designing a workable Public–Private Partnership model.

Subsequently, a Request-For-Proposal (RFP) was called, where vendors submitted their respective proposals based on certain requirements and guidelines specified in the RFP. In the hope of offering more flexibility to the vendors in coming up with highly creative proposals, the specifications in the RFP were intentionally kept to a minimum. A Project Manager clarified, "We gave a lot of leeway for them to come back with lots of creative ideas. So… the RFP was not prescriptive. This was to give them more leeway to come back with innovative proposals."

Throughout the entire process of working out a possible partnership model, LTA adopted a highly consultative stance and had been accommodative in adjusting some of their stated pre-requisites

---

[19] MIW is the abbreviation for "My Internet World" (http://www.miw.com.sg).

in light of the feedback received from the private vendors. Such an approach was distinctively different from typical IT initiatives undertaken by government agencies in Singapore. In most typical IT initiatives, the requirement was often well defined and the responsibilities of the private vendor were clearly demarcated. An incident which perhaps best exemplified the consultative approach adopted by the LTA was its willingness to change the contractual term from an initial three years to five years. This was in response to the feedback from the private vendors that three years would be too short for them to recoup their investment.

Notwithstanding the flexibility, there were also certain things that LTA stood firm and these were clearly laid out. An example was the intellectual property rights (IPR) of the resultant portal. Given that this was a Public–Private Partnership and the portal was to be jointly developed, there was undoubtedly going to be confusion over the ownership of the intellectual property of the resultant portal. To pre-empt such confusion from occurring, it was determined that any background IPR would be retained by the respective parties that brought them into the partnership. However, any foreground IPR will fall under the ownership of LTA.[20]

IDENTIFYING THE PARTNER

After the RFP was sent, a number of vendors subsequently responded with their respective proposals. However, given the rather open nature of the RFP, the scrutiny involved in the selection of a potential partner was certainly anything but straightforward. As this was the first time that they were handling such an innovative initiative, there was also an absence of appropriate reference models to fall back on.

One key distinction of this RFP as compared to most typical outsourcing venture was the nature of the proposal submitted by the

---

[20] Background IPR refers to any intellectual property that was already created prior to the contract. On the contrary, foreground IPR refers to the intellectual property that was created in conjunction to the contractual requirements and was created after the contractual agreement was established.

vendors. In a typical outsourcing venture, the vendor would state explicitly whether they were able to satisfy certain requirements stated in the RFP. However, given the open nature of this RFP, where the vendors were given a lot of leeway in coming up with creative proposals, LTA found itself comparing different comprehensive business proposals for the ONE.MOTORING Portal. Although this presented a steep learning curve for the evaluation committee, they eventually scaled it after putting in much hard work.

Needless to say, a key consideration was placed on how well the proposal from the private vendors fitted with the ONE.MOTORING Portal envision by LTA. In addition to evaluating how well the proposal fitted in with the vision, LTA was also concerned with how the vendor could assure the subsequent sustainability of the portal as well as how they intended to generate revenue through the portal. Another key quality that LTA was searching for in a vendor was how much initiative they were willing to take in further developing the portal. A manager who was involved in the evaluation of the submitted proposal shared, "We were looking for people who can partner with us, because I didn't want to be in a situation where we would keep telling them to move from step A to Z. We wanted them to take more initiative. So that became an evaluation criterion."

Another key consideration in identifying a suitable partner was the comprehensiveness of the proposed marketing plan in the proposal. This was driven by the belief that publicity was key in creating an awareness of the portal and the subsequent adoption of it by the public. In their attempt to be comprehensive in their evaluation process, LTA also requested the vendors to submit some estimated figures on the revenue and volume that they were expecting from the portal. This was found to be helpful as it enabled the evaluation committee to assess how realistic each of the proposals was. However, in order to do a competent assessment of the submitted figures, the committee also had to do its due diligence by carrying out their own research on the requested figures.

Apart from the key evaluation criteria, there were also some secondary considerations that were appraised in the partner selection process. One secondary consideration was the assurance that the good name and image of LTA will be in no way tarnished by a mis-management of the ONE.MOTORING Portal. In all, much care was expended in the evaluation process and every proposal was scruti-nised with considerable depth.

Besides the actual evaluation process, a lot of background work was also invested in bringing about a corresponding mindset change among all the different officers involved in dealing with this novel "contracting" process. Eventually, after many sessions of evaluation, which often occurred late into the evening, the proposal submitted by GDIS was identified as best suited to the needs of LTA. The part-nership contract was thus awarded to GDIS at the end of January 2003, after two and a half months of evaluation.

WORKING WITH THE PARTNER

In expediting the development of the ONE.MOTORING Portal, two distinct teams were formed in LTA to handle the project. One team was a typical IT project management team, which oversaw the smooth development and operation of the ONE.MOTORING Portal, and the exploration of further technical enhancements of the portal. The other was the business team which focused on the commercial aspects of the portal, such as studying the interest and predilection of the market demand and bringing this information to the drawing board in deciding whether or not to implement certain new features. As the partnership with GDIS progressed, GDIS began to take on the lead in developing the commercial aspect of the portal, bringing LTA's inten-tion of embarking on this Public–Private Partnership to fruition.

For instance, when there were requests and suggestions from the public for certain new services to be added to the portal, LTA would discuss these with GDIS. When necessary, GDIS would carry out a more detailed exploration by evaluating the technical feasibility and conducting market research. GDIS would then propose some appro-priate recommendation to LTA who would then make the final deci-sion on whether to implement their recommendation.

As with all new partnerships, the mutual understanding that was needed to drive the partnership forward needed some time to be inculcated. In this instance, the meetings and discussions became the platforms where the foundation of this partnership was established. Through these meetings and discussions, both parties gained a better understanding of each other's concerns and styles of working and they made necessary adjustments in adapting to each other.

Being the owner of the regulatory portion of the ONE.MOTORING Portal, LTA naturally retained the final say with regards to the regulatory aspect of the portal. But for the commercial aspect of the portal, GDIS was given much freedom in its planning and operation. For example, while the LTA had strict guidelines on the regulatory services and information which were hosted on the portal, GDIS was free to make recommendations on how they intended to provide additional channels for accessing the regulatory services and information (e.g., through mobile devices). To further expedite the decision-making process and to speed up the development of the portal, both parties also established certain guidelines for developing the commercial content of the portal. As long as it was within the broad framework of the guidelines, GDIS could decide how they wanted to proceed. On its part, GDIS also ensured that LTA was kept in the loop of these decisions as LTA was still ultimately responsible for what was available on the portal.

RE-LAUNCH OF ONE.MOTORING PORTAL

On 25 August 2004, approximately six months into the Public–Private Partnership between LTA and GDIS, the newly vitalised ONE.MOTORING Portal was successfully launched. The event was well-covered by the local media, with the major local broadsheet running a special section to feature the newly re-launched ONE. MOTORING Portal. The event was attended by the CEOs of both LTA as well as GDIS. In his speech made during the event, the CEO of LTA noted, "By collaborating with a private sector partner, we hope to deliver a more vibrant content and service rich portal to our motorist and the motoring industry.... Whilst the LTA would continue to provide the regulatory content and services for the portal, we need a partner who will drive commercial initiatives such as marketing and collaboration with other interested product and service providers."

In terms of the layout of its content, the ONE.MOTORING Portal was segregated into a few segments, which encompassed applications like e-transactions, e-payments, road traffic information, general motoring information, as well as lifestyle information and interest groups.

On top of the web-based information and services, ONE.MOTORING also offered Wireless Application Protocol (WAP) services to anyone with a General Packet Radio Services (GPRS) enabled mobile phone or Personal Digital Assistant (PDA) with a WAP browser that supported the WAP 2.0 specification. Some of the information and services available through WAP included traffic news alert, traffic camera images, road tax payment enquiry, vehicle transfer fees enquiry, and PARF Value Rebate enquiry.

To date, the ONE.MOTORING Portal has already won a number of awards since the time it was initially launched in October 2000. These included the Minister Innovation Award twice in 2002 and 2004 from the Ministry of Transport and the CIO Award in 2003. Since the re-launch of the portal in 2004, it has attracted an average of five million hits a month. Based on official figures, LTA has enjoyed a 40% savings in cost through the new ONE.MOTORING Portal. More importantly, users who were polled had also been positive in their comments on the new portal. One of them said, "The new website is very user-friendly. You don't have to spend time guessing which link will lead you to the right application or information." A car salesman remarked: "The portal has saved car dealers a lot of time. We do not have to go all the way down to LTA to complete the paperwork. Vehicle transfer forms and deregistration forms are all now downloadable from the website."

REFLECTING ON THE JOURNEY

The ONE.MOTORING Portal and the Public–Private Partnership model had indeed provided LTA with the means to enhance their services to the public. What was perhaps more remarkable was that these improvements were attained without any increase in resources.

Reflecting on the journey thus far, one of the Project Managers expressed that the experience gained from undergoing the first phase of development before embarking on the Public–Private Partnership had helped LTA to harness a better working knowledge of the tasks which GDIS encountered when they took over the management of the portal. Through the experience of the first phase, LTA obtained a first-hand account of all that was required to operate the portal.

Thus, when GDIS raised certain issues pertaining to the operation of the portal, LTA had a good appreciation of what GDIS meant. This had not only facilitated the communication between the two parties, but it has also facilitated the development of the much needed trust and understanding for the partnership to work.

Looking back at the learning journey, the GDIIT added that it started way back when government agencies began to buy manpower headcounts from IT firms to support their IT operations. Since then, it had progressed through different stages of development before evolving into what is now known as the Public–Private Partnership. From the purchase of manpower headcounts, the next stage was the outsourcing of IT projects, where the vendors were managed by service level agreements. This evolved into the current new stage of Public–Private Partnership.

In addition, from the perspectives of the private partner, it was also expressed that communication was key in making the Public–Private Partnership work. It was through communication that GDIS got a better understanding of LTA and this eventually led to the alignment of the priorities of both parties. This was revealed by the Senior Vice President of Business in GDIS, "We indeed went through that communication process. I think GDIS learned a lot in the process and that helped us to progress on…. You learned more about each other, understood their businesses better. After a while, you start to get into the hang of things. These were the priorities. So… the priorities were totally aligned."

MOVING AHEAD

The establishment of the Public–Private Partnership with GDIS has helped the ONE.MOTORING Portal to advance into a new phase of development in e-service delivery. For instance, e-services are accessible via multiple electronic channels such as SMS, WAP and iMode. Further work is also currently in progress to expand the range of e-services available and further enhance the user experience of interacting with the LTA. An example is the registration of new vehicles, which needs to be conducted at specified physical locations. In the near future, new vehicle owners will be able to conduct the registration online. Indeed, being a forward looking organisation, it can be trusted that LTA will not rest on its laurels and will continue to strive for greater success, building upon their past experience, and acquiring new knowledge as it continues to break new grounds.

DISCUSSION QUESTIONS

1. Why did LTA decide to implement ONE.MOTORING Portal? What were the advantages of the new system? Give your opinions.
2. How did LTA change its strategy towards implementing the ONE. MOTORING Portal?
3. What kind of actions did LTA take in implementing its portal?
4. What do you think were the key challenges faced by the LTA in implementing the Portal? How would you recommend that LTA address these challenges?

Case 11

IT IMPLEMENTATION: LESSONS FROM GRAND MERCURE ROXY HOTEL

Sitoh Mun Kiat and Pan Shan Ling

National University of Singapore

BACKGROUND

Mercure is one of the 15 complementary brands housed under Accor — Europe's largest hotel group and leading hotel employer that has about 145,000 employees across its 4,200 hotel properties in 90 countries. With 45 years of industrial experience in the hospitality sector, Accor's properties operate under various business models (e.g., direct owning, variable leasing, managing, and franchising), with varying levels of the business standardised and controlled by the group's headquarter. Under its belt, Mercure is positioned as one of Accor's midscale brands, boasting 681 hotels across 49 countries, with its operations less standardised as compared with Accor's other brands, such as Novotel and IBIS.

In Singapore, the Mercure brand is managed by Grand Mercure Roxy Hotel (GMRH), a local property that provides a unique blend of local experience for both leisure and business travellers. With a speedy 15-minute ride from the Changi International Airport and city centre, GMRH's strategic location has drawn travellers alike to its property parked at the east coast of Singapore. Furnished with 558 rooms, 4 restaurants and 2 bars, Mercure is an ideal destination for guests on business trips or leisure.

GMRH is owned by Roxy-Pacific Holdings Limited — a home grown speciality property and hospitality group established in May

1967 and listed on SGX Mainboard on March 2008. The organisation is principally engaged in the development and sale of residential properties and other investment properties.

Whilst GMRH's average occupancy rate (AOR) decreased marginally from 94.4% in the first nine months of 2010 (9M2010) to 94.1% in the first nine months of 2011 (9M2011), its average room rate (ARR) went up by 14% to S$188.4 in 9M2011, as compared with S$165.2 in 9M2010, as seen in Figure 11.1. As a result, the revenue per available room (RevPar) registered an increase of 14% from S$155.9 in 9M2010 to S$177.3 in 9M2011. Further, its hotel revenue rose by 9% from S$33.0 million in 9M201 to S$36.1 million in 9M2011.

David Lane — the Resident Manager of GMRH since 2001 — is the main person responsible for the overall business strategies and decisions of the hotel. The hotel has five major departments, namely engineering, housekeeping, front office, F&B and security — the structure of which has been summarised in Figure 11.2. At GMRH, marketing offers and online sales are made on four websites: two of them are operated by the Accor group, and the other two by GMRH itself.

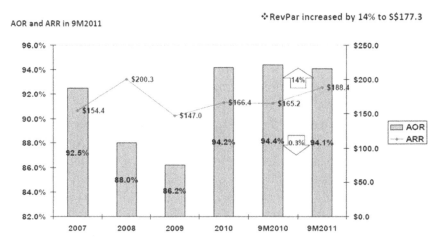

Figure 11.1:   Grand Mercure Roxy Hotel's average occupancy rate (AOR), average room rate (ARR), and revenue per available room (RevPar) from 2007 to 9M2011.

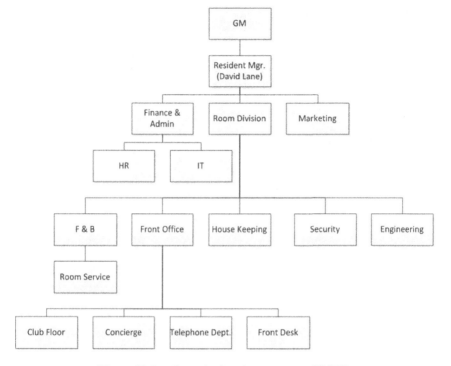

Figure 11.2:   Organisational structure at GMRH.

Accorhotels.com is the main online booking site that serves all hotels under the Accor group. Through this global site, economies of scale are achieved, with 183 million web visitors generated in 2010 alone. Further, the site contributes 23%, slightly more than a fifth, of total sales accrued for Accor. A mobile version of the website — in the form of an iPhone application — has garnered downloads of more than 500,000 copies and counting. To ride on the wave of Web 2.0, Accorhotels.com has also made its presence on social media platform giants Facebook and Twitter (see Figure 11.3).

Mercure.com is a brand-specific site, catered to promote the Mercure brand. The site builds guest loyalty by allowing guests to register as members, who are privileged to enjoy exclusive offers and benefits such as the personalised productivity tool that simplifies reservations for repeat customers.

Source: www.accorhotels.com   Source: www.mercure.com

Figure 11.3:   Accor managed sites.

Grandmercureroxy.com.sg is a site owned and managed by GMRH directly. The site is custom developed and hosted by a regional IT vendor located in Australia. With full control over the site, GMRH is able to update the site more frequently and exercise greater flexibility in terms of comprehensiveness and dynamics of site content. For example, the site includes detailed information on the 4 restaurants and 2 bars offered within the hotel. For actual room booking, however, this site will still redirect users to accorhotel.com, the main booking engine for the entire Accor group.

Grandmercureroxyvenues.com is a micro site designed to promote MICE[21] services offered by GMRH. Similar to grandmercureroxy.com.sg, the site is custom developed, but provides comprehensive content related to MICE. The main target audience of this site is business travellers who are looking for venues to hold business events (see Figure 11.4).

As with most other hotels in Singapore, if a hotel is managed by a global operator such as Accor, generally only one or two IT professionals are needed to manage and coordinate the IT tasks within the hotel. Mr. Lo Chee Keat, the IT manager of GMRH, brings with him 15 years of IT experience in the hospitality

---

[21] MICE stands for Meetings, Incentives, Conferences and Exhibitions.

Source: www.grandmercureroxy.com.sg   *Source*: www.grandmercureroxyvenues.com

Figure 11.4:   GMRH managed sites.

industry, of which 10 years were spent at GMRH. Mr. Lo's main role lies in coordinating with external vendors, Accor's IT team, as well as the daily operations within GMRH. As he puts it, "The most important things are the network and the server, the operations, [and] customer satisfaction."

Under the management control of Accor, GMRH needs to adhere to strict IT policies in its management of computer networks and IT systems installed at the local property. Currently, Mr. Lo is in charge of monitoring the 13 IT systems at GMRH, which range from mission-critical applications such as the Property Management System (PMS) to smaller applications such as the door key system. With all these systems under his sole supervision, it is no doubt that Mr. Lo's daily responsibility lies in monitoring and maintaining system health checks to ensure operational availability for the business.

On the other hand, Ms. Tika Larasati, the Assistant Manager of E-commerce & Marketing and who joined the hotel in early 2011, takes on a very different role. As a result of her previous work experiences, Ms. Larasati has developed a great passion for search engine optimisation (SEO) and website marketing. Tasked as the only person to oversee GMRH's online strategies, she is in charge of planning, implementation, and maintenance of the hotel's websites, aided by support rendered from Accor-appointed external agencies. The current platforms used by GMRH have enabled Ms. Larasati with minimal difficulty and restrictions in managing the sites, as she noted, "Basically I control everything, I change the content, [and] I change everything that needs to be changed... for all the bookings and all that stuff."

OPPORTUNITIES AND CHALLENGES

Reaching Out to Customers

The proliferation of Internet users across the globe has tendered hotels the opportunity to reach out to global customers directly. At the same time, advancements in IT have moulded similar opportunities for new online agents to link up potential business and leisure travellers with hotels, as well as pairing them up with other complementary services such as air flights.

In May 2009, GMRH upgraded its infrastructure to connect to the travel agent's reservation system known as TARS, which is a centralised booking engine owned by Accor to link to global distribution systems (GDS). The system allows booking orders received from GDSs to feed all the way to GMRH's local PMS without any human intervention. However, this automation has not proven its cost savings yet. As expressed by David Lane, "In my view, we thought we will get more savings out of it but we haven't. To be honest, we thought we could reduce a little manpower on the reservation part. We were going to — it was something that we could have enjoyed — but hasn't proven to be the case."

Although GMRH leverages on TARS to generate online booking sales from Accorhotels.com or from its collaborations with other OTAs and GDSs, GMRH reserves little control over how much sales actually comes from TARS. Hence, eventually GMRH is diverting its attention to its own websites to attract prospects and drive sales. However, as is the usual case for website marketing, the key challenges confronting the hotel are how to attract visitors and how to build an effective website that can drive sales conversion.

GMRH's websites are laden with many SEO issues, including the heavy use of Flash objects and insufficient "relevant" links that can push the website to the top few in search results. Together, these issues greatly reduced the effectiveness in bringing prospects and customers alike to the site. This in turn puts a strain on the potential profits that can be generated, given that the profits made from direct sales can be way higher than those from indirect sales through the OTA or GDS. The potential of direct online sales is irrefutable, and most clear-cut in terms of tracking, as seen by David Lane's remark, "The best thing about online is it's the 'most clean' revenue, apart from the phone call coming directly to hotel."

Improving Guest Experience

Much coordination is needed among staff, in particular the room service attendants, to ensure that hotel guests are served with everything they need while enjoying their stay at the hotel. Yet, when coordination takes the form of verbal communication, it is inevitably more prone to human errors arising from misunderstanding and uncertainty. This can cause poor service delivery that is not only cumbersome in terms of accountability tracking, but also puts a dent on guest satisfaction. An interviewee, aptly illustrates the challenge as follows: "When we call to a staff, they might hear wrongly and go to the wrong room. If they press the bell in the wrong room and the guest is resting and doesn't require a service, it would cause a nuisance. So when a person receives a request from guest, they have a big book to record what time received and who they passed the message to, so there is a lot of paper work. We are really looking forward to the day that everything is paperless so that everything can be accounted for in the system."

Although having a paperless system is seen as a means of minimising such communication errors and the subsequent undesirable service quality, actualising it is not easy, given the constraints of the business.

Firstly, one of the core strategies in the service industry has always been to keep operational costs low, since a significant portion of the operational budget is usually allocated to both human resource and property, thereby leaving limited funds for new technological investments. GMRH mirrors this situation, as David Lane pointed out, "It was basically in hospitality industry [that] we feel that we're constantly behind the technology". Also, technology adoption is usually slower among international chain hotels as compared with independent hotels and regional chains, owed in part by differences in implementation complexity, whereby international chains need to consider issues (e.g., cost, technical, and compliance) on a larger scale.

Secondly, a typical requirement of newly deployed hotel IT systems is to possess the ability to retrieve or exchange data with the hotel's existing PMS, which is the central system that contains the most up-to-date treasure trove of guest information. Without integrating to the PMS, hoteliers would be unable to leverage the new system at its fullest potential — or may even fail to make it work. However, the cost to such integration can be high, and may not even be feasible if the solution violates the hotel's security policies or runs into platform compatibility issues.

Hence, the key challenge for GMRH rests on finding a solution that is not only cost-effective in culling its coordination weakness, but which is also capable of integrating with its existing PMS — the system at the heart of the hotel's IT infrastructure.

Online Strategy

In GMRH's online strategy, GMRH aims to increase its share of direct sales and foster long-lasting customer relationships. To achieve this, GMRH engages in effective website marketing through the use of search engine optimization (SEO) and analytics techniques.

IT Decision

"One of the challenges now is to get people, who actually book through OLTAs to book through our booking engine instead because when you go through OLTAs, there is commission for them." — David Lane

Just as what the hotel's Resident Manager expressed, revenue is often split between hoteliers and the online travel agents, of whom the latter gains their share of the sales pie through commissions. In order to wrestle the share of this pie, GMRH knows that it will need to play an entirely different ball game altogether; to be successful in the online competition means that GMRH must not only know how to attract online users' eyeballs, but also it must know how to sustain their clicks from the website's landing page all the way to booking payment completion page.

Yet, to account for such high website traffic and conversion rates, investments in this area can be expensive. This is because the dynamics of the online market would necessitate the hotel to constantly keep its eyes and ears open to key developments and emerging trends in order to advance successfully. To this end, GMRH has invested in two websites and hired a person to dedicate in this area, and the hotel has made good progress so far. As noted by David Lane, "Our internet [sales] online has gone from about 10% three years ago to about 24% now; but having said that, our marketing spent on this area has gone from S$0 to S$800,000 a year." Some of these costs were spent on CMS and network upgrade.

Ms. Larasati, the personnel appointed for this role, observed that on the overall, the industry has heightened its sensitivity to the benefits of improving direct sales, with more hoteliers stepping up their efforts in capitalising on opportunities online, "Yes, more and more hotels you can see that now, with all the training seminars that they are doing, it's really pushing direct sales online."

However, there is no magic bullet to achieving this. While there are vendors who offer such strategic online services (e.g., SEO, online marketing, social media monitoring), vendors themselves are withholding the guarantee that they can deliver results as expected by hoteliers. Some vendors are even willing to provide full refund for their SEO services in cases where the results fall behind certain expectations, showing how unpredictable the effects of such online efforts can be.

On the other hand, certain online strategies need to be executed in-house rather than outsourced to vendors. The case of maintaining the hotel's presence on social media platforms such as Facebook and Twitter elicits this. It is difficult for a third party agent to engage with the customer who probably had an unpleasant encounter at the hotel on a particular day, when the agent most likely was not even familiar with the operations of the hotel. This lack of personal touch could go against the hotel's branding that it promotes, with repercussions anyone in the hospitality industry could easily imagine.

As Ms. Larasati explained, "It's hard to outsource to an agent. The thing is that it is social media; you have to know what the culture of the hotel is, to be able to represent the hotel.... How can you relate it when you're not working for the hotel? How you relate when you don't know what happened that day when the guest complain or something, you know that personal relationship, that touch you don't have."

For GMRH, it is now geared up with a series of routine activities slated to push its online strategy to a greater level. These include: electronic direct marketing (EDM), online marketing (SEO and promotions), frequent website updating to improve search results, e-commerce with pre-order facility, social media support, and later in the pipeline, creating individual F&B micro sites to promote individual branding. GMRH believes in the importance of dedication and specialisation to make its activities tick. As stressed by Ms. Larasati, the hotel's key person working on the online arena, "[It] requires a lot of energy and resources to take direct booking because you need somebody to keep updating it, refreshing it, you know it has to do with doing content, layout, SEO. So you got to have a dedicated person to do it."

IT Implementation

Before taking actions to improve the hotel's websites, Ms. Larasati built various technical mechanisms to monitor web traffic performance. Achieved using the concept of link tracking in which she could track the number of clicks on a certain key word on the page, she discovered various strengths and weaknesses of the sites, as she recounted, "I created a lot more tracking links now as compared to previously, so now we have got the details, conversions for all the different packages we put online."

Also, by using the latest version of Google Analytics, which is a web solution offered by Google that provides detailed statistics about visitors to a website, Ms. Larasati studied in detail on user behaviour patterns that could lead to customer conversion, time to conversion, and hot spots that induce conversion. Based on the analysis, she obtains great insights on various aspects. She highlighted an example of how she could see the difference in time taken for different users to make a booking, "So you could see that some people might take a longer to decide and some other people might just take one day, within the same day they would straight away book, so it would go through like probably 3, 6 clicks, so it's actually good, if the numbers are good." Ms. Larasati is particularly impressed with how the analytics features of the solution have given her valuable information such as path tracking of visitors, which has helped in reducing the bounced rate of their website significantly. The website serves as the platform for GMRH to experiment new ways of optimisation, with the analytics tool equipping Ms. Larasati with insights to evaluate their efforts. Experience and learning feedback obtained from the evaluation are then propagated back to testbed other ways for further improvement.

As Ms. Larasati explains, "I see what the other trends are and what other people are doing to make it more efficient and I try to implement others into ours and also learn from our mistakes, with Google analytics you can see the productivity of your website so which parts are useful, which parts are not and then you sort of work around that and the lead things that you don't need to put on your website and put more things that people are actually looking for."

To get ahead with her job, Ms. Larasati actively seeks the resources to acquire the information and knowledge she needs. For instance, information related to SEO and Google analytics can be found easily on the web. In addition, Google has been actively promoting its tools to web masters. By attending Google's organised events, Ms. Larasati gets to know more people working in this fledgling area, whereby there are few local professionals who have experience dealing with SEO. Hence, it is important to know where to get the necessary resources. According to Ms. Larasati, knowledge begets knowledge in a compounding manner: "You can find it online. You can ask friends like have you heard about this, you know how to this, that sort of thing, it's about who you know and you use the knowledge of others."

On the option of outsourcing SEO to vendors in the area, GMRH is confident of achieving the results in-house. Ms. Larasati agreed, citing reasons such as inability of vendor guarantees in the desired outcome, "There is no guarantee, so what's the point of paying that amount of money if [the vendor] can't guarantee anything. Might as well do it yourself and find out whether it works or not."

That said, she conceded it is a time, skill, and effort consuming task to build and maintain an effective website. In terms of optimisation, one has to be "really precise and detailed with all the key words." Not only that, care must be taken in deciding where the key words should be placed and linked to facilitate web tracking subsequently. As Ms. Larasati emphasised, "So page titles, this and that, a lot of html involved as well, it's not easy but you can do, you don't need to optimize all the pages on your website, you got to find the niche, which pages you really need to push on the google search engines." As optimising all pages is unnecessary, GMRH has chosen its landing page, home page, special deals page, and room description page as the heavyweights of its website SEO efforts.

Besides the judgement in placing tracking links, some of the optimisation tasks require certain technical knowledge such as JQuery and JavaScripts, hence there is a need to also understand how these technologies can impact the search effectiveness. Further, the CMS that supports these websites should allow GMRH to re-arrange the menu items, banners, and content layout easily so that they can be adjusted according to the way the site is normally explored by users. As an example, menu items that are more frequently clicked on are generally placed closer together to facilitate ease of navigation for the user.

Apart from website effectiveness in driving direct sales, Ms. Larasati primes social media as the other online strategy that

GMRH should focus on, and which she acceded the hotel should gather steam in seriously, "People think social media is a hobby thing, is easy to do, and they underestimate the importance of social media, which I think we do as well."

Routinely, GMRH has to reply to comments from Trip Advisor (tripadvisor.com.sg), a platform that allows the online community to share reviews on hotels, flights and restaurants. Based on this single website alone, GMRH has to respond to an average of 15–20 comments per week — a number that has tripled from the initial 5–6 comments per week. Moreover, as all replies are shown to the public, GMRH entrusts one of its senior managers to personally vet through each reply rather than using a standardised "copy-and-paste, template response." The reason for doing so is clearly understood, as Ms. Larasati explains, "I think others don't put attention to each, [but for] every review that comes in, for us, every positive or negative comment, we reply to them because they have taken their time to say something about our hotel. Whether it's bad or good, it's our responsibility to appreciate the time they have taken to do so."

Given the masses of the online communities, it is a huge challenge for hotels to carry out social media monitoring, especially without the support of certain IT tools to provide response promptly. As Ms. Larasati reiterated on the challenge of social media strategy, "Social media is real time customer engagement, so if somebody says something you've got to respond." Thus, to consolidate its efforts for ease of tracking and support purposes, GMRH is hosting a single Facebook page for all the departments, restaurants and bars under its property, rather than having a separate one for each.

IT Value Realisation

Through its online strategic efforts, GMRH has witnessed a double increase in its online sales from 10% to 24% over the last three years. In addition, the data collected from its websites has been used to further fine-tune the website effectiveness. Currently, at least the online users and guests stored in PMS and all other contacts collected from the sales and various touch points are compiled for electronic data marketing (EDM) purposes. The analysis of EDM outcomes helps GMRH in criteria-based customer segmentation for a variety of mass and targeted marketing purposes.

Beyond this use, however, the valuable data collected from other sources have not been mined and systematically utilised for other informational purposes. To illustrate, another type of valuable data lies in the transaction records kept in some of the 13 IT systems. The IT manager, Mr. Lo, automates the integration of these records to a central place for all departments and staff to extract and use. Some departments will outsource data processing when they need further data manipulation.

The skills and experiences accumulated from the website SEO efforts can be further extended in the area of mobile SEO quickly. This will give GMRH an edge over competitors in terms of mobile effectiveness since the penetration rates of mobile usage have caught up tremendously with traditional web usage. In this case, however, the mobile template has to be greatly simplified to suit the scale afforded by the mobile, which is seen as the rising trend, as Ms. Larasati remarked, "… You [are] going to take out all the things that are not necessary and make it thumb-friendly, because it [the mobile trend] is going to be bigger [than the web]."

In order to create synergy out of these opportunities, it seems that GMRH's impending task would be to source for a next-generation CMS that can support both web and mobile infrastructure amid the growing mobile trend, while at the same time derive innovative ways to craft advantages out of social media without the need for too much additional headcount to maintain their social presence.

Guest Experience Strategy

While the online strategy pursued by GMRH is meant to bolster the hotel at the virtual fronts, in terms of increasing online direct sales and managing customer relations at the online community space, it is insufficient for GMRH to park its efforts here. Internally, GMRH understands the importance of consistently improving its customer service to levels that will maintain, if not exceed, guests' expectations.

To this end, GMRH has enacted on a guest experience strategy to keep guests satisfied with the hospitality provided by the host, so as to induce repeat patronisations in the future. GMRH does so by exploiting the information accuracy, workflow coordination, convenience, and efficiency enabled by the US-based workflow software (UWS) deployed across its departments.

IT Decision

To improve coordination among staff, GMRH sought for a suitable workflow solution that can integrate to both its existing infrastructure and the PMS. However, due to various technical constraints (e.g., compatibility issues), as well as compliance issues pertaining to the hotel's IT security policies, there were only a select few off-the-shelf products that GMRH could choose from. Although a customised solution — developed from scratch — was an alternative, it would require system integration to GMRH's existing infrastructure — an option too costly to consider.

GMRH had to balance the quality of the solution against the requirements of a low entry and running cost. For instance, it is important that the solution is able to connect directly to the hotel's current Opera version of the PMS, and avoid the need to procure costly hardware equipment. In terms of running, the solution should be able to operate using the hotel's newly upgraded wireless infrastructure, obviating the need to subscribe to telephone lines for communication among staff.

At the end of the decision-making process, David Lane recalled that "it was designed to make us more efficient as well as more accountable... " and he was optimistic about the management choice. The selected US-based workflow software (UWS) is specially designed to help hotel operators in coordinating their daily workflow, which includes the assignment of tasks to on-duty staff to tend to the needs of guests. A prominent capability of the software is that it can track and trace every request, thereby giving detailed insights of each response.

The UWS painted an efficient picture of streamlined workflow within the hotel's daily operations. Firstly, it would enable GMRH to configure reservation rules and staff schedules, which would allow GMRH to automatically dispatch staff to perform certain tasks or services based on the rules set. Secondly, it would also make integration of the UWS to the hotel's infrastructure possible. Most importantly, the UWS is able to connect to the hotel's existing PMS directly. Communication could also be easily carried onto the wireless network, thus facilitating on-duty staff, each supplied with a wireless-enabled PDA, to communicate with one another using the device. With that, GMRH went ahead with the procurement of 65 PDA devices to be shared among its 300 staff working in shifts.

For managers who carry a personal iPhone, they are able to access UWS outside of the hotel's premises. This external access to the UWS is necessary so that managers can be alerted to any urgent incidents that have escalated to pressing levels that reach them. Overall, the UWS could aid the hotel in daily operational areas, such as automation of message passing, preventive maintenance, as well as servicing of orders and guests' requests.

Beyond delivering these essentials, however, the UWS also provides strategic value by empowering the hotel with bits and pieces of information about each guest, drip-irrigated through data retrieved from the PDAs. GMRH could use this accumulated knowledge about each guest to deliver innovative acts to create a unique, personalised guest experience, exactly reverberating the marketing slogan of UWS — "Don't just give your guests a room. Give them what they want. Give them an experience!"

The ability to mine every single piece of new information into diamond opportunities to delight each guest will provide GMRH the platform to edge their services. At this point, the management's eye is fixed on getting its staff to be familiarised with using UWS. After which, they will be looking at new modules that can further improve their operations. For instance, a possible module would be the quality inspection module that allows GMRH to systematically design quality inspection processes and which would aid supervisors in spotting quality issues, such as room cleanliness.

IT Implementation

By far, the implementation journey of UWS has not been easy. Foremost, the hotel had to integrate the software with the PMS, as well as connect it to the internal computer network including all wireless devices within the property premises. As all these work were executed on the hotel's existing IT network, Accor's IT department had to evaluate the product and mitigate risks that could occur when external systems were added to their internal environment. As a result, it took GMRH close to a year from the point the UWS decision was made to the point of system go-live; as David Lane asserted, "We actually have been trying to get this installed in the company for nine months or more, but we have a lot of hurdles with our company and we have a lot of challenges with the funding process as well."

After the system was installed successfully, the management conducted training for all 300 staff, each undergoing four hours per session over a period of three weeks. Workflow rules were also set up to accustom the system to their operations. One example of the workflow, as described by David Lane: "Norhaini received from the guest room that they want extra towel. She just needs to send [a message that] this room requests an extra towel. She doesn't have to care who this request will be sent to, but the system will automatically find out the floor, who is on duty on this floor, and send [a message] to the particular handset. So if Haze is on duty on the fifth floor today and the fifth floor room [made the] requests, her handset will receive…. If she did not answer her supervisor, it will be warned within 10 minutes. If her supervisor also ignored that request, half an hour's time, I will be notified that it's already half an hour and nobody has answered to this request and I will call them and find out what's happening."

The workflow described above has been applied to many other processes within the hotel. In turn this means that staff response time has to be prompt in all their service areas, so as to avoid escalating the event to their superiors, as explained by a manager, who said "… because if [the alert] comes to us, we will be the ones upset." Due to the design of the system, it is able to support many layers of "safety nets" that help ensure service quality is adequately maintained or improved.

With the UWS, many task-related communications between staff have been replaced by technology. While it yields efficiency benefits mentioned above, during implementation there was a challenge of standardising common search terms. As users have to input short text messages or select from a standard list of service items, different users may enter or interpret a message differently. This may limit the effectiveness of the search filter. For instance, as illustrated by David Lane, the search filter may be unable to return tasks related to "leaking toilet" if "toilet leaking" were entered instead, "You need to have a common search term and if you are going to search for a complaint, whether it's a leaking toilet or toilet leaking, [it] makes a big difference, leaking toilet or toilet leaking you can't find it, you have to get some sort of commonality, which is not easy." To overcome this, all users and department heads worked together to standardise a list of terms commonly used in their operations and services.

On the people side, not all staff were convinced that the UWS would be a productive tool for them. During the training, some of them gave excuses to reject the system, as one staff member by the name of Priscilla said, "During the training, half of us were quite negative. They say that 'you know my finger is too big.'" However, eventually the user-friendliness of the device interface won them over, and they have since become very comfortable with the device, except for two major drawbacks. Firstly, the device does not vibrate, and hence it sometimes causes missed "calls" when kept in the pocket. Secondly, the device is fragile, thus the hotel staff need to take special care of it while doing their rounds.

Apart from the guest related workflows, GMRH has in place workflows supporting both routine and *ad hoc* based non-guest related issues. The difference between guest and non-guest related workflows lies in the way in which escalation will be handled; non-guest-related issues are less urgent and typically do not need to be handled immediately.

IT Value Realisation

After using the UWS for just two months, GMRH is experiencing promising outcomes. Not only has it helped to coordinate more than 300 daily tasks more effectively, the hotel's overall service level has also improved tremendously. This can be gauged from the influx of positive comments by guests on the hotel's front desk staff, housekeeping staff, bellboy and concierge, such as "[staffs] are all doing a very good job, very efficient, [and] they delivered what I want." As Mr. Lo recounted, he acknowledges that these have been greatly enabled by the newly deployed workflow system, "there are a lot of these kind of good comments, but they [guests] didn't know behind the mechanism is [our workflow system]."

One of the greatest benefits is that the system helps to "surprise" guests when they see how fast the services can be delivered. The culture of the working environment has been positive as well, as Mr. Lo commented, "I think they [the staff] obtain more job satisfaction.... It's more on the ball actually." Even for older staff who were initially afraid they could not cope with the device (citing resistance such as "I used to fold towels. Now you ask me to use computers") their attitudes towards technology have taken a turn for the better after using it for a few weeks. That said, job satisfaction is still very much dependent on the individual. In order to encourage staff to be more proactive in creating service orders and responding to UWS alerts promptly, the management is currently considering rolling out reward programmes. Yet, the challenge lies in how they can create measurements that can track individual or departmental performance accurately and fairly. If the reward programme is not well thought out, it can easily create unnecessary dissent among staff. David Lane highlights the implications of the reward structure, "It should be taken very positively if we do it right. If not, [it] can have a whole department of people looking for a new job; and in the Singapore market, I will find a job in a day."

In terms of business analytics, data collected from the UWS provides good insights into operational issues and guest profiles. Linking past issues or requests made from an individual guest can give the hotel the opportunity to serve him or her better. Priscilla explained, "Any request will go back into the guest profile history, so that we will know this particular guest, third time, fourth time and still requesting certain issue; and we put alert to it." GMRH notes that it can further enhance its service if the profile histories of the stays across different hotels can be linked, in which case it can delight the guests with "surprising" moments even further.

With the effective workflow system in place now, GMRH is hunting for a fulltime Quality Manager to administrate the system, design workflows, analysis data, and cultivate staff to be proactive in the creation of and response towards service orders.

CONCLUSION

GMRH has capitalised IT to deliver both of its online and guest experience strategies. The online strategy ensures that websites are effective in engaging existing customers and reaching out to global target customers. On the other hand, the guest experience strategy is designed to ensure that staffs are able to coordinate efficiently and thus play an excellent host to guests by building high levels of guest satisfaction. This case study has illustrated several themes identified during the hotel focus group discussion. The online strategy has been designed to capture the growing trends of internet, mobile usage, as well as those of social media. It takes time and in-house resources for one to acquire sufficient experience and necessary know-how to be effective in the highly complex and dynamics cyber space. One essential skill is to analyse the behaviour of how surfers visit their websites. By bridging the data from websites and internal database, GMRH has implemented EDM campaigns to further engage customers.

The guest experience strategy helps to cultivate the organisational service excellence mindset. Users with different backgrounds have to adapt to new ways of working with technology, whereby staff on the move can be communicated real-time via PDA devices. Both guest and non-guest issues are now coordinated efficiently using pre-defined workflows based on the nature of these issues. The customer profile that keeps track of past transactions and past requests becomes valuable knowledge when made available to staff. The workflow system collected valuable data that can be further analysed for greater use in subsequent strategic marketing and operational purposes.

In conclusion, GMRH's focus on global reach and unique guest experience has improved the hotel's overall performance, enabled by the synergies created using cost-effective IT strategies. This, in turn, has allowed GMRH to gain overall marketing effectiveness and operational productivity.

DISCUSSION QUESTIONS

1. What were the areas of concern that GMRH identified?
2. What were the steps that GMRH took to implement the IT systems?
3. What were some challenges GMRH faced while implementing the various IT systems?
4. How useful were the implemented systems and what are the future directions for GMRH?

Case 12

IT IN SUPPLY CHAIN MANAGEMENT: BATAMINDO SHIPPING & WAREHOUSE PTE LTD

Leong Mei Ling and Pan Shan Ling

National University of Singapore

BACKGROUND

Consumers like you and I may not realise the importance and significance of logistics in our lives as it is often a behind-the-scenes function integrated in the supply chain and distribution network. Simple examples of a logistics would be the processes triggered after you drop a greeting card to your beloved in the postbox, or when you send your faulty iPhone back for servicing. In business terms, logistics refers to a set of processes, capabilities, and capacities used to completely fulfill customer orders in a timely and cost efficient way. Although logistics is often seen as a standalone industry, it is fundamental to the commercial operations of various companies across manufacturing and retail industry sectors, which has varying logistics needs. Referring to the familiar Supply Chain Operations Reference (SCOR) model steps (see Figure 12.1), logistics can occur anywhere in the process of planning, sourcing, making, delivering and even the returning (known as reverse logistics) but certain types of companies may require a more established reverse logistics capability (e.g., office equipment and mobile handsets). On the other hand, non-manufacturing scenarios, such as retail and wholesale distribution, may not be as concerned with the movement of raw materials or components into a production process but, rather, the movement of finished goods from a supply network to the consumer and back again if returns are involved.

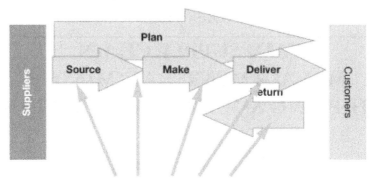

Figure 12.1:   Logistics needs across the supply chain.

In Singapore, logistics is one of the key industries. Strategically located between the East and West, Singapore is well positioned to deliver sustainable logistics solutions for companies' global operations. In fact, it is the world's busiest port and the largest transshipment hub. The Port of Singapore Authority's (PSA) Singapore Terminals are connected by 200 shipping lines to 600 ports in 123 countries, with daily sailings to every major port of call in the world, while Singapore's Changi Airport is amongst Asia's largest cargo airport, served by about 5,400 flights connecting to 200 cities in 60 countries. A 2010 World Bank report ranked Singapore as the Number Two logistics hub in the world, ahead of Netherlands, Sweden and Asian heavyweights such as Japan, Hong Kong and China. In the face of highly competitive environment with rising fuel prices, changing business models, and an increasing demand for sustainable logistics solutions, industry players have to innovate to stay ahead and even to survive in the field. Information technology is one of the vital weapons.

Located on the Batam Island about 20 km away from Singapore is the Batamindo Industrial Park, a pioneer industrial park on this Indonesia island which originated from an economic cooperation agreement between the government of the two countries. Its success singlehandedly transformed the economy of the island, attracting global manufacturers and creating employment for more than

60,000 workers. Leveraging on Singapore's international connectivity, one of the special features of the industrial park is the satellite concept, where companies establish their headquarters in Singapore and manufacturing in Batam. Tapping on this niche market, Batamindo Shipping & Warehouse Pte Ltd (Batamindo) was incorporated in January 1990.

Batamindo is a privately-owned joint venture between SembCorp Parks Management, CWT Limited, Toll, Mitsui, and Timsco. It provides logistics support to manufacturers and traders in Batam, specifically door-to-door shipping and transport services for raw material and finished goods between Singapore and Indonesia, and also warehousing, project cargo, and international freight forwarding services. It is the leading player in the Batamindo Industrial Park in volume of containers handled, with staff strength of about 80 being stationed at Singapore and Batam, and operating two derrick crane barges of 130 TEUS capacity each, handling more than 250 units of containers owned by the company and managing a total fleet of over 100 trucks of its contractors.

Starting from feeder vessel services, Batamindo has extended its capabilities to other areas of the supply chain. Its warehouses in Singapore and Batam enable Batamindo to deliver a whole suite of supply chain services including cargo consolidation and inventory management, to further value add to the customers. In 2010, the company extended its capability in local distribution by purchasing its own lorry trucks. It also provides services for bulk and project cargo handling for the oil and gas, and marine industry, which requires specialised capability and knowledge.

Batamindo's operations are based in PSA port, allowing them to make faster transshipment services for both inbound and outbound sea cargo via Singapore to international destinations. It has Connecting Carriers Agreement with a number of shipping lines for Batam service. By working seamlessly with them, Batamindo is able to provide one single Bill of Lading (BL) and therefore offering customers a higher level of convenience with lower cost and fewer hassles of coordination. Figure 12.2 illustrates Batamindo's door-to-door services for its manufacturing and trading customers. Through

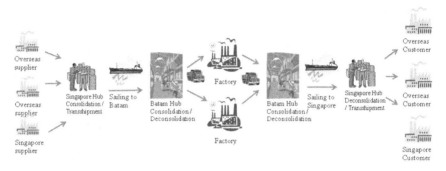

Figure 12.2:   End to end supply chain service offering.

creating this seamless service offering, it is better able to serve companies which use Batam as a hinterland to Singapore.

For the past 20 years, Batamindo has tided over the ups and downs of the global and regional macroeconomy. To stay afloat and ahead of its competitors, the company has to understand its own ability and the environment it is competing in. According to Mr. Goh Puay Guan, the General Manager of Batamindo, "We work with our customers to offer an end-to-end solution in and out of Batam. We try to synchronise with customers' production schedules and are able position inventory in and out through coordinating our shipping, warehouse, and container depot operations. Operationally, we are focused on our service level and delivery timings to customers."

Similar to any shipping line, the management of the company has to ensure adequate vessel utilisation to sustain the business. Puay Guan explained the situation, "We also monitor things like vessel loading to make sure that we have an adequate utilization. As with any other shipping line, because fixed cost of bunker, fixed cost of manpower, fixed cost of charter, leasing… so we have to achieve certain loading per trip voyage."

Looking beyond the company, as the lead player today, Batamindo faces stiff competition from competitors who try to emulate them in the service offerings. Batamindo is able to emerge as the dominant provider in the industrial park, handling the highest number of containers, due to several reasons. Being the first mover in this segment, it is acknowledged that Batamindo has laid a solid foundation and establish a good brand name. The trust and credibility that the company has instituted in its customers in the long term working relationship becomes a valuable asset. Being a Singapore-based company, the customers are likely to associate its brand with stability and reliability. When it comes to a decision point, this certainly benefits the company as it creates a brand preference induced by consumers' confidence.

There are quite a number of parties involved in the operation of the door-to-door supply chain. These include shipping lines, customs, freight agents, truckers, customers, yard operators and warehouses, of which some are under the direct control of Batamindo while some are subcontractors or agents which need to be managed. Batamindo thus has to coordinate these parties to meet customer needs and to react quickly to changes. To do so, it has implemented an Integrated Shipping Management System to facilitate the information flow, generation of documents, and responsiveness to changes.

OPERATIONS WORKFLOW

Currently, there are five sales personnel in Batamindo. After a deal is sealed, the sales personnel would have to bring the customer information, as well as the details of the quotation agreed, to share with their colleagues so they could follow up on the operation and then proceed to billing. Figure 12.3 shows the workflow within Batamindo.

When the operation staff receives a booking enquiry, they would have to first check the validity of the customer. Before they commit to the customer on the vessel timing, they would have to ensure the availability of the voyage. Occasionally, they would outsource the business by loading the container on other companies' vessel due to overloading. In this case, they would call up the contractors to check the vessel availability. Once the availability is confirmed, the booking can be made in the system.

Information such as container and cargo details, haulier, additional service required, will be entered into the system. The same information will be submitted in Portnet as well. Next, the job order will be generated and sent to the haulier to pick up the containers

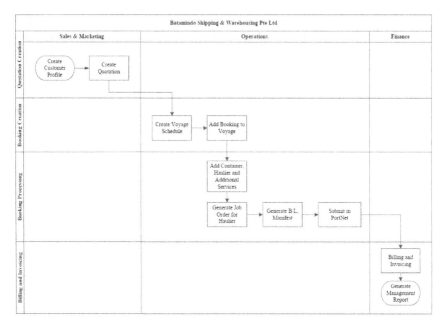

Figure 12.3: Batamindo's internal operations workflow.

from the locations indicated. Before the shipment, the BL and manifest will be generated and handed over to Batam agents for custom clearance. The operations staff will select from a checklist on what services have been provided to a customer for a particular job.

When all these are completed, the Finance department will take over to do the invoicing. Based on the quotation information shared by the Sales department and the order made by the Operation department, the Finance staff can generate a bill to the customer. In the event that a job is incomplete in the system, this would be highlighted so that the appropriate documents and services can be entered in the system to close the job.

Unlike long haul ocean freight, the distance between Batam and Singapore is much shorter. The sailing time is about four hours. The turnaround is very fast and delays in delivery can affect the availability of materials for the customer's production line. The same delay in hours would likely to have minimal impact long haul on ocean freight which takes days or weeks. Batamindo thus has to monitor closely on service levels, or notify the customer in the event of any changes in daily schedule. In case of exceptions, Batamindo will also activate contingency plans such as working with customers to re-schedule freight, expedite truck delivery, or to load on alternative vessels. It has visibility of key customer shipping schedules in order to enable better planning.

IT AS AN ENABLER

Without the use of IT, it would be difficult to manage daily shipments and monitor different customer requirements. Figure 12.4 illustrates the evolution of systems in the company over 20 years.

Phase 1: The Beginning — Data Capture with DOS (1990–1999)

In the beginning, Batamindo's team of less than 10 employees used typewriters to perform business tasks such as typing manifest, BL and

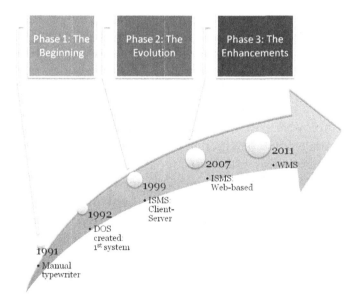

Figure 12.4:   The evolution of Batamindo's inhouse IT systems.

invoices. As Batamindo progressed, improvements in productivity quickly became a concern among the General Manager at that time, Mr. Tan, and employees of Batamindo. In particular, as typewriters were used, documentation hindered efficiency since the same data had to be re-typed for various purposes across booking to invoicing. According to Ms. Tham Yee Fun, Finance and Administration Manager, "When we were talking [about] how to improve our productivity, we were suggesting that because we were using typewriter to type and later, we had to invoice. Basically, they [need] the same information, same data. So we suggested that why don't we create one system so that we can link from booking all the way to invoicing."

In 1992, the suggestion was put into reality when a simple DOS system — termed "Data Capture" — was developed by a vendor using Dbase to support Batamindo's employees in business operations, such as creating booking. As Yee Fun recalled, "Initially we were using typewriter to type our manifest, BL, invoices. Subsequently, when we started to use the system [which is] DOS version — it is a very simple system that allows us to create quotation, booking and BL."

Apart from linking the operations from booking to invoicing, the Data Capture brought about serendipitous time savings as well, as Yee Fun explained, "If [a] mistake [was made], then we don't have to re-type everything again. [The system was] considered quite smooth."

While the Data Capture catered to the needs of the nascent logistic firm, a major issue that remained was the need for "double work." Employees had to write down their input on paper first before the data could be keyed in to the Data Capture. Fadil and Yee Fun concurred this was due to Batamindo's process-driven organisation. As Fadil pointed out, "We need to write first before we can key in. Remember when we do our booking, we need to write on our booking form and then our loading list, discharging list then later on someone can key in one by one. Basically someone needs to do everything in paper first, then transfer to the system."

As the operations were carried out in a "process driven" manner, starting from beginning (booking) up to the end (invoicing), certain information were pre-requisite of subsequent steps. As an example, Yee

Fun illustrated, "Because when we did the booking, we had to fill in some necessary information before we could enter into the system."

In terms of documentation, only BL, manifest and invoices were printed. Other documents were all handwritten. During this phase, Batamindo already had a separate IPAC accounting system to which the invoice information could be interfaced. During this era, Batamindo was considered advanced as compared with its competitors.

Phase 2: The Evolution — Proprietary In-House IT System (1999–2007)

As Batamindo progressed, its business needs outgrew the capabilities of the Data Capture. It resulted in a predicament where the Data Capture was unable to handle the increased volume of operations required. As mentioned by Yee Fun, "It caused [the system] to slow down and always hang." Secondly, the Data Capture did not have a search functionality which the business needed for tracking purposes. In the 1990s, if a customer called, they would have to go through much hassle of manual checking to trace the container location using T-card. Fadil said, "It is a card in the T-shape where delivery [information] was written on the card. Every time you move a container, you write the date, BL number and all the particulars there. So you have a few columns. Any container that is in Singapore, we put a card here [to represent it]. That means this container is in Singapore. So a card denotes one container. When this container is out from the yard into a customer premise [and] when we receive a report that this is now with customer, we move it to the customer [slot] on that day. From customer [place], he stuff cargo and export to PSA then we move it to PSA [slot]. When it is loaded, we bundled it up and give it to another person to input all the data inside. So there is a story there — date of release, date of stuffing, date of input into the port…. We need to write the card. And when it is full, then we stapled [the cards] together."

With the T-card in different colour codes representing varying container types and sizes, the employees were then able to count the number of containers on hand and track the location of each container. However, without the search functions, the staff had to rely on the T-card to tracking purposes and consequently, they had to bear with the pain to maintain the data on the T-card and later on transfer it to the system for other purposes such as billing. Yee Fun commented, "There is no function for us to do the search but the data was actually inside. It was a very simple system." In terms of reporting, only BL, manifest and invoices were printed. Other documents were all handwritten. Quotation was done manually using word processors; hence information had to be re-typed again. The existing system and process put a restrain on the efficiency, productivity, and accuracy of the operations.

In view of the above limitations, Batamindo saw the need for enhancements to the then near decade old Data Capture system, and its ex-General Manager, Mr. Tan Choon Wei, made the decision to transit to a new system in 1999. This transition marked the evolution of Batamindo's inhouse IT system, with its Integrated Shipping Management System (ISMS). With the decision to embark on its ISMS, Batamindo engaged a vendor, who had previous experience in developing for other big players in the market, to customise the system for the logistic firm. A project team consists of representatives from all departments who has a share in the system setup and led by Yee Fun. With requirements gathered from each department, the new system included several modules customised to Batamindo's business needs. These include the Customer Module, Quotation Module, Rates Module, Booking Module, Billing Module, Voyage Module, Container Module, and Report Module, underpinned by Oracle database. Instead of booking, the new system workflow started at customer profile and quotation creation. Employees were able to print out quotations directly from the system without duplication of work faced in the Data Capture era.

Validation checks were greatly enhanced. For Batamindo, their booking process is controlled by existing quotation. A booking from a customer has to be checked against the quotation for validity. If the quotation is invalid, that booking will in turn be invalid and therefore not be processed. Prior to the implementation of the IS, employees at Batamindo were unable to follow up with the check and they had no choice but to process the booking based on their memory and relationship with the customer. Fadil explained the difficulty, "We don't know whether this guy exist (existing customer) or is he under our black list because there is nothing for them (staff) to follow up. We just based on the relationship."

After the ISMS was implemented, such uncertain situations were eradicated as the necessary business validation checks had been customized and incorporated into the modules. For instance, when a particular customer called to make a booking, the employee could easily check if the customer was a valid customer, blacklisted customer, or if the quotation had expired. Only pre-approved customers would be able to make bookings. As illustrated by Fadil, "Say Customer A call to make a booking. We just key in a few characters and it will appear. There will be drop-down [menu] for us to choose the correct customer. And when we try to save, if it is not a valid quotation, you cannot save. So it helped us as a check [that] this is our valid customer, not blacklisted customers or [customer with] expired quotation. So we control by quotation. Anybody can just call and book. If there is no valid quotation, we cannot process the booking."

Phase 3: The Enhancements (2007–2011)

The beginning version of ISMS was client-server based until 2007, when it was changed to web-based by a different vendor using MySQL, where the system accessibility was no longer confined to the office. Figure 12.5 shows the screen shot of the ISMS home page. There was a need to enhance the ISMS and move to the web in order to speed up the work flow and improve business operations, which was put forth by the Management team.

Firstly, as Batamindo's lifting capacity increased, work efficiency, and productivity were greatly compromised as the ISMS could not handle the increasing volume of multi-users concurrent work processing. Operation was encumbered by the system limitation and it caused frustration in the users who had to wait to use the system.

Figure 12.5:   Screen-shot of the ISMS home page.

As illustrated by Fadil, "The decision to change is to improve our work because our lifting capacity also increases. So when a guy was doing enquiry, e.g., on container history and if another girl was doing processing, it would affect her processing as the system was trying to check and you asked it to do something [else], then it became very slow. It could not support…. But the moment when you enter the data and have to wait for the processing then it becomes frustrating."

Further, the ISMS moved to the web during this period. Besides benefiting users as they could use the system from home, the main reason for the change was to allow Batamindo's counterparts based in Batam to access the ISMS independently rather than calling on employees based in Singapore to check on services. As pointed out by Fadil, "We can allow our counterpart in Batam to access the system for information. Rather than they call us and check, they can view from the system, so this improves the coordination."

Secondly, the ISMS was enhanced to improve the ease of use. A system is designed for and ultimately used by the end user in order to reap the greatest benefit for the organisation. The usability and user-friendliness are thereby key design considerations. The users sat down together with the vendor of Batamindo and went through the workflow, step-by-step, and screen-by-screen. The flow was improved when toggling functionality was added, such that employees could perform their tasks more smoothly. As corroborated by Ms. Wendy Soo, the Operations Executive, "From one module, e.g., booking, sometimes we have to go to billing or from billing we want to go back to booking, we have to exit, then enter. Now we can toggle between the modules."

Previously, the Container Module required that employees maintain the Rates Management Module (RMM) cost by keying in the container one by one, activity based. With the upgrade, employees are now able to upload the information by batch, which increased the efficiency greatly. The vendor applied the same design concepts to the entry of container in the booking module, so that the users enjoy the option to do away with the to-and-fro navigation and edit the containers' information for one booking on the same screen. An example is shown in Figure 12.6 below.

Apparently, it does not always cause the pain to change the business process flow to improve productivity. The astute use of heuristic approach in designing the user interface enables intuitive navigation of a complex system like ISMS and facilitates efficiency and accuracy of data entry.

Thirdly, while the initial ISMS allowed employees to download information to process their statistic reports, the enhanced ISMS implemented in 2007 further provided them with the ability to churn out all the statistical reports required for management reporting.

The reporting functionalities of the ISMS help the management team in its strategic planning and execution. This is due to the comprehensive information that can be retrieved from the reports. Mr. Sam Yu, Sales & Marketing Manager, illustrates this example, "We have a weekly variance report which looks at how our loading

Figure 12.6:　Booking screen in ISMS.

has increased or decreased over one month period. We can also query by daily loading and we can query by customer over whatever time period you specified, one day, one week.... Basically it allows you to track customer variances and react to any customer changes or requirements."

USER ACCESS AND CONTROL

In a web application, other than authenticating the user' identity, the login ID and password control allow the company to maintain the control over the module access based on the predefined user roles and privileges. Depending on the company policy, some of the information e.g., rates and quotations are confidential and must not be shared with all staff. After all, not all the staff would need the information to execute their tasks. This is exactly what happened in

Batamindo. An example would be the RMM which is only accessible by the Sales and Finance staff. Tables 12.1 and 12.2 clearly outline the access rights of different user groups and departments. Some other controls implemented including the valid period of user password, which will expire every 90 days, and the password can only be recycled after one year. These are the features built in the system to enforce a good information security practice.

The enhanced ISMS has impacted the way Batamindo employees use the system to perform their work. One of the notable changes pertains to loading list. During the client-server era, the Singapore and Batam based counterparts used different file formats to input and store delivery information. Thus there was a need for more frequent overheads in information transfer. However after the ISMS was enhanced, both counterparts used the same excel file to communicate the delivery information, thereby reducing data duplication and the mistakes that could accompany with it. As brought up by Yee Fun, "Last time we had to inform Batam side to use pdf form but now we are allowed to download information to excel and pass the file over to them so they can make use of the excel file to key in those info like delivery time, where to deliver. We even use that same info — we gave the info to Batam side, they will fill in the data like delivery, where we deliver, where we collect then they will send [it] back to us." Overall, as a customized inhouse system that combines the features of both freight forwarding and shipping management systems. The ISMS has contributed to securing Batamindo's advanced position in its industry.

Table 12.1: Module-user access.

Sales & marketing	Operations	Finance and administration	Management
• Customer Module • Quotation Module • Rates Management Module	• Booking Module • Container Module • Vessel Module • Voyage Module	• Billing Module • Rates Management Module	• System Administration • Report Module

Table 12.2:   Roles and privileges of user groups.

Level	User	Roles/Privileges
1	System Administrator	• Administrator of system common resources. • For company security, the System Administrator cannot log into any company. He is able to create/delete companies and user IDs only. • In the event when users forget their passwords, only the default System Administrator can change other users' passwords. Any other users (Company Administrator, supervisors, and normal users) can only change their own passwords.
2	Company Administrator	1. Administrator of all data of the managing company he/she is assigned to. 2. Access to all modules with read/write privileges of the set of data for his/her managing company. 3. A company Administrator has the access rights and privileges of a supervisor.
3	Supervisor	• Supervisor of a module under a managing company. • Read/Write privileges for the module he/she is assigned to. • Can overwrite rules build into the system, for example, a supervisor of the booking module can allow booking to be processed for a black-listed billing party. Re-prints of controlled documents are done by the supervisor.
4	Operator	• User of a module. • Read/Write privilege to the module is based on what the rights he/she is given. There are two access rights: Read Only, Operator. • Read Only means that this user can only view the data displayed in the module, and he cannot create new data, amend or delete existing data. • Operator means that this user has 'read and write' privileges.

CONSIDERATIONS AND CHALLENGES FACED

Over the past two decades, Batamindo has altogether engaged three different vendors to accompany each generation of its IT systems, from the Data Capture in the 1990s, to its first proprietary inhouse

ISMS in 1999, to the current enhanced ISMS in 2007, excluding the upcoming WMS which would involve another vendor as well. Notwithstanding the implementation successes, Batamindo has inevitably faced internal difficulties during the course of the systems transition journey.

Firstly, as with other organisations in general, budget remained one important criterion in deciding on system requirements, as there is a budget approved by the board of directors. When asked about the main decision factors to purchase new software, Yee Fun emphasised, "Price, Budget [is] of course number one. We have constraint."

To that, Fadil followed up by pointing out the need for trade-off in making system functionalities decisions, "Shaun (ex-General Manager of Batamindo) always says, 'Good to have, nice to have and must have... which one you want to choose?' Because there is a budget constraint. Of course [our] staff wants everything."

While budget was noted as a key concern, it was highlighted that the ability of the system in meeting the business requirements was a factor that should not be overlooked too. Yee Fun stated, "Of course for this vendor that we selected, I think they can meet our requirement first — very important. Besides the price, we also look at the system, the functions, is it user-friendly, and whether their support is good."

The situation was elicited by Yee Fun, who said that due to the fact that standard WMS functions were not suitable for Batamindo's business needs, they chose a vendor (out of a total of three vendors) who was willing to customise the system for them, "Actually we short-listed three [vendors]. One of them is standard WMS system. Then this one we selected on is actually more flexible. The third one seems like they are not very keen. So left two and of course we select the one which is more flexible. Because standard WMS functions is not suitable for us. As an example, the vendor selected was willing to make system changes, such as adding timing fields and to allow users to produce KPI reports from the WMS system, which was a business need of Batamindo."

Secondly, there has been a presence of resistance among certain internal employees from different departments towards the system during each of the phases. This resistance takes on two ends of the pendulum; while some employees who have previously worked in IT-intensive environment would criticise the system for its inability to do certain functions, there remains another group who resisted change and preferred the old way. As mentioned by Yee Fun, in the initial computerisation in 1990, "Someone even told me, 'Give me typewriter, I prefer typewriter.'"

The project team has tried to solicit the user feedback in order to improve the system. However, very often, the users were only passing remarks before they familiarise themselves with the system. Hence, the implementation strategy adopted by the team is to mandate the implementation and phase out the old system after one month of parallel run. Fadil said, "Sometimes we have to force it down the throat. After a while when they get used to it, they will love it."

CONCLUSION (2010 AND BEYOND)

With the strong foundation built over the years in the region, the company is exploring different possibilities of strategic expansion, and further improving its processes and operating efficiency. It has launched a 2,400 sqm Batam Logistics Hub and invested in trucks for loose cargo distribution in Singapore in 2010. It has also increased its sailing schedule and looking at increasing its vessel fleet in 2012. The ISMS continues to be enhanced with new management reporting features, and to integrate with external systems.

To establish its strength in warehouse management and inventory management, Batamindo is now implementing the Warehouse Management System (WMS). In the past, Batamindo used excel for its internal warehouse management. For customers that engage in end-to-end full logistics service, Batamindo consolidates the goods received in their Singapore and Batam distribution centres, after which they would prepare shipping documents, followed by sending the containers to their warehouse for storage.

Due to the level of complexity and work involved in managing the storage up to the component level, there has been a consideration to enhance this with a WMS, which is expected to go live in

July 2011. A promising feature in the upcoming WMS implementation will be the ability to interface with the existing ISMS to allow for certain information transfer between the two systems. The implementation of the WMS, together with its existing ISMS, will support the end-to-end supply chain by helping manufacturers with the whole process to do their manufacturing in Batam and regional HQ functions out of Singapore, including import and export out of Singapore. The need for integration and how it would aid the end-to-end supply chain operations is illustrated by Yee Fun, "We need to control goods received in warehouse — how many shipments sent out or received from Batam, how many of them already delivered or collected. Basically we have same info like for one pallet we received and shipped to Batam, we need to enter into our ISMS to produce our shipping docs like BL, so we hope to share the info by download from ISMS and input to WMS so warehouse can simply do a goods receipt to check against the incoming cargo. So no need to key in again when they receive the cargo. This actually saves time on data input...."

DISCUSSION QUESTIONS

1. What were Batamindo's challenges in different phases of system development and how did the company overcome the problem?
2. What are the IS capabilities that Batamindo has developed over the past 20 years and how does it contribute to the competitive advantage of the company?

Case 13

HEALTHWAY MEDICAL GROUP'S CLINICAL MANAGEMENT SYSTEM

Anand Ramchand and Leong Mei Ling

National University of Singapore

HEALTHWAY MEDICAL GROUP

The Healthway Medical Group (HMG) is a leading private healthcare provider with strong presence in Singapore and China. It has one of the largest networks of medical centres and clinics in Singapore serving about one million patient visits per year, and  a fast developing network in China, providing medical, wellness, dental, and specialist healthcare services to a great number of patients in the community. HMG is also developing medical services related facilities like hospitals, medical resorts, retirement villages and large medical centres. To maintain the high quality, accessibility and affordability of their services, HMG leverages on computing and information technologies in various ways, including networking their various clinics and integrating with their patients, to revolutionise the healthcare experience for both their patients and doctors.

BACKGROUND

Singapore is consistently recognised as having one of the finest healthcare systems in the world. Basic healthcare and medical services are easily accessible by all citizens, and being provided by both public and private healthcare institutions keeps healthcare affordable and cost-effective, without putting undue strain on the

PRIMARY CARE	ACUTE CARE	LONG TERM CARE
Private Institutions	**Private Institutions**	**Private Institutions**
2,000 Outpatient Clinics	16 General Hospitals & Specialty Centres	53 Nursing Homes
		27 Rehabilitation Centres
		9 Community & Chronic Sick Hospitals
Public Institutions	**Public Institutions**	**Public Institutions**
18 Outpatient Polyclinics	5 General Hospitals	4 Geriatric Units in Public Hospitals
	2 Specialty Hospitals	
	6 Specialty Centres	

Figure 13.1:   Public and private healthcare institutions in Singapore.

healthcare system. Figure 13.1 depicts how both public and private healthcare providers form Singapore's healthcare industry. For instance, 80% of Singapore's primary care needs are addressed by the 2,000 private outpatient clinics, while 20% are addressed by the 18 government-run polyclinics. The converse is true for acute care, with 72% being addressed by government hospitals and specialty centres, and the remaining by the private sector.

Many of the healthcare institutions in Singapore choose to work together in a medical group. As a group, the institutions are able to enjoy several benefits and offer better services to their patients. Raffles Medical Group, for example, is a medical group that consists of a hospital, 74 clinics and a network of specialty centres. HMG is one of the largest private medical groups in Singapore, owning, operating and managing over 100 medical centres and clinics and 120 permanent doctors at housing estates, commercial hubs as well as within all major private hospitals. Founded in 1990 as a partnership among a few physicians, the GP chain expanded rapidly and now includes specialists and dental chains, as well as health wellness centres, after new investor came onboard in 2006. HMG has also expanded to China in 2009 and the International Finance Corporation (IFC, a member of the World Bank Group) became a shareholder of HMG in 2010.

HMG strongly believed that better healthcare service provision can be driven through IT connectivity. As resonated by Dr. Jong Hee Sen, Director in charge of strategic and innovative IT planning, in his interview with ZDNet Asia, "Healthcare is about information. Better healthcare comes from better availability of information linkages, and this can be life-saving."

Underlying HMG's success is a driving philosophy that healthcare should be patient-centric and integrated across various medical activities. From patients' initial health checks, primary care, prescriptions and payments, to specialist services, surgeries and even hospitalisation. To support these patient-centric goals, HMG leverages heavily on the power of computing and information technologies, recognising the importance of IT as a key enabler of many business and service needs.

This is palpable in their IT development in recent years. A networked platform that allows the Group to share patient information among their medical specialities, thus better meeting the healthcare needs of their patients, was put in place. Patients at one HMG clinic are able to visit other HMG clinics and have their previous medical records electronically and readily available for doctors to use. The networked platform also allows the Group to share resources between clinics. For example, rather than each clinic independently tracking the price of medication, staff at each clinic can obtain accurate price information from the Group itself, allowing patients to obtain the same prices at any of HMG's clinics. Figure 13.2 lists some of the key systems used by HMG.

THE HMG CLINICAL MANAGEMENT SYSTEM (CMS)

The Clinical Management System (CMS) is a key application system used to automate, simplify and computerise the operations of a clinic (such as patient registration, appointment management, inventory control and billing) into a single integrated system, thus relieving physicians and clinical assistants from tedious manual, paper-based and error-prone processes and allowing them to focus on delivering

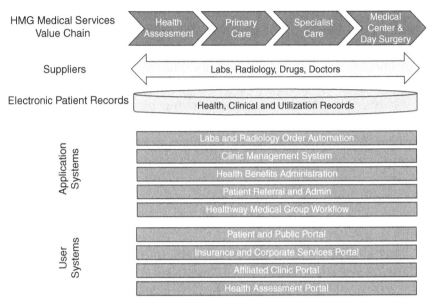

Figure 13.2:   Key information systems at HMG.

better healthcare to patients. The CMS processes, stores and accesses all the information needed by the clinic for its daily operations, instantly and accurately, providing doctors with more efficient and effective control over the clinic and their patients' needs.

HMG needed CMS at each of their GP and specialist clinics for several reasons:

(a) Obsolescence of existing systems

When clinics and centres first joined or were acquired by HMG, they were typically using independent, older systems and IT infrastructures, if at all. These systems were not just obsolete, they served the need of the individual clinic and hence were not robust and could not integrate with other HMG group-level systems.

(b) Increasing data volume and complexity

When an increasing number of clinics joined HMG, particularly after 2007, it became clear that a system would be required to store, process, and manage the increasing volume of data generated by the clinics. Some newer clinics also had their own systems and existing data to be incorporated into HMG. The existing systems used by HMG were inadequate to handle the migration of data effectively.

(c) Tighter linkage between management and clinics
It is not good enough if each clinic has a system that only serves its needs. As a group, there need to be communication established between the management and the clinics. HMG sees IT a potential tool to provide seamless information exchange, and facilitate control over the clinics without minimising or even reducing overhead.

(d) Regulatory requirements
Introducing CMS at each clinic was also a response to regulatory requirements by the Ministry of Health (MOH) for the online reporting of cases involving infectious diseases, allergies, immunisations, and claims from patients' Central Provident Fund (CPF). When such cases occur, the CMS would send the relevant data to government agencies electronically, rather than via fax.

With over one million patient visits to its clinics in Singapore, there is a critical need for doctors to have accurate and easily accessible patient medical information available in real-time. HMG knew that they are looking for not just a CMS system for the clinics, but a system that could form a network of communication to channel information to clinics, as well as between clinics and management.

In 2007, HMG began to design a CMS to support the operations of the clinics, as well as to provide decision-making support and interface with suppliers, healthcare partners, health authorities and insurance companies. Rather than developing the application system in-house, its 5-person IT department studied available commercial off-the-shelf (COTS) software, with the desire to find a cost-effective solution in a shorter time, using less of the group's IT resources.

CMS FOR GP CLINICS

After an extensive search, HMG met a local IT solutions provider, CrimsonLogic, who demonstrated a prototype system, ClinicWeaver clinic management system suite, which partially met their requirements for GP's system. Figure 13.3 shows how the data may flow from clinics to HMG.

At the same time, HMG carried out a "gap analysis," to locate differences between the functionalities offered by a system and sought by its users. The analysis identified the need to conduct considerable customisations in CrimsonLogic's CMS solution so as to meet HMG's requirements. One of the examples cited by Mr. Kyaw Kyaw Thein, the Head, System and IT of HMG is the drug transfer module. According to him, "We have a central purchasing mechanism. If there is no electronic drug transfer module, you have to transfer the inventory information and drugs manually. Both ends have to update their inventory record. With the system, the information can be transmitted electronically. The receiving end only has to verify the drugs physically and the record can now be validated electronically."

Within eight months, they developed several features, complementing the standard software, e.g., the Electronic Medical Record, Inventory System, synchronisation mechanism with central server etc. Before the rollout, HMG conducted a trial run with CrimsonLogic's

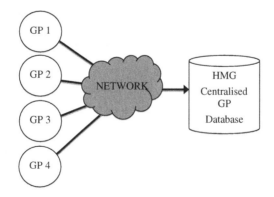

Figure 13.3:   HMG centralised GP database system.

solution in two clinics, to further identify issues and incompatibilities that would arise in its use. Two clinics with lower patient traffic were selected to conduct the trial run to avoid disruption of services to the patients.

During the trial run, one of the emphases is the network quality which determines the service reliability and continuity. In order for the clinic to operate at the high service levels expected from customers, the system could not afford any decline in connectivity in the secured network connection. A loss of connection would mean a GP's system not able to communicate with the HMG central database, thus impairing the clinic's operations. As a result, CrimsonLogic and HMG needed to ensure that the GP's operations would still continue, even in the event of temporary network loss or other disconnect from the centralised database. Besides reliability, speed is another key factor because some HMG clinics have to attend to about 200 patients a day. A lagged response will unavoidably result in frustration among clinical assistants.

To resolve this issue, the companies employed a "hybrid model." As Kyaw explained in simple terms: "When internet is down, the system can still run on local server. When internet is up, they will be automatically synchronised to the central server… the hybrid system has no performance or response issue at all."

This model comprises Microsoft SQL Server-based servers located at each clinic (this computer was called the "local server"), and a centralised Sun server and Oracle database hosted by CrimsonLogic, with the clinics access over the Web. Data between the local and central servers is synced in real time with updated data between local and central databases via a secured network connection to the Centralised GP Database. In the event that the connection was lost, the clinic could still operate as per normal on its local database. The regular uploading of the local database to the centralised database would resume when the connection was again operational. The corollary is a data redundancy with copies of all data stored in the central system.

Figure 13.4 details this hybrid network application model. The hybrid model for the networked application would therefore allow

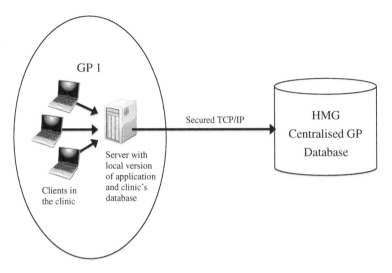

Figure 13.4: Alleviating network application issues with a hybrid model that synchronises data.

each clinic in HMG to connect and sync operational data to the centralised database. As an untested model for networked applications in Singapore's healthcare industry, HMG and CrimsonLogic spent considerable effort to ensure the system met their expectations before implementing it.

In April 2008, HMG IT team and CrimsonLogic team migrated the legacy system to CMS in the first clinic. Subsequently, they went through a two-month fine-tuning process, leading them to a smoother execution of the migration plan that saw one or two clinics started using the CMS each month. It was not a painless process. The management recognised that without the support of doctors and clinical assistant, no system could be adopted. HMG's IT addressed this by gaining staffs' trust and support. Resources were deployed to ensure users' enquiry or complaints were addressed and solved promptly during the migration. Furthermore, as a pre-emptive measure, CrimsonLogic was requested to make changes to the user interface in order to facilitate usability — instead of toggling 2–3 pages, user should be able to view and enter the data in one screen. By end of first quarter in 2010, HMG completed the migration for the 55 clinics. Figure 13.5 shows user interface for clinical assistants.

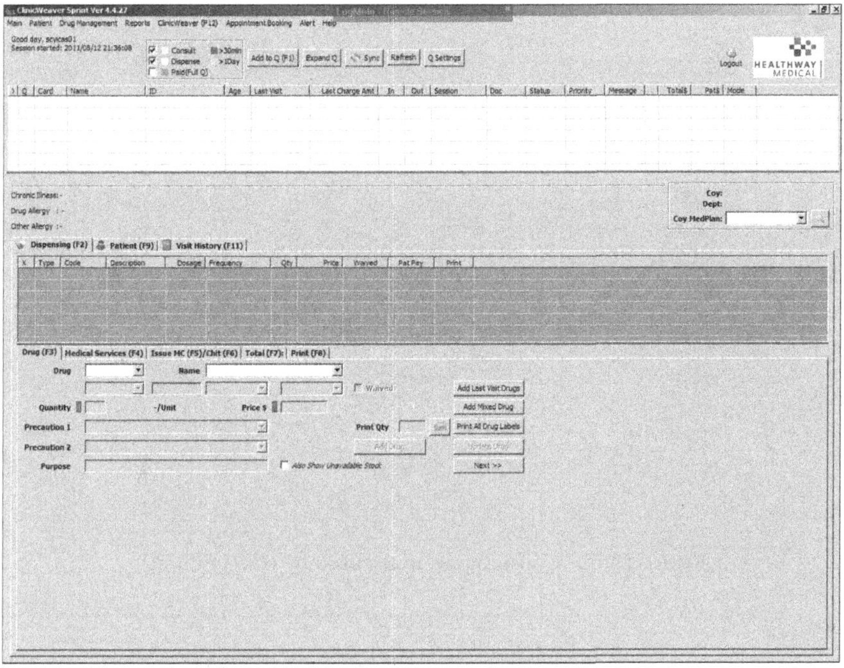

Figure 13.5: User interface for clinical assistants.

CMS FOR SPECIALIST CLINICS

An in-depth analysis revealed that the specialist and wellness clinics would not be able to utilise the same package as GP due to the distinction in practices — a patient seeking medical attention at eye specialist centre is bound to undergo different screening steps with a patient seeing an Ear Nose Throat (ENT) Specialist. Different specialist clinics would require patients to undergo different types of tests, carry different inventories of medication, and require information captured about patients to be more specific to the specialisation. The CMS for specialist and wellness business unit has to be developed in-house. As mentioned by Kyaw, "It is difficult for specialist to suit their system (CrimsonLogic system). We cannot change every single unit to suit the system. Even they can change it, it will take a long time and the cost will be too high. That's why we — develop the proprietary system ourselves."

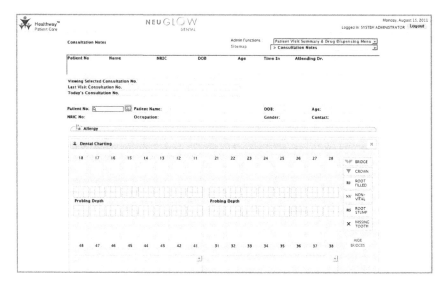

Figure 13.6:   Consultation notes used by HMG dental.

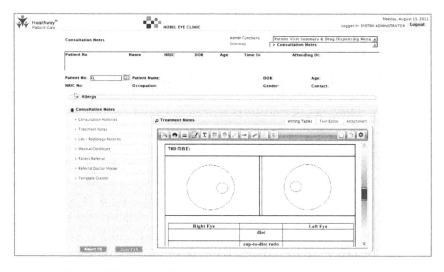

Figure 13.7:   Consultation notes used by HMG eye specialist.

Figures 13.6 and 13.7 show the CMS used by dental and eye specialist, where user interface and data captured are very different.

This posed a problem for data collection and synchronisation across the HMG clinics. Data from the specialist clinics would be

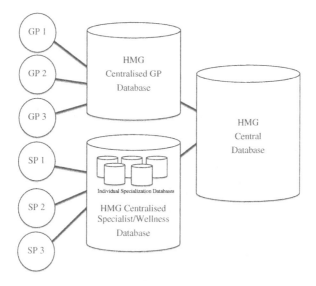

Figure 13.8:   Data flow between all GP and wellness/specialist networked clinics to multiple centralised databases.

different from data captured in GP clinics, and thus would not easily be stored in an integrated database. To resolve this problem, HMG introduced a new centralised database for specialist clinics, and another to store all the information needed by HMG for analysis. Figure 13.8 depicts the data flow management.

The efforts paid off. The CMS with a hybrid model allowed information to be stored, processed, and accessed centrally at HMG, rather than independently at each individual clinic. Management and geographically dispersed clinics can now "talk" to one another. Efficiency, transparency and control over the clinics improved by leap and bounds. As mentioned by Kyaw, "We have full control over the server... for example, if we add new procedure or new drug [to CMS], we do not need to add each and every one to the clinics, we simply have to add at server, then enables a real time update."

With centralised database, there is no more strenuous and time-consuming information extraction and consolidation. HMG would be able to obtain and analyse data from each clinic effortlessly while consolidating financial and performance reports across the entire group.

Information that flows through them could be utilised to enhance patients' experience at the clinic. Updated medical records of patient are immediately accessible for attending doctors at any HMG clinics. Imagine this scenario — a patient has done health screening at one of the group clinic. If he/she visits another clinic and the doctor is able to access the result of his/her health screening to provide a comprehensive diagnosis. This would certainly enhance patient's experience and boost their confidence. In short, the CMS provides the platform for the central database of HMG's electronic medical records, enabling viewing of lab results and patient records electronically.

ELECTRONIC MEDICAL RECORDS

In order to better serve their patients, HMG embarked on the development of electronic medical records (EMR), where patient information, diagnoses, and treatments could be electronically stored, recalled and shared between clinics. To date, HMG has successfully implemented EMR within the business units (within GP, specialist and wellness), and are working towards sharing the information across the units.

This information exchange would ultimately extend beyond the group. As part of MediNet (Singapore's nationwide computer network for the medical and healthcare community), HMG is able to communicate and submit details required by government agencies like Ministry of Health (MOH) and Central Provident Fund (CPF) Board behind the desk. "For example for dengue case — You have to report [to MOH] within 24 hours.[22] If you do not submit through the system, you would have to fax in… [with linkage to MediNet] hence making the information flow faster and easier…."

Implementing the EMR, however, demands several considerations. Patients' medical records are highly sensitive documents, and

---

[22] All medical practitioners are required by the Infectious Diseases Act to report all clinically-diagnosed and laboratory-confirmed dengue cases and deaths to the Ministry of Health by facsimile or by online electronic notification within 24 hours.

required HMG to adhere to medical and legal frameworks within the country. While the Singapore government is also simultaneously undertaking an EMR initiative for its polyclinics and public hospitals, it did not stop private medical groups like HMG from innovating with its own efforts.

HMG recognised the importance of EMR in providing higher quality healthcare for patients, but realised its responsibility to its both its patients and doctors to keep those records secure, and available to only the right people at the right time. Not only were legal issues involved, the integration and use of electronic medical records also brought up several privacy and ethical issues. For instance, could HMG systems administrators view patients' records stored in the centralised database? Could doctors view the treatment options provided by other doctors? What information could be shared if a patient is referred from one unit to another? How would the records be stored securely to prevent loss or modifications of the data by other parties, while in storage or in transmission? Apparently, professional views from medical practitioners and policy makers would have to be elicited in assessing the various risks.

In managing these issues, HMG has approached the design of the EMR, and the user interfaces that employ these records, with great level of discretion and sensitivity. Password and access controls are used to ensure that only the right authorities are able to view details in records. For instance, based on their log-in credentials, physicians logged into a client terminal in a clinic are able to access different levels of detail than other clinical assistants.

"We have the log file [that keeps track] of who changes the records.... We should have some standards.... Not all information are allowed to be modified. Even if we allow changes, we have to log it," said Kyaw in explaining how they safeguard the integrity of the patient medical data and organisational transactional data e.g. cash and drug inventory.

To further mitigate the risk of data leakage or loss, users of the systems are not allowed to use portable storage media. For HMG IT staff, the data would be encrypted when data are transferred to the storage media. Querying and downloading of data would be logged too.

The IT department at HMG also recognised that doctors could not peruse patients' entire histories in their electronic medical records, as doing so would consume too much time. To aid in the responsible use of this information the IT department worked with CrimsonLogic and HMG doctors to design and test new user interfaces for presenting existing patient information from their EMRs to doctors.

ELECTRONIC CONSULT MODULE (PAPERLESS MODULE)

In 2010, HMG took a step further to leverage on IT to enhance service delivery and process efficiency. "Paperless Module" was introduced for physicians to store and retrieve their diagnosis and prescription in the system as the management of HMG believed that paper is neither an effective way of storing information needed for clinical governance, nor an efficient way of recalling the information when needed. The interface which doctors would to enter their diagnoses is shown in Figure 13.9.

Dr. Jong Kee Sen said, "Healthway Medical is strongly committed to improving patient care services. For our doctors to operate effectively and deliver better patient care, a key part of our strategy is to move away from a paper-based approach towards the adoption of electronic medical records systems in our clinics."

Dr. Jong explained, "this seems like a mundane thing. But if you visit a GP clinic, you will find that medical cards take up two-thirds or half of the clinic space because [under Singapore] law, you have to store them for seven years — and you may have a patient that sees you only once in those seven years."

The doctors saw the need for embracing the new technology, be it clinically or financially. Altogether 34 clinics adopted "Paperless Module" in 2011 and another 20 were implemented in the year 2012. Instead of flipping through papers, doctors can view the patients records on two screens, with one displaying the past records and the other displaying the current one. The information is organised and displayed to facilitate ease of retrieval and analysis. For example, the permanent details such as blood type and chronic

Figure 13.9:   Electronic consult module.

disease are segregated from visit details like temperature, on the display device. Compared to papers and cards, another key benefit is the ability of the computer system to prompt or alert the patients' drug allergies, if any, thus lowering the chances of doctors missing that important information.

By providing a dual mode of data entry and intuitive user interface, HMG's IT team applied the lessons learnt from their previous experience of managing different stakeholders' needs to gain support. Physicians can choose to either use the keyboard or write on the tablet in order to keep the data. This helps the doctors who may not be technology-savvy. Now, with prescription created directly by doctors in the system, the likelihood of clinical assistants making mistake in deciphering doctors' writing is much lowered. It also automates the key clinical procedures, and improves the productivity and patients' waiting time, without compromising the quality of service.

CONCLUSION — SMARTER HEALTHCARE FOR THE FUTURE

As the Healthway Medical Group continues to innovate with medical records, networked applications and user interfaces, it is also looking into how these information technologies can be combined with smarter processing to further improve healthcare provision. The group is currently examining the technologies available for intelligent Decision Support Systems (DSS) that will be able to help doctors diagnose illnesses and prescribe medications, based on patient histories, existing symptoms, drugs interaction database, and current epidemics.

While such innovations will open a new era in healthcare, several questions arise on the safety and ethics of using computing technology to diagnose patients. Is it truly safe, and will it lead to a commonplace acceptance of tele-medicine, where doctors are able to diagnose patients without meeting them in person?

In the meantime, the Healthway Medical Group continues to work toward ensuring a more secured, convenient, and patient-centric healthcare experience for both its physicians and its patients, hence living up to the group's objectives of leveraging IT: Healthway Medical strives to continuously provide quality medical care at affordable rates. They aim to improve patients' health and increase productivity at the workplace for their valued clients.

DISCUSSION QUESTIONS

1. What are the benefits and critical design considerations of a "hybrid model" in Healthway?
2. Implementing electronic medical records requires capturing, storing, and transmitting sensitive patient information. What are the technical and ethical concerns in implementing such a system? How did HMG address these concerns?
3. Security is critical in network applications design and implementation, and more so for healthcare industry due to the privacy and sensitivity of information. What are some of the elements that a CIO or Head of IT must address?

ABOUT THE EDITOR

Associate Professor **Gary Pan** is the Associate Dean (Student Matters) at School of Accountancy, Singapore Management University. Gary was awarded Student Life Recognition Awards in 2012 and 2013; Most Outstanding Teacher, Master of Professional Accounting Teaching Award in 2010; School of Accountancy Most Promising Researcher Award in 2009 and Best Paper (*Honourable Mention*), Journal of Strategic Information Systems in 2009. His research and teaching focus on areas of accounting information systems, strategic implementation of IT systems and corporate governance. Gary's research has been published in various premier academic journals such as *MISQ Executive, Journal of the Association for Information Systems, IEEE Transactions on Engineering Management, European Journal of Operational Research, Information & Management, Decision Support Systems, Information Systems Journal, Journal of Strategic Information Systems,* and the *Journal of the American Society for Information Systems and Technology.* Gary is currently a member of FCPA Australia, CPA Singapore, and ICMA. He is also Associate Editor for *Journal of Information & Management.*

INDEX